THE MARXIST THEORY OF SCHOOLING

A Study of Epistemology and Education

THE MARXIST THEORY OF SCHOOLING

A Study of Epistemology and Education

MICHAEL R MATTHEWS
Lecturer in Education, University of New South Wales

HARVESTER PRESS · SUSSEX
HUMANITIES PRESS · NEW JERSEY

First published in Great Britain in 1980 by
THE HARVESTER PRESS LIMITED
Publishers: John Spiers and Margaret A. Boden
16 Ship Street, Brighton, Sussex

and in the USA by
HUMANITIES PRESS INC.,
Atlantic Highlands, New Jersey 07716

© Michael R. Matthews, 1980

British Library Cataloguing in Publication Data
Matthews, Michael R.
    The marxist theory of schooling. —(Harvester
    studies in philosophy).
    1. Education—Philosophy
    I. Title
    370.1   LB880.M3/
    ISBN 0-85527-443-3

Humanities Press Inc.
ISBN 0-391-01801-9

Photoset in Great Britain by
Rowland Phototypesetting Limited, Bury St Edmunds, Suffolk
and printed by
St Edmundsbury Press, Bury St Edmunds, Suffolk

To

Wal Suchting, Friend and Teacher

CONTENTS

PREFACE

This is a work in philosophy of education. It attempts to bring to bear a Marxist epistemology on some issues in educational theory and practice. My conviction is that epistemology, or theory of knowledge, is best elucidated in terms of the philosophy of science. To this end I have used examples from the history of science to prove and illustrate many of the positions argued for. I beg the indulgence of those for whom science is not familiar. I have tried my best to be clear and to avoid particularly esoteric concerns which are the province of specialists. If we can be moderately clear about the epistemology of natural science then disputes in social science, education, theology and the like can be conducted in a more informed and sophisticated manner.

I am explicitly opposed to the dominant philosophy of education in the Anglo-Saxon world—Analytic Philosophy of Education. I am aware of the 'Pauline Effect'—those brought up in a tradition overreact to it when they leave. I acknowledge the personal hospitality and encouragement of both Richard Peters and Paul Hirst in this project. I hope I have done justice to their epistemology and social philosophy in my criticism.

My Marxism is of a catholic variety—I believe that the kernel of Historical Materialism contained in Marx's and Engel's works can be elaborated by research within and without the Marxist tradition. Marxists do have things to say to other traditions; but they also have things to learn from other traditions. This catholicity was well attested to by Bob Cohen and Marx Wartofsky of Boston University, with whom I had the great pleasure of spending a sabbatical leave and from whom I learnt so much. Catholicity and tolerance are not to be confused with vacuity. The importance of having something to say, and then saying it clearly, was impressed upon me by my friend, and first teacher of Marxism, Wal Suchting of Sydney University.

The philosophy of science contained here is an anti-empiricist one. I can only admire and respect the vigour with which many in the empiricist tradition have pursued their research; however, science must be seen as being penetrated much more by social, historical and cultural influences than logical empiricism and positivism have been prepared to admit. Having said this, I do not wish to collapse the science/ideology distinction or to discount the cognitive claims of science. It is primarily a cognitive enterprise, but the process of production of its intellectual claims is more complex than often admitted. In these matters I have learnt much from Alan Chalmers of Sydney University, Randall Albury of the University of New South Wales, and Roy Bhaskar of Edinburgh University. My interest in Galileo was sparked by Abner Shimony of Boston University, a gentle and tolerant person who is a scholar in both physics and philosophy. He is eloquent testimony to the need for philosophy to be studied in conjunction with science.

My development in philosophy of education has been dependent upon the work of my friends and colleagues in Australia—Jim Walker, Peter Stevens, Bill Andersen, Kevin Harris, John Kleinig, Philip Steedman and Bob Mackie. I should especially like to thank Bob for his continual support and encouragement in the project of producing this book from a vast collection of lectures I had written over a space of two years.

I have argued for an account of knowledge as intellectual production. Until I came to put this book together, I had no conception of it as entailing a process of material labour and craft production. By virtue of the painstaking labour of many readers, what was originally a rambling script littered with errors has become a much more precise work containing significantly fewer errors. I have a debt here to Wal Suchting, Bob Petersen, Ralph Hall, Randall Albury, Michael Howard, John O'Brien, Margaret Jolly and Marie Zuvich. A special debt is owed to Des Burke and Jim Lonergan whose skill and diligence in proof-reading the manuscript brought to light innumerable grammatical and syntactical blunders. Their command of the English language is remarkable.

My final debt is to Dympna Casey, who gave up a month of her time to type the manuscript. She brought not only competence to the task, but joy and good humour to the 'family' for the duration of her stay.

CHAPTER 1
INTRODUCTION

All great philosophers in the Western tradition have recognised that an epistemology, or a theory of knowledge, is of crucial importance for the elaboration of coherent world views, and for intelligent and reflective action in the world. This book is written with the same conviction. It is with good reason that philosophers concerned with education have regarded epistemology in the same manner in which carpenters might regard their saws—epistemology has to be good, it has to be attended to, it will inevitably be put to use in practical programmes and in the creation of eductional theories. Plato, Augustine, Aquinas, John Henry Newman, Alfred North Whitehead are just some of the classical figures for whom this claim is clearly true. In contemporary philosophy of education Paul Hirst at Cambridge, Israel Scheffler at Harvard and Paulo Freire, the once exiled Brazilian, all see that epistemology is the way to bring rigour to their theorising, and relevance to their proposals for the practical conduct of education. This book is a contribution to philosophy of education; its epistemology is in the Marxist tradition; it will underpin the analyses and proposals of the now mushrooming radical sociological and historical studies of schooling.

Teachers are involved in the process of producing, transmitting and justifying public knowledge. They do this explicitly via the curricula and implicitly via the hidden curricula. Course content, teaching styles, grading procedures, power relations entered into, are all means whereby the school makes its contribution to the consciousness of students and to the store of public knowledge, public values, public culture. School children recite the Lord's Prayer; line up at assemblies; salute the flag; attend History and English lessons; put on musicals; go on excursions; join cadet corps; segregate according to sex to use toilets, participate in sport, and attend certain lessons; hand work to teachers; sit exams and gain certificates. Children are born into a society, and through their experience of particular social relations, first in the family and then in the school, they become socialised. Children variously learn the language, skills, competencies, knowledge and myths necessary for them to participate in society. When teachers select texts and poems; when they give explanations of the Depression and of the reactions of acids on metals; when they talk about current affairs; when they grade exercises; and when they do innumerable other things, they presuppose in one form or another a theory of knowledge. They presuppose answers to questions such as: Are there right and wrong opinions? How do we judge between competing accounts of matters? What separates myth and ideology from knowledge? Is knowledge apolitical and interest-free, or is it impregnated with ethical and political commitment? What are the appropriate ways to acquire knowledge? As with many other matters, this is a case where what is implicit benefits from being made explicit. A theory of knowledge is of great assistance to teachers in going about their business, and in understanding what, indeed, that business is which they are going about.

People engage in varied practices in society and enter into varied relations. They play sport, cook, entertain, seek love and earn a living. They become husbands, wives, mothers, employees, buyers, sellers, learners, teachers. These practices and relations are variously ritualised and legalised or legitimised. The marriage ceremony is an example of a highly ritualised practice which creates specific legal relations between people. Social consciousness develops out of this base of practices and relations. They can be adequately or inadequately understood. Some understandings are obviously inadequate. The woman who believes that her practice of incessant hand-washing is motivated by a desire for clean hands has an inadequate understanding of the activity. Similarly, if she fails to see her daily housework practices as being linked to the productive processes of the society (it is partly responsible for the creation of society's labour power) then her consciousness is inadequate. But here it is less obviously inadequate. An alternative theory is required to display the inadequacy. Science and critical thinking are concerned in part with producing correct accounts of the practices and relations in which people are engaged. This will involve displacing everyday, commonsense, immediate intuitions and conceptualisations. It does appear that the sun revolves around the earth; it does appear that bodies need an applied force to maintain them in motion. Science tells us that these appearances are false. There are many equally immediate, and equally inadequate, conceptualisations of the varied practices and relations that constitute schooling. This work aims to provide more adequate ones.

Knowledge has to be seen as a product with social and historical dimensions. People who create knowledge are themselves created. The 'we think' establishes the limits of the 'I think'. People are children of their time and circumstance. However, to acknowledge the contingency of human consciousness, is not tantamount to acknowledging a relativism, or much less a scepticism, about consciousness. There are good and bad theories, adequate and inadequate conceptualisations, competent and incompetent techniques. Further, the differences can be established. It is not the case that 'anything goes' in the attempt intellectually to appropriate the world. Some phenomenologists and other anti-empiricist thinkers who have forced the recognition of the 'human factor' in cognition and who have stressed the 'social construction of reality' have unfortunately collapsed into a debilitating relativism. Teachers need to recognise that not all ideas are as good as each other. The theory of knowledge developed here aims to assist this recognition.

No important epistemology has ever been proposed which ignores scientific practice and the process of theory appraisal in science. Aristotle, Francis Bacon, David Hume, Immanuel Kant all based their epistemology upon an understanding of science. Although difficult, and prone to error, this procedure is a wise one. Much contemporary Anglo-Saxon epistemology is simply aberrant in this respect. It is a departure from the great tradition. It is of particular note that Paul Hirst's 'Forms of Knowledge' theory, so influential in British philosophy of education, is altogether bereft of considerations of the history and philosophy of science. This is not the least of the reasons why Hirst's epistemology is rejected in this work. We will argue that considerations in the philosophy of science force the rejection of all seriously empiricist epistemologies. Galileo's achievements in physics will be returned to repeatedly to help establish the inadequacy of empiricism. If empiricism is rejected, then popular educational slogans such as 'learn by experience', 'discovery learning is the best learning', 'experience is the best judge' all need to be reinterpreted or rejected.

Karl Marx, in his early writings, saw clearly that human practice had to be a key element in any theory of human knowledge—in practice the truth is to be proved. He further saw that posing the question of knowledge in terms of some isolated *Robinson Crusoe* figure making direct immediate contact with the world and then writing up the results of this contact was pure fantasy. Francis Bacon's metaphor of entry to the kingdom of knowledge being akin to entry to the kingdom of heaven, in that one has first to be free of the fruits of all civilisation, has unfortunately mesmerised much Western philosophy. Thankfully, Marx was never under this spell. Contrary to empiricists, he believed that the virgin perception was a myth. All perception has a theoretical component, a fact which is now widely acknowledged. Contrary to rationalists, he saw practice and experimentation as the prerequisites of knowledge. There are no essences of things which are discoverable by processes of intellectual abstraction. His later writings provide the basis of the epistemology developed in this work. This is an epistemology which sees consciousness generally as the product of processes of intellectual production. The raw materials are already theorised concepts, observation statements and theories of varying universality. Knowledge does not have, and does not need foundations. There is no Archimedean point from which by correct reasoning the corpus of human knowledge can be constructed. This model of consciousness, of the intellectual conceptions and theories of a society, enables us to isolate the place where ideology and mystification enter into public knowledge—in the raw materials, in the productive process, in the products or in the productive relations governing the process. The model also enables us to accommodate the insights into knowledge that have been made in a variety of traditions. It is a catholic, not a sectarian epistemology. There are certain affinities with Karl Popper's *objectivist*, third-world theory. Specifically, to see knowledge as the product of theoretical productive processes is to discount second world episodes such as the individual's beliefs, experiences and the like. Inasmuch as products can be reworked as raw materials in another process, then this epistemology shares the *Fallibilism* of theorists such as Stephen Toulmin. Fallibilism means that although we can choose the best account among a number of rivals, we are not committed to that being the only possible account. It itself can be superseded. Good methodology leaves all cognition open to revision. It was a mistake of Immanuel Kant's to regard Newton's achievements in mechanics, towering though they were, as true for all time and not susceptible to overhaul. In the theological tradition this feature, this intellectual modesty, is Newman's thesis of the 'development of doctrine'. There are other affinities to which we will point.

A universally accepted aim for educational processes is that they should develop rational thinking by students. This is somewhat like the injunction to 'do good'; or the advice that under capitalism, if you wish to get rich, then 'buy cheap and sell dear'; or the Republican politician whose platform was 'Backward never, Forward ever'. There are no disagreements at this level of abstraction; there are, however, serious disagreements as we move from principles to policies to practices. Unfortunately for those who seek easy and neat answers to complex problems, there is no purely formal answer to what rational thinking is. To teach someone logic is not to guarantee rational thinking. To argue with utmost vigour and validity from stupid and absurd premises is not the hallmark of rationality. Given certain premises, the Ku Klux Klan might argue validly to the conclusion that Negroes ought to be hanged. Validity is not equivalent to rationality. Rationality has to move beyond the purely formal realm of rules of inference and come to terms with substantive issues of the adequacy or correctness of beliefs. The contention here is that these substantive issues of how evidence relates to beliefs are best examined in the crucible of science and its history. A common view is that rationality consists of holding just those beliefs for which you have evidence. This is known as *Inductivism*. It is well illustrated in the spectre of Dickens' Mr Gradgrind, who stood over his students insisting that they believe only the facts. He was dedicated to planting nothing else and rooting out everything else but facts from the minds of the pupils. Such an account of rationality results in standard ongoing scientific practices being irrational. This is a *reductio ad absurdum* argument, the inference from which is that our account of rationality has to change. Another common view is that rationality consists in *not* holding beliefs against which there is evidence. This is known as *Falsificationism*. Once more the history of science is the testing-place for this opinion, and when we test it, we find it wanting. The philosopher Imre Lakatos has developed an account of scientific rationality known as the *Methodology of Scientific Research Programmes* (MSRP), which holds most hope of guiding people in their *inevitable* chore of weighing up and appraising alternative bodies of opinion, and rival world views and theoretical discourses. This is outlined here, and it is utilised in appraising liberal and Marxist theories of schooling. Rationality as an aim of education cannot be divorced from practicality. People have natural and social needs; they are faced with objective problems that require solutions. Rational thinking is not to be identified with idle jottings on paper concerning some subject or other. How do we deal with unemployment? How do we bake a cake? Should we have abortion law reform? Why did America wage war in Vietnam? Which party will I vote for and does it matter anyway? We think and exercise intelligence in order to do things—things which for the most part are solutions to practical and theoretical problems which are thrust upon us by virtue of the specific social, economic, intellectual milieu in which we are placed. Coming to terms with analytic philosophy of education is a problem for us in 1980; it was not a problem in 1950.

The complement to a theory of knowledge is a theory of ignorance. As well as insights, we have outsights. We need to understand both, particularly as some outsights recur systematically in society and are generated by the very fabric of our social institutions. Insight into insight gives us a theory of knowledge; insight into outsight gives us a theory of ideology. This is of the utmost importance in education, as schools are the chief loci for the reproduction and inculcation of the ideologies of society. The doctrine of 'Manifest Destiny' was taught in all schools in the United States until the recent past, and indeed is still widely taught. People do learn that England went to war in 1914 to defend the rights of small nations to determine their own affairs. Ideology is taught explicitly in Civics classes and implicitly in English Literature, History, Economics and Science classes. It is also conveyed by the structures and practices of schooling. Girls who see all senior positions in a school filled by males do pick up messages about a woman's place in the world.

The theme of 'Ideology and Education' has been a much canvassed one in recent times. Unfortunately a lot of social science writing on the theme has been glib and unsystematic. The characterisation of ideology as 'muddy thinking' is not very informative. A recent work in analytic philosophy of education seeks to develop an account of ideology by a conceptual analysis of four sentences in which 'ideology' occurs. This is no more informative. Some French and English works which say that all systematised thought—science included—is ideology also leave us where we began. To destroy the distinction is to jettison the programme of trying intellectually to appropriate the world and to act intelligently for its transformation. The theory of ideology developed here is a Marxist one. It locates ideology in human practices, and particularly in the practices of social production and the economy.

The theory and practice of IQ testing, and its utilisation in school systems, provide an opportunity to illustrate the themes developed in this book. The origins and early history of IQ testing illustrate clearly the ideological and political nature of the practice. In understanding most things, an historical perspective is a decided advantage. IQ theory arose out of the Eugenics Movement in England and the United States and was consciously an instrument for class control and legitimation of class privilege. The fact that there were numbers sprinkled around, and sophisticated covariances worked out, gives the lie to the view that having measurements and numbers is tantamount to having science. IQ theory is not scientific. People who developed the tests were themselves developed. They intruded into the tests their particular biases, prejudices and class positions. As with so much social science theory, it was like a Rorschach test —it tells us more about the person who creates it than it does about the reality with which it is ostensibly concerned. Later IQ theorising illustrates innumerable faulty positions in the philosophy of science.

An adequate understanding of IQ theorising requires that we jettison a much ingrained position in philosophy, namely the context of discovery/context of justification distinction. A recent review of the IQ controversy, which is very sophisticated in its methodology, is entirely concerned with the justification of the nature versus nurture sides of the argument. It altogether fails to locate and analyse the IQ argument in its context as a political and ideological weapon. Once this is done, then other questions emerge and demand our attention. When Cyril Burt attributed success in life to the 'degree of intelligence with which any particular child is endowed', we are not dealing simply with a scientific hypothesis whose justification is to be examined. We have here ideology, and the contexts in which it is generated need to be scrutinised, and its absorption into the consciousness and practices of school-teachers counteracted.

On the basis of the dictum 'by their fruits ye shall know them' I shall examine the contribution of philosophers of education of the 'London Institute' variety to the IQ debate. It will be pointed out that their methodology precludes their having much of significance to say. One recent London Institute contribution was concerned with, in part, establishing that there was a 'conceptual connection between intelligence and flexible behaviour' and to argue that 'disparateness is not written into the concept'. Such an endeavour is futile. 'Intelligence' is a theoretical term whose meaning is given within the theory in which it is articulated. There are as many different concepts of intelligence as there are theories of intelligence. There is no place for conceptual analysis across theories. 'Mass' means something different in Aristotelian, Newtonian and Einsteinian mechanics. To engage in the enterprise of analysing everyday usage of the term and then proposing a concept of mass is plainly absurd. Interestingly enough, one other London Institute contributor to the debate says that science takes up the commonsense understanding of mass. It does no such thing. 'Weight' is common-sensical, and it does not figure in mechanics. 'Inertial mass' figures in mechanics and has little to do with common sense. The chapter on the IQ controversy can be regarded as a case study for the research programme in philosophy of education which we are proposing.

Since the late '50s, analytic philosophy of education has developed a powerful and influential presence in teacher training establishments, in the deliberations of numerous committees and in the editorial boards and policies of major journals in education. It is given shape and definition in the work of D. J. O'Connor, Israel Scheffler, Paul Hirst, Richard Peters and many others. It was consciously the extension into philosophy of education of the 'Revolution' in philosophy which overwhelmed so much of Anglo-Saxon philosophy during this century. This was the revolution of the conceptual analysts, of those for whom philosophy was a second-order activity concerned with clarifying the concepts and logic of first-order discourses such as science, history and mathematics. In England, analytic philosophy of education can be referred to as 'London Institute' philosophy of education. Peters took a chair at the London Institute of Education in 1963; Paul Hirst and R. F. Dearden were his early colleagues. The Institute was the alma mater of hundreds who have taken up university teaching appointments throughout the world and of thousands who have taken up school teaching appointments. This book is in fundamental opposition to analytic philosophy of education (or 'APE', as my colleague Jim Walker has referred to it). It rejects the philosophical *method* of APE as being not only puerile, but intrinsically ideological. It rejects the *epistemology* of APE, particularly as that epistemology is coextensive with Paul Hirst's 'forms of knowledge' theory. It rejects the liberal-rationalist political and social ideology which lies behind and informs its conception of schooling. Popper's advice to philosophers to turn from the analysis of concepts and the search for meanings and concentrate on the search for truths via the appraisal of competing theories is followed here.

Educational theory has often been produced on the cheap; it has been utopian and idealistic theory; it has frequently been prescriptive or normative theory. As such it consisted of various nostrums and remedies for practical problems and various high-flown goals to which education should aspire. Educational theory had become a secular form of theology. But a theology is not a theory of religion. It is educational theory in this latter sense with which we are primarily concerned. Why were schools established? What are their functions in society? How are these functions achieved? These are broadly empirical questions and are the subject of rival theories. It is idle to talk of what should happen in schools and classrooms independently of what does happen and what can happen. Progressivists in education have too frequently suffered from this 'blah, blah, blah' malady. Marx's strictures against the utopian socialists who did not bother to analyse the actual mechanisms of capitalism, nor to provide any guidelines for the creation of socialism, can equally be applied to Utopian educational theorists. There has been a plethora of informative analyses of schooling in recent socio-logical and economic literature. The extensive works of Samuel Bowles and Herbert Gintis stand out. The research of radical historians such as Joel Spring and Clarence Karier have forced a reappraisal of the simple-minded view that schools were estab-lished to initiate children into the forms of knowledge, or the many mansions of our heritage. One mistake with radical analyses is that they have often overlooked the contradictions within schooling. There is no neat fit between the class structure of society and the structure of schooling. A fit, yes; a neat fit, no. This is a point brought out clearly in the work of Paul Willis and others at the Birmingham Centre for Cultural Studies. In schools strong counter-school cultures have developed. Radicals in schools certainly have plenty of reasons for pessimism, but there are some reasons for optimism. Few now maintain that changing schools will significantly alter the structures of oppres-sion in the wider society. Ivan Illich was correct in stating this. However, not all engagement and commitment in schools is pointless. A certain tragic sense of life helps, but even without it there can be rewards for committed actions. Dominant ideol-ogies can be penetrated; a socialist consciousness can be created.

Broadly speaking, there have been two approaches to radical school reform. The first is content-focused, the second pro-cedure-focused. The first is concerned with curricula content— with exposing myth, nonsense and ideology in school pro-grammes and substituting class analyses and socialist values. For instance, a social science text published in 1972 by the Center for the Study of Instruction in California announces, amid the pictures and glossy pages, that 'economic progress in Venezuela is threatened by communist revolutionaries'. The curricula radicals know they can do better than this. They relate the economy of Venezuela to its class structure, to its long history of imperialist exploitation and to its economy's being currently controlled by multinational corporations. The procedure radicals, or strategy radicals, believe that altering the relations of power and control within schools is the key to altering consciousness. Thus we aim to abolish uniforms; give more power to student councils; break down assessment procedures; do away with the hundred and one little mystifying practices which teachers also are trapped in, and to which they cling. This is the group that says that if Peking University seems to be structured and run exactly the same as Harvard University then something has gone wrong. As with most dichotomies, the correct answer lies somewhere in between. But that is a fairly glib reply. If forced to be characterised on the content/procedure classification, this work lies in the tradition of the former.

CHAPTER 2

PLATO AND THE RATIONALIST TRADITION IN EPISTEMOLOGY AND EDUCATION

With considerable justification, Alfred North Whitehead once described the history of philosophy as a 'series of footnotes to Plato'. This is certainly true in epistemology. Plato's questions, at least (if not, always, his answers), have been returned to again and again. In large measure he pegged out the terrain for subsequent discussion about the nature, origin, scope and limits of human knowledge. He has exercised a similar influence in educational theory and practice. Not only in education, however: his rationalism has cast a long shadow over Western religion—witness St Augustine and John Calvin, both acknowledged admirers of Plato. The Platonic heritage is assuredly something with which we must come to terms. This chapter will isolate various features of his epistemology and begin defining our own epistemology in opposition to these features. Plato's individualism, his foundationalism, his intellectualism and his intuitionism will be rejected. His anti-empiricism—at least inasmuch as he opposes immediacy and obviousness as criteria for knowledge, and the senses alone as the instruments of knowledge creation—will be endorsed. His doctrine of knowledge as recollection will be given a social reinterpretation and the core of it—namely, that knowledge predates the individual—retained. There are attractive features of his educational proposals which can be endorsed. In particular, his stress upon disturbing commonsensical, everyday, immediate impressions and conceptualisations as a prerequisite for knowledge acquisition is well placed. His stress upon understanding as distinct from rote learning, or any behaviourist variant of it, is also well placed. There are unattractive features of his pedagogy which will be outlined.

There is no pretence of doing justice to one of the greatest thinkers of our race. All thought has to be situated in its time, and this cannot be done here.[1] However there is virtue in isolating recurrent motifs, particularly in isolating them at their source. The necessity of an historical sense for understanding is one of the main claims of this work. It is not sufficient, of course. Hitler is just one of many who extolled a sense of history, but who seemed to have benefited little from such a sense.

KNOWLEDGE AS RECOLLECTION

The *Meno* is an early dialogue of Plato's containing the well-known episode of Socrates' eliciting from an ignorant slave boy the understanding of a Pythagorean theorem. The question put to the boy is that of how to double the area of a square garden plot. By deft questioning, and with the active engagement of the boy, Socrates leads him to the recognition that a square on the diagonal of the original will result in doubling the area. The episode is a paradigm for epistemologies based upon the knowing-subject, the individual. It is also a paradigm for the child-centred learning approaches of progressive educationalists. Plato interprets the event of the boy coming to have knowledge, seemingly without it being given to him, in terms of his recollecting something that was once in the mind. This is the doctrine of *Anamnesis*, or recollection. As an account of how we acquire knowledge, anamnesis is untenable. But, instead of dismissing it outright, we can gain from seeing what Plato was getting at, and what led him to the postulation of the doctrine. If we take the group rather than the individual, and objective, external theories rather than private, subjective thoughts as our epistemological focus, then something of epistemological value can be retrieved from the doctrine. Knowledge predates the individual coming to know. Individuals are born into a human society which has built up mastery of certain practical tasks, and a body of varied intellectual achievements. In coming to know, the individual does not recollect, or bring into focus something he or she once knew, but something which has been known in the society. We serve an intellectual and practical apprentice-ship. In the objectivist terms of Karl Popper, there is an existing theory (say classical mechanics) which predates the individual who comes to know it. What is *a priori* for the individual is *a posteriori* for human society.

Crucially for Popper, and for the epistemology of this work, the objective theory—the laws, formulae, suppositions—has itself to be knowledge in order for the individual then to have knowledge. If the theory of classical mechanics or Christian theology or whatever is not in itself knowledge, then in-dividuals believing it cannot be said to be knowledgeable. Individual, subjective knowledge (states of mind and beliefs of people) is parasitic upon objective, external knowledge (theories which exist independently of whether people happen to be currently believing them or not). The important nexus between objective knowledge and subjective knowledge will be elucidated in subsequent sections. The hallmark of empiricism, and indeed of most rationalisms, is that their epistemology is a subject-centred one. It focuses on the beliefs, reasons, convictions of individuals. The 'knower and the known' is the characteristic epistemological couple. Our epistemology rejects this couple.

Anamnesis under any description does not tell us how *new* knowledge is created, and surely any epistemology has to do this. Further, it does not explain how we separate putative knowledge from all the stupidities, superstitions, ignorances, incompetencies which also predate the individual and into which people are systematically introduced—often by courtesy of educational systems.

FOUNDATIONALISM
Later in the *Meno* Plato introduces the distinction between knowledge and true belief, a pivotal distinction for subsequent epistemology. What is the difference between a knowledgeable guide who directs a party on its journey and who leads them safely to their destination and another guide who happens simply to guess the route correctly and achieves the same result? Socrates answers:

True opinions are a fine thing and do all sorts of good so long as they stay in their place; but they will not stay long. They run away from a man's mind, so they are not worth much until you tether them by working out the reason . . . knowledge is something more valuable than right opinion. What distinguishes one from the other is the tether.[2]

The distinction is repeated and argued for in the *Theaetetus*.[3] The tether, or chain of supports, for a belief must be anchored; if not, then the exercise loses its point. This leads Plato to formulate a *foundationalist* account of knowledge. Knowledge implies sure foundations. If we take '*p*' as a proposition expressing a subject's belief, then we can systematise Plato's analysis of what it is for *p* to be knowledge, as:

'*A* knows *p*' ≡ i) *p* is true—Truth condition
　　　　　　　 ii) *A* believes *p*—Belief condition
　　　　　　　iii) *A* has good reasons for believing *p*—
　　　　　　　　　 Evidence condition.

This analysis recurs throughout the history of epistemological theorising; discussion in terms of it has dominated twentieth-century Anglo-Saxon philosophy. We can find the analysis in the work of A. J. Ayer,[4] R. M. Chisholm,[5] D. M. Armstrong,[6] Israel Scheffler,[7] to name just a few. Paul Hirst gives the analysis a complete endorsement. 'In spite of much debate about the precise wording of these conditions, they do seem to me to express the nub of the matter and all that I have to say about knowledge . . . is based on this approach'.[8]

All three conditions of the analysis have been extensively debated and refined. Subject-centred epistemologies have had, of necessity, to address the second. Indeed, when talk about beliefs figure in epistemology we know that we are dealing with a subject-centred, empiricist epistemology. A. J. Ayer, for instance, claims that knowledge requires a subjective state of certainty on the part of the knower. Using standard notation, he claims: Kap → Cap. That is, A knows p implies A is certain about p. Others claim that knowledge is consistent with lack of certainty regarding our beliefs. Here we have: ~(Kap → Cap). That is, it is *not* the case that A knows p implies A has certainty about p. Still other philosophers argue that the belief condition should be abandoned, as knowledge is a state of mind which is, technically, inconsistent with belief states. This because 'belief' implies the possibility of error. These maintain that ~(Kap → Bap). J. L. Austin, in a much anthologised paper, draws a connection between believing and promising and utilises this in his explication of knowledge.[9]

All of these disputes are necessary ones with which a subjectivist (subject-centred) epistemology must engage. On the whole, they are not questions which are generated by an objectivist epistemology; an objectivist epistemology can decline to engage with them. We will maintain an account of knowledge which is independent of subjective wishes, beliefs, mind states, hopes, opinions and the like. Wave theories of light do not have to discuss the mass of light particles. Non-Natural Law theories of ethics can decline to answer the question of whether extra vaginal deposition of semen is unnatural. Questions which arise for one theory need not arise for another. As Lenin once said, 'we discuss whether devils are red or green only if we first believe in devils.'

The third condition of the analysis, the evidence condition, has been the most important and most debated one. It is what generates the issue of *Scepticism*. If the tether cannot be tied securely, then there can be no claims to knowledge. In the *Theaetetus*, Plato recognises the first problem with the condition —namely, that it appears to introduce circularity. If 'A knows p' implies 'A has reason q for p' then, it appears, we have to say that 'A knows q'. Then we have knowledge of p explicated in terms of knowledge of q, and this in turn in terms of knowledge of r. An immediate response has been to search for statements expressing non-inferential knowledge (NIK), which could be used as an anchor for the series. These have been of either an empiricist or a rationalist variety. A. J. Ayer regarded 'I have a red patch before my eyes' as NIK for empiricism. René Descartes regarded 'I think, therefore I am' as NIK for rationalism. The spectre of scepticism begins to loom over the classical analysis of knowledge. It sets out to explicate what is necessary and sufficient for the truth of the sentence '*A* knows *p*', and it ends up saying that '*A* cannot know *p*'. We can see in Bertrand Russell's work the sway that this search for a secure tether has had. For him, physics could not be regarded as validly based upon empirical data until, for example, light waves 'have been expressed as functions of the colours and other sense-data'.[10] D. M. Armstrong, in his *Belief Truth and Knowledge* turns to the simpler judgments of perception and introspection for NIK. The following can be said about the search for secure foundations of knowledge:

(i) Any ostensive foundation will have to be expressible in language, in words and concepts. Thus it will no longer be non-*inferential* knowledge. It will be subject to questions about the adequacy of the language.

(ii) Any observational foundation will be undermined by the theory-dependence-of-observation argument, which will be developed in a subsequent action.

(iii) Because the search cannot in principle be successful, the requirement of finding NIK is equally, in principle, an unnecessary requirement to place on knowledge claims. Things cannot be impugned by virtue of lacking something they cannot possibly possess. A geometrical system is not to be thought deficient by virtue of its failing to square the circle.

(iv) Contrary to Russell's argument, the search has little, if any, bearing on science. Consider commonplace scientific claims such as: 'the kinetic energy of the ball is 25 kilojoules'; 'plastids are the cellular site of starch accumulation'; 'if a body absorbs energy E, its mass increases by E/c_2.' The justification of these claims is important, but they are justified in terms of the theory in which they are embedded. Justification is molecular, not atomic. It will have nothing to do with individuals having red patches before their eyes, or currently believing that they are in pain. The choice is between a foundationalist epistemology which is irrelevant for scientific claims, or an epistemology relevant to science which will be non-foundationalist. The answer is clear.

INDIVIDUALISM

Plato poses the problem of knowledge in individualist terms—what is it for *A* to know *p*? But this is a mistaken formulation. Knowledge necessarily has a social dimension. Karl Mannheim states the matter this way: 'Strictly speaking, it is incorrect to say that the individual thinks. Rather it is more correct to insist that he participates in thinking further what other men have thought before him'.[11] The 'we think' is prior, temporally and epistemologically, to the 'I think'. This is in part what Ludwig Wittgenstein was saying in his arguments against private language. David Hume, John Locke, René Descartes all contributed to this asocial tradition in epistemology. It is a *Robinson Crusoe* model. The individual goes about the world entertaining propositions and asking him or herself whether he or she is possessing knowledge. Marx, in the *1844 Manuscripts*, insists that 'the individual is the social being'.[12] In the Introduction to the *Grundrisse* he writes against the individualist, *Robinson Crusoe* assumptions of Adam Smith and Ricardo in political economy.[13] Those arguments are well heeded in epistemology. Focusing upon the individual, and asking questions as to how he can singlehandedly arrive at, and test, valid ideas and truths, has distracted attention from the social character of knowledge and the necessarily communal criteria of truth. This is a point made by Stephen Toulmin, among others.[14]

ISOMORPHISM

Plato had a tripartite conception of human beings: they consisted of body, mind and soul. The body senses, the mind believes and the soul knows. Plato and Aristotle were rationalists; it was exercise of the faculties of the soul which constituted the highest good. Contemplation was the *Summum Bonum*, or supreme good. Corresponding to this ordering of the components of an individual, there was an ordering of the components of the world. The hierarchy of levels in the individual was isomorphic with the hierarchy of Being. The objects of sense were not the objects of knowledge. They are in constant flux, they come into being and pass away, they have no perfection. The objects of knowledge had to be unchanging. These were the forms or essences which it was the mind's function to grasp in the act of contemplation. The highest form was God, and it was the soul's contemplation of God which was the highest state to which people could aspire.[15] Not everyone, of course, could attain this goal: it was the preserve of the philosophers.

There is a second isomorphism in Plato. This is between the social structure and the structure of Being. Corresponding to the gods were the philosophers, the best of whom became the Philosopher-rulers. Underneath these came the Guardians; then the artisans, workers and farmers; then slaves. The social hierarchy was not a meritocracy. One's place in it was ordained at birth. Plato expressed this in his story of God making some people with gold, other people with silver, others with brass and the rest with base metals. Occasionally some gold was mixed with silver, and some silver with brass. Thus there was slight social mobility. This fable is a paradigm of ideology. It is but one instance of the widespread practice in the ancient world of contingent social circumstances, stratifications and practices being valorised and justified by members of the class of intellectuals whom the social division of labour liberated.[16] For Aristotle, the position of slaves and women was a 'natural' one; it was part of the 'order of things' and hence unalterable. The doctrine of natural place in physics was transferable to a doctrine of natural place in sociology. A feature of ideology is that it is a closed system: it has its answers and merely looks for questions. Kant had free will, God and morality *before* he constructed his *Critiques*, and not surprisingly the *Critiques* made rational conjoined belief in free will, God and morality. The nineteenth-century popular hymn 'All Things Bright And Beautiful' can be seen as a continuation of this Platonic tradition of using the gods to make necessary circumstances which are in fact contingent. We all know the infamous verse:

> The rich man in his castle
> The poor man at his gate
> God made them high and lowly
> And ordered their estate.

The ideology of IQ is a secular version of this. Plato's gold, silver and brass are replaced by Burt's varying amounts of intelligence, which then explain a person's social position.

The Platonic isomorphisms are found in a slightly disguised form in the liberal-rationalist theories of Richard Peters and Paul Hirst. They are explicit in rejecting Platonic metaphysics,[17] but are committed to there being Reason written into the fabric of the world; it is the cultivation of reasoning in accord with

Reason which is constitutive of the educated person. Reason breaks up into seven forms of knowledge (which just happen to be the subject departments of the English Grammar Schools) and the development of one's mind 'involves coming to have experience articulated by means of the various conceptual schema'[18] embodied in each of the forms. Without such a structure in one's mental life, all forms of consciousness become 'unintelligible'.[19] Because knowledge is both intrinsically valuable, and is indeed valued, educators are justified for being the equivalents of Plato's Guardians (with professors, presumably, being the Philosopher-rulers). Authority is justified by virtue of being necessary for the initiation of the children into the seven mansions of Reason.

INTELLECTUALISM

For Plato, what unites people to the natural world—their body and its senses—is a liability for the speculative affairs of the mind. The progressive ascent of the mind, from the transient objects of sense to the intuition of the Forms and the final contemplation of the Good, is *also* the progressive shedding of the hold of the body on the individual. In Book VII of the *Republic*, Plato speaks of cutting the mind free from the 'dead weight of worldliness fastened on to it by sensual indulgence'. The natural world is anarchic and impulsive; the intellect has to free itself from these ravages and bring order to the chaos. The mystical and contemplative traditions in both the East and the West echo this sentiment.

Plato's intellectualism devalued experimentation and discounted practice. The idea of knowing the world by the physical transformation of it, by the use of tools and effort and labour, was as foreign to intellectuals of the ancient world as work is to the modern judge who believed 'manual labour' was the name of a Spanish bullfighter. Plato even upbraids mathematicians who have recourse to diagrams and models. Artisans and labourers are excluded from the company of philosophers; sculptors who expend energy and strain muscles on their creations are regarded as lower artists. Aristotle, in his *Metaphysics*, says that in an ideal State citizens would not lead the life of shopkeepers, mechanics, or even farmers.

Undoubtedly, the dominance of the contemplative stance in ancient Greece was related to it being a slave-owning society, where work was regarded as less than honourable. John Dewey was a tireless critic of the dualism between thought and action enshrined in that tradition. He saw the source of the dualism 'in the division of society into a class labouring with their muscles for material sustenance and a class which, relieved from economic pressure, devotes itself to the arts of expression and social direction'.[20] Marx regarded the social separation of labour in ancient Greece as being responsible for Aristotle's failure, in economics, to grasp human labour as being the source of value. The dichotomy was an obstacle to knowledge. Democritus, Lucretius, Plato and Aristotle all believed ice to be heavier and denser than water. When water froze it was supposed to have contracted. This is wrong, and artisans at the time knew it was wrong. Whilst the philosophers were saying that water contracted, they were leaving expansion chambers in water vessels which were subject to freezing!

ESSENTIALISM

The objects of knowledge were to be things perfect, immutable and unchanging; they were the Forms. For instance, no physical objects have the properties of the objects of Euclidean geometry, yet we talk of knowledge of circles and straight lines. In this world we see only approximations to Justice, yet in ethics we lay claim to knowledge of it. To have knowledge is to grasp the essence of things, an essence which is something other than, and lies behind, the world of appearances.

Plato holds an anti-empiricist position in the *Theaetetus*: he argues against the proposition that knowledge is nothing but perception. There, many of the well-known arguments of later philosophers against empiricism can be found—the subjectivity of perceptions; the fluidity of the objects of perceptions; perceptual illusions. Plato poses the rhetorical question: 'Is it more correct to say that we see and hear *with* our eyes and ears or *through* them?'[21] He would agree with the anti-empiricism of Norwood Russell Hanson, who held that 'There is more to seeing than meets the eyeball'.[22]

Plato's anti-empiricism is correct, but his essentialism is incorrect. The search for essences is mistaken, despite having exercised a mesmeric effect on philosophers. Searching for the essence of human beings, trying to ascertain what human nature is, has been the most persistent essentialist quest. Marx, in his *Theses on Feuerbach*, says of this that 'the human essence is no abstraction, inherent in each single individual. In its reality it is the ensemble of the social relations'.[23] There is no essence of the State, of women, of blacks, of burning bodies. Things, processes and institutions have properties and characteristics by virtue of the network of relations and causal processes in which they are enmeshed. The expectation is that these will alter with history. Essentialism is a close relation of ideology: those who search for essences usually find ideologies. Thus some maintain that it is of the essence of women that they be in the home and devote themselves to their husbands. Others maintain that particular races are in essence dumb or that schools are in essence vehicles for knowledge transmission. It is essentialism to think that science is characterised by some unique feature which is invariant over time and place. Paulo Freire writes against the essentialism of those who attribute the poverty of Latin American countries to the peasants' being in essence lazy. These social circumstances are not a product of any eternal essences which manifest themselves in the social world. They are, rather, the consequence of contingent, economic circumstances: imperialist and neo-imperialist domination. Jean-Paul Sartre's claim that 'existence precedes essence' is in pointed contrast to the metaphysics of Plato and Aristotle. For Sartre there are no eternal, fixed essences which predate their embodiment in material existence, and which determine the form or properties of those material bodies. For Sartre there is no essence of a person which is fixed at birth and which subsequently determines their behaviour. A person's 'essence' is the product of their choices through life.

The rejection of essentialism was a prerequisite for the Scientific Revolution. Robert Boyle, in chemistry, proposed a non-essentialist account of chemical, compounds and reactions.[24] There was no essence of salt which was responsible for the properties of salt, because salt could be artificially produced from two very un-salt-like liquids. Essences were to be unchanging things. Thus in the language of essences, once we have an acid essence and a base essence, there is simply no room for a salt essence. The essence chemistry of Aristotelianism is therefore inconsistent with the artificial production of salt from the reaction of an acid and a base. Likewise he argued against explaining the sourness of lemons in terms of the essence of the lemon tree. He did this by grafting on to a lemon tree the branch of a pear tree. The grafted branch bore sweet fruit. Instead of essences (or substances, as they were for Boyle) being responsible for manifest appearances, he proposed to account for appearances in terms of the rearrangement of the fundamental corpuscles of nature.

Galileo's achievement was, in part, to break with the essen-

the goal of education. Understanding was sought, not merely correct answers. There is a commendable anti-behaviourism in Plato. Knowledgeable guides were wanted, not just guides who could get to the destination. Plato's account of what it is to understand and explain can be rejected without impugning understanding as a desirable goal. Plato would reject the teaching of, for instance, the mineral compositions of granite and basalt as separate entities without the intention or attempt to give an account of why there are differences and why there are similarities. For us this would be done in terms of Bowen's Reaction Series for the order of crystallisation of minerals from a magma. It will not be done in terms of the essences of granite and basalt. We do want children to understand wars in terms of underlying political and economic realities. Richard Peters echoes this concern in his talk about the educated person 'understanding the reason why of things'.

Unattractive Aspects

Plato is a creature of his own circumstances; his educational theory bears the imprint of its material and intellectual origins. Plato posits, but he himself is posited. He transcended his circumstances in many respects—he argued for the education of women; despite his intellectualism he argued for gymnastics and play as curriculum components. But he also cemented and justified his circumstances. We expect this mixture of transcendence and immanence in any thought system. Some of the negative features of the Platonic system which have had an enduring history are:

(i) *Salvationism*. An entrenched human fallacy is 'educational salvationism'. This is the hope and commitment that the proper education of individuals is the solution to the personal and social problems and evils which have plagued human society through its history. Plato, in his *Laws*, says that if the young generation is, and continues to be, well brought up, then the ship of state will have a fair voyage. If this is not the case, then he says that the 'consequences are better left unspoken'. Dewey echoes Plato when he says that 'sin is ignorance and knowledge is salvation'. This notion of salvation through education is endemic in the liberal-rationalist tradition. It puts out of focus the objective clash of interests which arises from structural features of our social relations. Capitalists must continue to expropriate surplus value or they cease to be capitalists. They are objectively locked into a deadly battle with Labour over the proportion they expropriate. Capitalism needs to locate raw materials for production, and it needs to find or create markets for its products. These are requirements of the system; they are utterly independent of wishes of individual operatives. Dewey says at one stage that what stands in the way of a planned economy in the United States is 'a lot of outworn traditions, moth-eaten slogans and catchwords that do substitute duty for thought'.[32] The explicit implication is that the overthrow of capitalism and the substitution of socialism is a matter of education. This is rampant idealism. As an astute theological critic of Dewey wrote, these educators and moralists 'do not recognise that when collective power, whether in the form of imperialism or class domination, exploits weakness, it can never be dislodged unless power is raised against it. If conscience and reason can be insinuated into the resulting struggle, they can only qualify, but not abolish it'.[33] Education has some part to play. In the first instance, it is a weapon in the struggle; it enables ends to be pursued more intelligently and attacks to be deflected more efficiently. The *Collected Works* of Lenin fill whole shelves. As Marx wrote, ideas can become a material force when they grip the masses. It is the notion of Reason as the arbiter between entrenched interests which has to be rejected.

(ii) *Closedness*. Insight epistemologies such as Plato's give rise to a lack of openness about intellectual appropriation of the world. To have insight is to have something which is not open to revision, particularly when the object of insight is some eternal, fixed and unchanging essence. Plato, of course, allows a dialectical series of approximations to the goal of insight, but once there, it is not revisable. This is a short way from dogmatism and authoritarianism. Those who have been up the mountain and have had insight can feel justified in legislating for the spread of their insight. It is frightening to contemplate all the nonsense taught to students under threat of failure, detention and punishment. To say that there are good and bad theories is not to say that there is some best and inviolable theory. Insight epistemology and its educational corollaries need to be replaced by a fallibilist epistemology and educational modesty.

CONCLUSION

Education has something to do with knowledge; thus education is going, explicitly or implicitly, to have something to do with a theory of knowledge, with epistemology. The nexus is very clear in Plato. The individualism, foundationalism, essentialism, intellectualism and ahistoricism of his epistemology are all things which have exercised a lasting influence. These are all features which any adequate epistemology needs to reject. In educational practice and theory Plato has cast a long shadow. Indeed, Richard Peters, in his Introduction to Paul Hirst's book *Knowledge and the Curriculum*[34] says that Hirst is the first curriculum theorist since Plato to make any significant contribution to the subject. Plato's educational theory has a number of strengths: in particular its anti-empiricism, its stress on understanding and its recognition of the need for students to be actively involved in the learning process. There are some enduring weaknesses in the theory. The stress on insight leads to a closure and absolutism about intellectual endeavour. This is to be avoided in favour of openness and fallibilism. Nowhere does Plato provide criteria for assessing *rival* claims to insight. In psychotherapy this is a common problem. Insight for a Freudian is different from insight for a Jungian, a Sullivanian, a Horneyite and many others. Who has insight and who has outsight? The argument of this book will be that insight is a matter of the adequacy of theories. The ascertaining of such adequacy is a matter of the appraisal of rival theories. In the following chapter, empiricism will be introduced. This is a rival of Platonic rationalism for influence in epistemology, and in educational theory and practice.

NOTES

1. See some standard commentaries such as A. E. Taylor, *Plato*, London, Methuen, 1926; I. M. Crombie, *An Examination of Plato's Doctrines*, London, Routledge & Kegan Paul, 1962.
2. The *Meno*, W. Guthrie (trans.), Harmondsworth, Penguin, 1956, p. 154.
3. *Plato's Theory of Knowledge*, F. M. Cornford (trans.), London, Routledge & Kegan Paul, 1935, pp. 141 ff.
4. *The Problem of Knowledge*, London, Macmillan, 1956.
5. *Perceiving: A Philosophical Study*, Ithaca, Cornell University Press, 1957.
6. *Belief Truth and Knowledge*, London, Cambridge University Press, 1973.
7. *Conditions of Knowledge*, New York, Scott, Foresman, 1965.
8. 'Human Movement, Knowledge and Education', *Journal of Philosophy of Education*, 13, 1979.
9. 'Other Minds' in A. G. N. Flew (ed.), *Logic and Language*, Vol. 2, Oxford, Blackwell, 1959.
10. *Mysticism and Logic*, London, George Allen & Unwin, 1963, p. 109.
11. *Ideology and Utopia*, London, Routledge & Kegan Paul, 1960, p. 3.
12. *The Economic and Philosophic Manuscripts of 1844*, Dirk Struik (ed.), New York, International Publishers, 1964, p. 137.
13. The *Grundrisse*, Martin Nicolaus (trans.), Harmondsworth, Penguin, 1973, p. 83.

14. *Human Understanding*, Oxford, Clarendon, 1972, p. 37.
15. In the *Nicomachean Ethics* Aristotle puts the classical view succinctly: 'Contemplation is the highest form of activity, since the intellect is the highest thing in us and the objects that come within its range are the highest that can be known' (Bk. X, Ch. 7).
16. See Henri Frankfort *et al. Before Philosophy*, Harmondsworth, Penguin, 1949.
17. Paul H. Hirst, 'Liberal Education and the Nature of Knowledge', in R. F. Dearden *et al.* (eds.) *Education and the Development of Reason*, London, Routledge & Kegan Paul, 1972. Pt. III, pp. 1 ff.
18. *ibid.* p. 12.
19. *ibid.* p. 11.
20. *Democracy and Education*, New York, Free Press, 1966, p. 336.
21. *Plato's Theory of Knowledge*, p. 103.
22. *Patterns of Discovery*, Cambridge, University Press, 1958, p. 7.
23. K. Marx and F. Engels, *Selected Works*, Moscow, Progress Publishers, 1969, Vol. I, p. 14.
24. See R. Harré, *Matter and Method*, London, Macmillan, 1964, pp. 79 ff.
25. See S. Gaukroger, *Explanatory Structures*, Hassocks, Harvester Press, 1978.
26. *Democracy and Education*, Ch. 24.
27. See R. C. Lodge, *Plato's Theory of Education*, London, Kegan Paul, 1947.
28. *The Republic*, H. D. P. Lee (trans.), Harmondsworth, Penguin, 1955, Pt. VII; Sect. 7.
29. The *Meno*, p. 135.
30. G. Ryle, *Dilemmas*, Cambridge, University Press, 1969, Ch. V, 'The World of Science and the Everyday World'. See also D. C. Bloor, 'Are Philosophers Averse to Science?' in D. O. Edge and J. N. Wolfe (eds.) *Meaning and Control*, London, Tavistock, 1973.
31. *ibid.* p. 71.
32. *Philosophy and Civilization*, New York, Minton, Balch, 1931, p. 329, Quoted in Reinhold Niebuhr, *Moral Man and Immoral Society*, New York, Scribners, 1932, p. xiii.
33. *ibid.* p. xii.
34. *Knowledge and the Curriculum*, London, Routledge & Kegan Paul, 1974.

CHAPTER 3

DAVID HUME AND THE EMPIRICIST TRADITION IN EDUCATION

Empiricism is a towering, many-headed giant whose influence on education, culture, science, morals, religion and philosophy has been profound. Intellectual systems are best understood at their source. Unlike rivers, they are not necessarily clearest at source, but there we can see the influences which give rise to and sustain them. British empiricism is distilled in the epistemology of David Hume. His crucial impressions/ideas distinction, or 'microscope' as he referred to it, has been used by empiricist and positivist philosophers with traumatising effect on theological, ethical and psychological discourses, to name just a few. British empiricism arises out of the Scientific Revolution. The work of Francis Bacon, John Locke and David Hume has to be interpreted in relation to the massive upheavals in the science of their time. The failure to do this has been widespread in philosophical commentaries. The fathers of empiricism set out to defend the new science with which they were so enthralled. Tragically, however, they misunderstood the role played by experience in this new science. The epistemology they created for science is the death of science. The case of Galileo is illustrative of this claim. Their project of making epistemology face up to scientific practice is, of course, commendable; there can be no good epistemology without attention to science. They got the methodology of science wrong; with hindsight, however, epistemologists can now do better. Empiricist epistemology has had an influence on educational theory and practice. 'Learning by experience' is just one of a host of empiricist slogans going the rounds among educators. In philosophy of education, empiricism has taken a more sophisticated form. Israel Scheffler and Paul Hirst are both committed to forms of empiricism. This commitment is in need of drastic revision. John Locke's *tabula rasa* theory of mind has guided numerous pedagogues concerned with the development of mind. In its most vulgar form, it issues forth in variants of the 'Banking' concept of education.

DAVID HUME

Hume was a child of the Scientific Revolution. He was born in 1711, only 70 years after Galileo's death; he was for a short time a contemporary of Newton. He was an enthusiast of the New World View. His justly famous and epochal *A Treatise of Human Nature* (1738) is subtitled: 'Being an attempt to introduce the experimental method of reasoning into moral subjects'. Of course, he did not begin his philosophical articulation of empiricism *de novo*. Francis Bacon, a contemporary of Galileo, had written his *Advancement of Learning* in 1606 and his *Novum Organum* (the New Method) in 1620. John Locke, the contemporary of Newton and self-styled 'underlabourer' in his garden (who was also a friend of the chemist Robert Boyle), had written his *Essay Concerning Human Understanding* in 1690. Hume made history, but he did not make it as he pleased, he made it 'under circumstances directly encountered, given and transmitted from the past'. There have been two great mistakes in the history of empiricist philosophy. The first was the inadequate grasp that the original empiricists had on the new science whose success exercised such a mesmeric effect on them. The second has been the subsequent elaboration of and commentary upon this empiricism where it is removed from its foundations in scientific methodology. Bacon, Locke and Hume are wrongly treated as philosophers of timeless, universal experience. I hope some of this traditional distortion can be corrected here; or rather, as space is limited, that enough might be indicated to bring into focus the main contours and encourage subsequent independent elaboration.

Hume, Berkeley and Locke all saw experience as the key element in the success of the marvellous science around them. Locke put this view forward together with his much celebrated *tabula rasa* account of the human mind:

Let us then suppose the mind to be, as we say, white paper, void of all characters, without any ideas; how comes it to be furnished? Whence comes it by that vast store, which the busy and boundless fancy of man has painted on it with an almost endless variety? When has it all the materials of reasons and knowledge? To this I answer, in one word, from Experience; in that all our knowledge is founded, and from that it ultimately derives itself. Our observation . . . supplies our understandings with all the materials of thinking.[1]

Knowledge is a picture etched in the mind by sensory inputs. There are no innate ideas, and the mind itself lacks capacities and powers of its own. Hume adopts and extends this conception. He divides the content of the mind into two classes— impressions and ideas: 'The former include all our sensations, passions and emotions as they make their first appearance in the soul. By "ideas" I mean faint images of these in thinking and reasoning'.[2] This is the crucial distinction between experience and our thoughts about experience; between sensations and ideas. It grows into the observation term and theoretical term distinction so pivotal for twentieth-century empiricism. Hume utilises the distinction for his theory of meaning. He likens it to the 'microscope' of the natural scientist. He uses the microscope to examine human intellectual products for sense or nonsense: 'When we entertain, therefore, any suspicion that a philosophical term is employed without any meaning or ideas (as it is but too frequently), we need but enquire, from what impression is that supposed idea derived? And if it be impossible to assign any, this will serve to confirm our suspicion'.[3] Hume's microscope has been handed down from generation to generation of empiricists and revered as a sacred instrument, indeed almost a holy relic. The Vienna Circle positivists made great use of it in their demarcation of science from non-science. Bertrand Russell and A. J. Ayer utilised it in their campaigns to discredit religious, moral and aesthetic statements as all meaningless. The only trouble with the weapon is that it cuts off the hand that feeds it: it is supposedly inspired by science, but its use destroys science.

Hume is justly famous for his doctrine of causality, which follows from the application of his microscope to causal relations. The doctrine has reverberated through subsequent centuries. He eliminates power or necessary connection from the notion of causality. When causal occurrences are observed, try as we might, we never observe the necessary connection between cause and effect. He regards 'efficacy', 'agency', 'power', 'force', 'energy', 'necessity', 'connection' and 'productive quality' as nearly all synonymous, and all ideas without foundation in impressions, and thus meaningless.[4] On the whole, 'necessity is something which exists in the mind, not in objects'.[5] Causality is reduced to relationships where objects are geographically and temporally contiguous and constantly conjoined. Philosophers have dined very well off this Humean offering. Or—to change analogies between courses—they have taken each other's washing on the subject in and out with alarming persistence. In some ways rightly so, as an understanding of causation is vital to science and philosophy, and it does not come easily. One should, however, be suspicious of the terms of reference of the debate.

We can already appreciate that there are problems looming here. What becomes of Galileo's 'frictionless surfaces', his 'bodies falling in vacuums', his 'weightless strings' and his 'point masses'? All of these end up as the equivalent of religious fictions, and their utilisation in science is banned. But there is much worse to follow. Some, F. C. Copleston for example, interpret Hume in a lenient way as saying there might be forces and powers and necessary connections in the real world but, unfortunately, we are never able to see them.[6] This is a mistaken reading. A. J. Ayer is correct when he says that there can be no such relation for Hume, because causes and effects are distinct events: 'If two events are distinct they are distinct'.[7] But if events are isolated, discrete and distinct there can be no continuity or identity of properties or qualities across changes; nor even continuity of qualities for unchanging objects.[8] What disastrous results this has for Newtonian experimental science! Bodies do possess momentum and energy; these are transferred and changed during interactions. For Newton, bodies have real quantities—mass, momentum, energy; it is these which are operative, and efficacious, in their motions and interactions. His laws state that bodies continue at rest or in constant motion unless acted upon by a force; the change in momentum of a body is proportional to the force applied. For Hume, when a moving billiard ball collides with a stationary one, the momentum of the first must be totally destroyed and the new momentum of the second created 'ex nihilo'—the loss of the first and creation of the second having nothing to do with each other. This is very odd. Indeed, his microscope denies us talk of momentum and force because we see only moving bodies. The general epistemology espoused is not only inconsistent with Newton's scientific achievement, but also, crucially, with Newton's methodology. Newton, dealt, as did Galileo, with simplified, abstracted models. His law of planetary motion was formulated on the basis of initially having a solar system consisting of the sun and one planet considered as point masses. Gradually, on the basis of theoretical, not observational, clashes, he complicated the model and worked out painfully the corresponding mathematics.

The early empiricist Francis Bacon opposed the Copernican hypothesis because he thought it contradicted the evidence of the senses. Locke and Hume were unknowingly inconsistent with Newton's science. The early twentieth-century empiricist Ernst Mach opposed Bohr's atomic theory, saying that atoms were unobservable fictions. Subsequent empiricists have been forced into an instrumentalism which puts a strait-jacket on science and precludes the development of concepts (Kelvin's absolute zero cannot be instrumentalised). They understood themselves as defenders of science. We have been intimating that if science has friends like these it doesn't need enemies. More generally, and less flippantly (hard-headed empiricism is on occasions more beneficial than fuzzy-headed idealism or entrenched obscurantism), we see, with Hume, two things:

(i) The fact that theories of knowledge are worked out in conjunction with, and under the influence of, interpretations of good science.

(ii) Where there prove to be clashes between epistemology and science, one has to alter. It is a safe bet to assume that the former should. 'Forces', 'fields' and 'energy' might be proscribed by an epistemology, but if they are required by science, then so be it.

Now these are not simple, cut-and-dried matters. The history of epistemology is characterised by lost, irrelevant theories wandering around in a fog altogether removed from science (much current analytic epistemology).[9] But it is also characterised by the corpses of epistemologies which tried to relate to science but misunderstood it (empiricism) or else related to a science which was subsequently overthrown (Kantianism). Our advice is to try to be relevant, even though this poses dangers, rather than be comfortably irrelevant and pass the days hiccuping about ordinary language and the grounds for believing that the Senior Common Room still exists. Karl Popper has put the matter clearly: 'The central problem of epistemology has always been and still is the problem of the growth of knowledge. *And the growth of knowledge can be studied best by studying the growth of scientific knowledge*'.[10]

GALILEO AND EMPIRICISM

Galileo is often pictured as the champion of sensory evidence against the blind and dogmatic Aristotelians, who were upholding the geocentric theory in astronomy. This is a false picture on both sides. Aristotle was committed to sensory evidence being the cornerstone of knowledge. He says that men who love knowledge delight in their senses, particularly their eyes.[11] He was a careful and untiring observer of social and natural events and a meticulous cataloguer of the natural world. Many of his taxonomical works are still the standard authority (a delicate part of the sea-urchin's digestive system is called 'Aristotle's

Lantern'). Any impediment to, dilution of or interference with the senses was regarded as compromising one's ability to know. Aristotle had an inductive-deductive scientific methodology. He induced general principles from particular sensory evidences and then made deductions from these to extended fields.

The medieval Aristotelians were, on the whole, faithful up-holders of Aristotle's advice. Some, as might be expected, short-circuited experiences. When they wanted to know of a particular matter they went to the table of contents of Aristotle's works. This is no different from current standard practice much in-stilled and authorised by the school system. The best of them were faithful followers of Aristotle. When Galileo asserted that the earth revolved around the sun and that, further, it spun on its axis, they appealed to sensory evidence to refute him. Why, they said, don't we fall off the earth? Why don't we feel always a strong wind from the east? Why can birds hover effortlessly above the same place for long stretches of time when they should be flapping furiously just to keep up? In the famous Tower Argument of Galileo the Aristotelian Simplicio asks: If the earth is spinning, why do objects dropped from towers fall straight to the ground below and not fall a great distance from the base? Galileo replies that they do in reality fall slantingly, but we do not see this, to which Simplicio replies: 'This is a bald denial of manifest sense; and if the senses ought not to be believed, by what other portal shall we enter into philos-ophising?'[12] Even the cardinal's dramatic decision not to look through the telescope was guided as much by the principle that it interfered with naked vision as by the principle of pigheaded-ness, which is the normal reason provided.

Many of Galileo's most famous demonstrations and dis-coveries were the result of 'thought experiments'. He had recourse to idealisations which could not be observed by the senses. Consider, for instance, his law of inertia—the law which says that moving bodies need not be subject to impressed forces. Aristotle held that all moving objects required a mover. This was a law based soundly on everyday experience. We, for the most part, never experience motion which is not maintained by applied forces; and our experience tells us that whenever the force is removed the motion will eventually cease. How then did Galileo establish his law against 'manifest sense'? He invited his listeners to consider a carriage being pushed along, and then the force removed from it. On a rough road it would not continue very far; on a marble floor it would continue much further; with greased axles even further; in the ideal limit situation, where all friction is removed, it would continue forever. But the idealised and abstracted situation could never be experienced; in the world there are no frictionless surfaces. Again, consider his law of free fall. This was vindicated by the movement of pendulums, such pendulums being considered as point masses and their strings being regarded as weightless; little wonder that Galileo was such an affront to the contemporary hard-headed scientists demanding sensory evidence.

Galileo was in many respects a Platonist. He shared the Platonic conviction that the sensory world was messy, confused, complicated. What we are given in experience is chaotic and opaque. Science has to go beyond this in order to discover the intelligibility which is there. Thus the idealisations and abstractions. Alexander Koyré has argued cogently for the need to recognise the Platonic dimension of Galileo's achievement. He says, against common accounts, that 'observation and experience, in the sense of brute, commonsense experience, did not play a major role—or if it did, it was a negative one, the role of obstacle—in the foundation of modern science.'[13] What lay behind these experimental procedures was a conviction on Galileo's part that the world was mathematical. In his *Il Saggiatore* he refers to Nature being an open book whose text is in mathematical symbols, and says that to understand Nature we have to read mathematics. This is a very Pythagorean and Platonic commitment. It enabled him to discount irrelevancies and the failure of experiments to match theoretical predictions.

In passing it is worth noting that the theory of society contained in Marx's *Capital* needs to be interpreted in the same way as the theory of mechanics in Galileo's *Dialogues*. Marx does not provide an empirical description of any particular society's economic structures and functionings; his is rather an abstracted, idealised, theoretical model which relates to the actual world only when certain stated assumptions are met. It establishes tendencies or potentials, whose actualisation is a contingent matter. To be scientific, the assumptions have to be stated as clearly as possible; to be of practical interest they have to be occasionally met or approximated to in the real world. In these respects Galileo and Marx are both scientific and practical. As the former said: 'our theorising has to relate to the world of facts not of words'.

Galileo's achievement was threefold:

(i) He quantified and mathematised physics. He introduced systematic measurements into science and utilised Euclidean geometry for the statement, development and interpretation of physical problems. Physical balls were treated as points; rods as lines; gross contacts as discrete angles. This was an abrupt break with Aristotelianism, for whom the science of mathematics was in one domain and the science of physics in another, and never the two were to meet. (Compare our own subject divisions, or P. H. Hirst's famous discrete Forms of Knowledge.)

(ii) He replaced simple sensory observation with controlled experimentation—both actual and idealised. Importantly, instrumentation was conceived as not just ancillary to the senses. Its function was to isolate and specify particular mechanisms in the world which were being investigated. Nature was tortured, not just observed. The reality dealt with by Galileo was not the reality of everyday gross experience; it was a manipulated, contrived, artificial reality. This was an important and vital prerequisite for the mathematisation of physical problems.[14]

(iii) He made it clear that sensory experience was already interpreted in implicit and explicit ways. Like Plato, he understood that we see *through* our eyes, not *with* our eyes; that there is more to seeing than meets the eyeball. Copernicus had posited the revolutionary claim that what we 'see' as the movement of the planets is a function of two movements, their movement and our own movement. Galileo endorsed Copernicus' claim and generalised it. He was constantly trying to unearth the assumptions and theoretical commitments underlying and generating the perceptions of his adversaries. The everyday, immediate perceptions are called 'natural interpretations'. These are the subject of all manner and means of scientific, ideological, social, political presuppositions. To bring these into focus and scrutinise them is in part the business of science. We shall argue also that, across the board, it is the business of education. Analytic philosophers who make science and common sense incommensurable are supporters of continuing social ignorance.

There is, of course, an enormous literature on Galileo and the Scientific Revolution.[15] In the mid-'60s there were over 6,000 titles in the *Bibliografia Galileiana*. Paul Feyerabend has written extensively on him as the basis for his attack on empiricism in philosophy of science.[16] This has generated hundreds of scholarly endeavours in rebuttal and support. The treatment here has no claim to originality or completeness; it is meant only to situate the epistemological contribution of British Empiricism, and to say enough to support the claim that its founding fathers did not adequately grasp or conceptualise what was going on in the Scientific Revolution.

EMPIRICISM, KNOWLEDGE AND EDUCATION

There have been consequences drawn from empiricist accounts of knowledge in the fields of both educational practice and educational philosophy. I hope that enough has been said to stimulate caution prior to enthusiastic endorsement of them.

In the *Republic*, Plato had said that we must reject the conception of education professed by those who say that they can put into the mind knowledge that was not there before. This is the antithesis of Locke's *tabula rasa*, which must receive all its knowledge from external sources. For hardline empiricism, the mind is empty and inert. It lends itself easily to a 'Banking' concept of education, where the teacher makes all the deposits, preferably in discrete, predigested, marshalled and organised form. Locke, in his own educational writings, advises teachers to begin 'with that which lies most obvious to the senses'. A constant refrain is: 'Begin with that which is plain and simple' and 'give them first one simple idea'. He endorses the Baconian inductivist view of the growth of knowledge and believes it ought to be replicated in the growth of the individual's knowledge. In Nature, movement and growth occur in slow steps from one place to the adjoining place and so it is in the mind, from the knowledge it stands possessed of already, to that which lies next and is coherent to it. The clearest possible statement of empiricism's most basic general regulative principle in regard to the development of children comes from Locke's own pen; children are 'as white paper or wax to be moulded and fashioned as one pleases'.[17] This finds contemporary expression in many variants of behaviourism. Skinner's reinforcement programmes for creating the beliefs, attitudes and behaviour patterns of people are a striking example. Other examples are the predigested programmed learning kits which constitute a multi-million dollar industry. In his time Locke was, it seems, an educational progressive. I do not wish to make anachronistic judgments about him. When schooling was largely rote Latin and Greek learning, he was advocating play, freedom, creativity. There are also some unexceptionable features in his advocacy of considered and piecemeal learning: we learn to walk before we can run. In general terms, however, the educational consequences are pernicious. The theory grossly underestimates self-directed learning and it fails to recognise the importance of practical involvement and participation in the learning process. It also overestimates the freedom of the teacher. Teachers who might aspire to fashion children are themselves fashioned. Marx puts the matter deftly in his third thesis on Feuerbach: 'The

materialist doctrine that men are products of circumstances and
upbringing, and that, therefore, changed men are products of
other circumstances and changed upbringing, forgets that it is
men that change circumstances and that the educator himself
needs educating'.[18]

A major oversight of this classical empiricism is that, by
stressing experience and sensation as the basis and building
blocks of knowledge, it neglects the fact that experience is con-
ceptualised in language. We are a part of a human community
which has a particular language, and our simplest and earliest
experiences are mediated and enveloped in this. We do not just
accumulate a vast array of impressions or sense data (as Russell,
Ayer and others termed primitive experiences). Rather it is an
interconnected and processed set of formalised or described
experiences, expectations, evaluations. We do not just begin
experiencing something yellowish, soft and moderately fibrous,
but rather 'food' and 'bananas' and 'good for you' and 'daddy
cares for you' and 'be a person whom mummy loves' and 'we
might have them tomorrow' and 'don't rub them in the carpet'
and 'they cost money'. Eventually, even the direct component
fades out, and our experiences are of reading and listening and
talking. We gradually become language users, and thus partake
in a society where there are knowledges and ignorances and all
things in between.

The foregoing considerations affect how we understand and
appraise such practical recommendations of empiricism as
'children should learn from experience' and such varied sophisticated forms of it as we have in 'discovery learning' programmes and the Collingwood-inspired *Verstehen* approaches to
history and literature. According to the latter, we understand
past situations by trying to place ourselves as closely as possible
in the way of the experiences people in the past or other cultures
have had. If we replicate their situation, then we will have their
experiences, and thus their feelings and views. In brief, this is
all too simple if the intention is to *understand* the circumstance.
This understanding depends on the development of theory.

EMPIRICISM AND PHILOSOPHERS OF EDUCATION

The foregoing considerations also affect how we understand
and appraise some influential assertions in the philosophy of
education. The two most important philosophers dealing with
epistemology and education are Israel Scheffler in America and
Paul Hirst in England. Both present empiricist accounts of

knowledge, though in modified form. Scheffler, in a much anthologised paper, 'Philosophical Models of Teaching', discusses empiricism, saying: 'It sets forth the appeal to experience as a general tool of criticism to be employed in the examination of all claims and doctrines, and it demands that they square with it. Surely such a demand is legitimate, for knowledge does rest upon experience in some way or other'.[19] Hirst, in his famous 'Liberal Education and the Nature of Knowledge' (1965), which has become the *locus classicus* of mainstream philosophy of education, writes that 'the major forms of knowledge, or disciplines, can each be distinguished by their dependence on some particular kind of test against experience for their distinctive expressions'. He particularly notes that the sciences 'depend crucially on empirical, experimental and observational tests'.[20] To be fair, he does subsequently modify this somewhat, substituting 'publicly testable' for 'experience'. Our point here is only to show that the classical empiricism of Locke and Hume has cast a long and influential shadow over both educational practice and educational philosophy; further, it has had unfortunate consequences. To situate and evaluate the major contributions of Scheffler and Hirst adequately, we must once again point to philosophy of science as the place where an understanding of the role of experience in knowledge claims can be explicated. To say that knowledge is based on experience is like saying we ought to pursue the good life; no one really disagrees. The interesting and fruitful discussion should be about the constituents of the good life. Similarly when one says that knowledge is based on experience—in a simple sense everyone agrees: the controversial questions are what in fact experience is, and how knowledge is based upon it. I shall now turn to some key issues in philosophy of science in search of what I hope will be interesting and fruitful discussion.

NOTES

1. John Locke, *Essay Concerning Human Understanding*, London, Dent & Sons, 1961. Bk. II, Ch. 1, Sect. 2.
2. *A Treatise of Human Nature*, L. A. Selby-Bigge (ed.) Oxford, Clarendon Press, 1888, p. 1.
3. *Enquiries Into Human Nature*, L. A. Selby-Bigge (ed.) Oxford, Clarendon Press, 1888, p. 22.
4. *Treatise*, p. 157.
5. *ibid.* p. 165.
6. *History of Philosophy*, New York, Doubleday, 1964. Vol. V, Pt. II, p. 92.

7. *The Concept of a Person*, London, Macmillan, 1963, p. 214.
8. We assume a great deal of Humean exegesis here. He does appear to argue from the discreteness of sensations to the discreteness of the world. He often conflates sensations with what they are sensations of. In the end he does hold an atomistic, discontinuous, fragmented acccount of the world. These are arguable interpretations. See J. Aronson, 'The Legacy of Hume's Analysis of Causation', *Studies in the History and Philosophy of Science*, 2, 1971.
9. Consider, for instance, an anthology of contemporary articles on epistemology which is widely used as a text in English universities. This is A. Phillips Griffith's *Knowledge and Belief* (Oxford, University Press, 1967). There are *no* articles on philosophy of science; in its list of 70-odd references there is no mention of Popper, Quine, Kuhn, Feyerabend, Hempel. The whole discussion is conducted in empiricist and ordinary language terms. There are articles on 'saying' and notes on 'believing and promising' and rejoinders to articles on 'knowledge and disbelief'. The knowing subject is not only at the centre, but occupies the entire epistemological stage. One commentator has pointed out that for the analyst P. Strawson, the essence of creative thought in the sciences is a paradigm of philosophical confusion. In such clashes, our money is with creative scientific thought.
10. *The Logic of Scientific Discovery*, London, Hutchinson, 1972, p. 15. His italics.
11. *Metaphysics*, Richard Hope (trans.), Ann Arbor, University of Michigan Press, 1968, p. 3.
12. *Dialogue Concerning the Two Chief World Systems*, Stillman Drake (trans.), Berkeley, University of California Press, 1962, p. 171.
13. *Metaphysics and Measurement*, Cambridge, Harvard University Press, 1968, p. 18.
14. On these matters see Stephen Gaukroger, *Explanatory Structures*, Hassocks, Harvester Press, 1978. For an account of scientific experimentation which clarifies what Galileo was doing, see Roy Bhaskar, *A Realist Theory of Science*, Hassocks, Harvester Press, 1978.
15. See E. McMullin (ed.) *Galileo: Man of Science*, New York, Basic Books, 1967.
16. *Against Method*, London, New Left Books, 1975.
17. In his *Some Thoughts Concerning Education*. This and other excerpts are from S. S. Curtis and M. E. A. Boultwood, *A Short History of Educational Ideas*, London, University Tutorial Press, 1953, Ch. 10.
18. K. Marx and F. Engels, *Selected Works*, Moscow, Progress Publishers, 1969. Vol. I, p. 13.
19. R. S. Peters (ed.) *The Concept of Education*, London, Routledge & Kegan Paul, 1967, p. 122.
20. R. F. Dearden *et al.* (eds.) *Education and the Development of Reason*, London, Routledge & Kegan Paul, 1972. Pt. III, p. 16.

CHAPTER 4

EDUCATION AND RATIONALITY: INDUCTIVISM AND FALSIFICATIONISM

There are many aims proposed for education. One of the most persistent is that it should produce people who are reasonable and rational in their thinking. This in turn is often interpreted as having one's thoughts swayed or determined by the evidence. To be reasonable is to believe what there is evidence for; to be unreasonable is to believe what there is no evidence for. It is anticipated that these qualities should be manifested in all the scientific, social, moral, political, historical and religious domains of our lives. This view requires that for each of the domains the evidence, or at least some significant sample of it, should be available to the student. This is what curricula content decisions are about. There are internal educational debates over liberal versus vocational education; and breadth versus selective depth in dividing up and organising the fields of knowledge into which schools induct pupils. But whether physics, Latin, geography, history, biology are all taught, or only a selection of them are taught, the educational aim remains the same—to try to have reasonable beliefs about the subject matter. This raises the epistemological question of what it means to have reasonable beliefs. This chapter will survey two strong candidates for accounts of reasonableness—*Inductivism* and *Falsificationism*. Both views have at different times been the ruling orthodoxy not only in science and social science, but also in school texts and programmes. Children have been taught either that reasonableness consists in having only beliefs for which there is a great deal of evidence, or that reasonableness consists in *not* having beliefs that there is evidence against. The first orientation generates a concern for supporting beliefs, for finding evidence that confirms our beliefs and theories. The second orientation generates a concern for testing beliefs, for finding evidence that disproves our beliefs and theories.

INDUCTIVISM

There has been a long-entrenched inductivist version of empiricism which sees evidence as, in the long run, facts, and reasonable belief as being belief in the facts, limiting conjectures and generalisations (if one has them at all) to the barest extension of the facts. Roughly, the business of research, and the extension of knowledge, was to be the ascertaining and ferreting out of more and more facts. The business of education was to be the passing on of some of these, and the training of individuals in how to do their own searching. The nineteenth-century British Academy was a great place for fact-finding. William Whewell, a contemporary of J. S. Mill, spoke of facts lying around 'like stones' waiting to be picked up. The 'un-civilised' and 'half-civilised' tribes had them before their eyes, but they lacked the 'process of the intellect' by which these could be picked up and the 'stately fabric of European physical philosophy' thereby created.[1] The historian Ranke adopted as his dictum that the task of history was 'simply to show how it really was'.

Historians like Acton, Gardiner and Bury were all faithful to this in their laborious compilations of the facts of history. Their hope was that with enough effort, from enough people, all the facts would be known and that would mark the successful completion of the historical exercise. In true Imperial fashion this view was exported to the colonies. A recent book on Australian history, which bears the title *The Second Year*, pur-ports to be an account of everything that happened in Australia in 1789. For those interested in everything that happened in 1788, the author's preface directs them to his other publication, *The First Year*. This crass inductivism in history has been criticised by E. H. Carr, among others.[2]

Inductivism is a thesis about how we discover scientific laws, generalisations and theories—about the context of discovery. It is also a thesis about how we justify, prove, confirm these laws, causal relations and the like—the context of justification.

I. **Discovery.** The seductive belief that there is a method, the ready application of which will unearth all of Nature's secrets, is stated most powerfully by Francis Bacon. As well as being a philosopher of the Scientific Revolution, he was a philosopher of the Industrial Revolution. His account of scientific labour is remarkably similar to accounts of current industrial labour—labour which was appearing as the harbinger of later full-blown capitalist industrial production.[3] Not only was capitalism to create material riches, but the scientific method was to create intellectual riches; indeed for Bacon the two were intimately connected. Science as the handmaiden of industry was to create a material paradise on earth. Thus, 'knowledge is power'. He pointed specifically to the discovery of gunpowder and its influence on warfare, the discovery of the printing press and its influence on literature and propaganda and the discovery of compasses and their influence on commerce and navigation as being the first practical fruits of the scientific revolution. We have here in embryo the scientific-military-industrial complex of the twentieth century.

What did Bacon recommend as the fail-safe scientific method? What were its features? It was to be, firstly, a collective enterprise; secondly, it was to be hierarchically organised; thirdly, it was to be fragmented, with various operations being the responsibility of different people; fourthly, there was to be a separation of intellectual and manual labour, with rules and guidelines being followed and not much critical involvement required of the scientist; fifthly, and finally, the scientific pursuit was to be a tightly disciplined undertaking. Bacon remarks: 'Men are very far from realising how strict and disciplined a thing is research into truth and nature, and how little it leaves to the judgment'.[4] The naive version of inductivism is in the end the admonition to make one's generalisations only after a wide range of particulars has been collected and examined in a wide variety of circumstances. After we look at many ravens in England, Australia and America we can reliably say: 'All ravens are black'. Bacon has been a whipping-boy for the anti-inductivists, notably Karl Popper and P. B. Medawar,[5] and it is perhaps only to be expected that perhaps not all the epistemological sins of later inductivism can be laid at his door.[6]

After Bacon, it is John Stuart Mill in the nineteenth century who is most closely connected and identified with the advocacy of inductivism as a method for discovering scientific generalisations. These are formalised as the famous 'Mill's Methods' in his *System of Logic* (1865). He claimed that every causal law known to science had been discovered by application of the methods he systematised.

There is an important principle underlying all these methods. It is expressed in Mill's prescriptions on how we are to use general terms or class names, for example 'ship', 'crow'. To have clear conceptions of these, and to use the terms in a scientifically rigorous manner, it is necessary that we have 'habits of attentive observation and extensive experience, and a memory which receives and retains an exact image of what is observed'. The clearness of our conceptions 'chiefly depends on the *carefulness* and *accuracy* of our observing and comparing faculties'.[7] Here we have the *sine qua non* of empiricism most generally, and inductivism more specifically. Knowledge comes from, and is justified in, individual experiences. The quality, accuracy and meticulousness of the observations guarantees and underpins the knowledge claims. This is carried over into textbooks and school classrooms as the central component of the scientific method; it is what is extolled for field excursion notes and laboratory class reports: 'observe, and observe well'.[8] Unfortunately, as we shall see, observation in this sense does not have so central a role to play in science. Indeed, the case might be quite the contrary.

Qualified Importance of Observation in Discovery
(i)   Things which observationally are very different are nevertheless related—moving needles, iron filings in configuration and electric currents are all instances of electromagnetism.
(ii) We need often to see forests where this advice encourages us to see trees. In geology, for instance, there are characteristically all manner of discrepant and locally disturbed dip and strike readings for rock strata. To get a picture of what is going on overall we have to ignore and discount these.
(iii) As will be illustrated, observations are guided and determined by the prior theory the scientist holds. It is the theory which enables the observations to be made and described.
(iv) As a matter of fact, numerous major breakthroughs in science have been made by people who did very little, if any, observing. Copernicus used the data of his Ptolemaic opponents for the formulation of his heliocentric theory of the solar system. His *On the Revolutions of the Heavenly Spheres* contains fewer than two dozen new observations. Indeed, he ignored observations contrary to his theory (a moving earth implies star parallax, which was absent). This was strikingly paralleled by Newton, the non-observer, in his rejection of the meticulous and voluminous observations of Flamsteed, the Astronomer Royal, because they conflicted with his theory of planetary motion.

We shall see that there are strong affinities between these critiques of inductivism as a method and Marx's methodological prescriptions in his 1857 Introduction to the *Grundrisse*. There he rejects collecting 'concretes' as the first step in science because he sees that the concretes (data, descriptions, etc.) will in fact embody theoretical abstractions. In its place he recommends beginning with a small number of abstractions such as 'division of labour', 'money', 'value', and then proceeding to immediate realities. Inductivism in broad terms says to go from the concrete to the abstract.

Inductivism as an account of the method for discovering scientific truths has to be rejected. Popper is correct in saying that the process of scientific discovery cannot be rationally reconstructed.

II. **Justification.** Inductivists have proposed varied accounts of how universal statements or laws can be justified in terms of finite bodies of evidence. The problem is how the truth of a generalisation can be warranted on the basis of a number of particular truths; how can we reasonably believe things about all falling bodies on the basis of knowing things about some falling bodies?

This is the Problem of Induction, which was given its clearest statement by David Hume. Hume noted that science and the common sense always maintained beliefs about unobserved and unexperienced things on the basis of observed and experienced things. This is scientific inference. He also noted that the conclusions of these inferences were not completely warranted by the premises. The truth of crow one being black and crow two being black, and so on and so forth, does not warrant the truth of 'the next crow will be black' or of 'all crows are black'. As is well known, Hume drew the sceptical conclusion that we could not have knowledge of universals, generalities, causal relations or laws. Once more the supposed philosophical friend of science mortally wounds it or, at least, mortally wounds a science which claims its justifications in observation and which identifies rational arguments with deductive arguments (those where, if the premises are true, the conclusion has to be true; characteristically arguments from 'all' to 'some'). If both assumptions are denied the problem of induction loses much of its thrust.[9]

Inductivism as an account of the justification of beliefs is inherently conservative. Its main thrust is to say that only beliefs, conjectures, theories for which we have a considerable amount of evidence are justified beliefs, conjectures and theories. 'Do not go beyond the evidence' is the repeated advice.

Classical empiricism holds three principles here:
(i)   That facts are independent of theories: anyone can pick

up the stones on the beach. Close scrutiny of Nature will yield the same collection of facts, irrespective of who is doing the scrutinising.

(ii) New theories are to be introduced in a domain only if they are consistent with the known facts in the domain and consistent with other established theories in the domain.

(iii) The meaning of concepts is not to change as the domain of a science is enlarged or deepened.

Paul Feyerabend has been the most influential recent critic of these principles.[10] What he correctly points out is that, historically, most important theories have been introduced despite the factual evidence and in the face of well-entrenched and supported existing theories. Furthermore, that facts and theories are much more intimately connected than the first principle (the Relative Autonomy of Facts principle) allows. Specifically, every fact will be described in terms of some theory or other; and some facts will be found only when exploration of alternative theories and conjectures is allowed.

These points can be illustrated by considering the corpuscularian and wave theories of light. As is known, Newton proposed the former account and shortly afterwards the Dutch physicist Huygens proposed the latter. Inductivist accounts of justification would suggest that Huygens should not have proposed the theory. Newton's theory was consistent with most of the known facts (light being different coloured; light showing deflection and refraction behaviour; light casting shadows; light travelling through vacuums). Further, it was consistent with the overall philosophy of atomism or corpuscularianism which so successfully underpinned the Scientific Revolution. Huygens proposed that light didn't travel; rather a wave enabled light energy to be transmitted without any light itself being transmitted (compare the 'movement' of waves across the sea: energy travels but the water particles themselves do not). The wave theory, however, did suggest new experiments, which unearthed new facts which eventually confirmed it and falsified the Newtonian theory. These were the experiments showing that extremely thin bodies cast no shadows and that light passing through small pinholes casts diffraction shadows. Young and Fresnel performed these experiments over a century after the theory was proposed. Here, facts which disproved one theory were available as evidence only when a contrary unjustified theory was allowed to be exploited.

Consider innovations in education, politics, child-raising. The entrenched standard practice will have most of the evidence, prestige and power on its side. Any new proposal will in the nature of things have no evidence for it, except perhaps analogical evidence. But it is often only as a result of instituting new practices that behaviours and outcomes become available to show the limitations of the entrenched practice and the validity of the novel practice. Inductivism says: 'Don't rock the boat'. The contrary view is: 'We don't know until we try'. Having children involved in school government has been much less 'unthinkable' since Neill demonstrated that it worked at Summerhill; staffs rejecting external inspections is much less unthinkable once it has been done by some schools; teachers not wearing suits and being addressed by their first names do not result in the school crashing down around their ears, as some dire prophesies predicted. What is today's utterly unjustified, unthinkable, impractical heresy is usually tomorrow's standard, dull, routine normalcy.

FALSIFICATION

If one doubts that having reasonable beliefs is the same as having beliefs for which there is evidence, then perhaps we could say that having unreasonable beliefs is having beliefs that there is evidence against. If evidence does not prove beliefs it should at least disprove them. In essence this is the view of Karl Popper who, from the '20s to the present, has led the main opposition to positivism, inductivism and logical empiricism in philosophy of science. Popper's falsificationism has had a great influence, not just in philosophy of science but in the practice of science and of social science. One philosopher has described him as the 'greatest philosopher of science that has ever been';[11] and a leading scientist's advice to his fellows is 'read and meditate upon Popper's writings on the philosophy of science and to adopt them as the basis of operation of one's scientific life'.[12] The extensive work of his students—John Watkins, Imre Lakatos, Paul Feyerabend, Joseph Agassi—although differing in degrees of fidelity to Popper, has ensured that the tradition is a lively one. Unlike inductivism, falsificationism has never pretended to give recipes for scientific discovery, it has never advocated any method for discovery. It is a thesis about the justification of beliefs and scientific theories. The following discussion is thus about falsificationism and the context of justification.

Austria, in the '20s, was bubbling with new and exciting

theories, all immense in their scope; all suggesting a break with previous conceptions; and all laying claim to legions of advocates. These were Marxism, Freud's Psychoanalysis, Adler's Individual Psychology and Einstein's Relativity Theory. There was much putative evidence *for* the first three theories, but this did not impress Popper; indeed, on the contrary, he regarded this apparent strength as their greatest weakness. The claim that they always fitted and were always confirmed disguised the fact that they were never critically put to the test; there was never any clearly specified state of affairs which, if it obtained, would be regarded as inconsistent with the theory. He saw Eddington's 1919 trial of Einstein's mass-energy equivalence thesis as a startling and exemplary model of how a theory should be put to the test. In advance it was determined that, if energy and mass are equivalent, then light from a far star passing the sun should be bent. Thus, readings of the star at half-yearly intervals should exhibit parallax. If they did not, then the theory would have to be abandoned. In the event the theory survived the test and received an incisive confirmation; Popper proposed a demarcation of science from non-science on this criterion of testability. 'A system is to be considered as scientific only if it makes assertions which may clash with observations; and a system is, in fact, tested by attempts to produce such clashes, that is to say by attempts to refute it. Thus testability is the same as refutability, and can therefore likewise be taken as a criterion of demarcation'.[13]

This was in contradiction to the positivist criterion of meaning which, following Hume, maintained that statements had meaning only if they referred to observables or were reducible to statements which did refer to observables. For them the criterion of meaning was also a criterion of the demarcation of science from non-science. Thus the positivists proposed a criterion of *meaning* such that

(i)　A statement S (which was not a statement of mathematics or logic) had meaning if, and only if, it could be verified.

(ii)　A statement S is verifiable if, and only if, it is deducible from some observation statements.

In contrast Popper proposed a criterion of *demarcation* of science from non-science such that

(i)　A statement S is scientific if, and only if, it is falsifiable.

(ii)　A statement S is falsifiable if, and only if, S is inconsistent with some possible observation statement.

Positivism and Science

Popper saw clearly the inconsistency between positivist doctrine and scientific achievement. Science outruns experience in three ways:

(i) *Law Statements*. To say: 'All metals expand when heated' or; 'All gases combine in simple proportions by volume' is to speak about metals and gases which have not been experienced. Hume was insistent upon this and Popper agreed with him. Hume drew sceptical conclusions and later positivists drew the conclusion that law statements were meaningless. Popper, in contrast, drew the conclusion that something was wrong with the positivists' criterion of meaning.

(ii) *Theoretical Terms*. To say: 'The magnetic field strength at X is 10 gauss' or: 'Electrons in pairs have opposite spin' is to speak about fields and electrons which are beyond experience. The history of science is a history of realism; it is one of seeking knowledge of entities and mechanisms beyond experience which are causally responsible for observed patterns and events at the level of experience. This is the basis of scientific instrumentation and measurement. The great French positivist, Pierre Duhem, spoke of science telling us nothing 'of the realities lying under the phenomena we are studying'.[14] His views were largely motivated by a desire to keep religion and science in separate spheres of authority. Perhaps it would have been appropriate for him to use the same words as the great English theologian and intellectual Cardinal Newman who, when told of the 1870 proclamation of Papal Infallibility, said: 'I believe in the dogma but I cannot reconcile it with the facts of history'.[15]

(iii) *Metaphysical concepts*. To say 'there is no empty space' or 'the real properties of bodies are bulk, figure, texture and motion' or 'there is no attraction at a distance' or 'space-time is a curved four-dimensional continuum' is to engage in discussion which does not make direct reference to experience. It is widely accepted that metaphysics has always played a central role in science. Aristotelian physics is intelligible only in the context of Aristotelian metaphysics—a metaphysics of actuality and potentiality, of substance and accidents; of the conception of the universe on an organismic model. Galilean and Newtonian physics is only intelligible in the context of a corpuscularian metaphysics—a mechanistic and atomistic world view. The attempt to render meaningless the doctrines of metaphysics is misguided and impossible.[16]

These types of consideration lead Popper to say of the verificationist criterion: 'This criterion excludes from the realm of meaning all scientific theories (or 'laws of nature'); for these are no more reducible to observation reports than the so-called metaphysical pseudo-propositions. Thus the criterion of meaning leads to the wrong demarcation of science and metaphysics'.[17]

Development of Falsificationism

In its simplest form, a form never held by Popper but held by some of his followers, falsificationism is the view that we propose bold theories or conjectures, draw deductive implications about states of affairs in the world and, if these states of affairs do not obtain, then we regard the conjecture as falsified and begin our search again. Schematically:

$$T \rightarrow O \quad \text{(theory implies an observation)}$$
$$\sim O \quad \text{(the observation does not occur)}$$
$$\therefore \sim T \quad (\therefore \text{ the theory is false})$$

This naive form of falsificationism is often touted about in supposedly sophisticated educational circles. A writer on school science objectives speaks about the scientific attitude being one which is prepared to jettison the oldest theory in the face of a single recalcitrant fact—'nothing can be called scientific which is not based upon such an attitude'.[18] As we shall see, this is not only a misinterpretation of Popper, but it is plainly ridiculous. It is the reason why Popper has often remarked that 'criticism of his alleged views was widespread and highly successful, but criticism of his actual views was much rarer'.

As early as 1934, in his book, *Logic of Scientific Discovery*,[19] Popper was allowing theories to escape death at the hands of recalcitrant experience by sanctioning the creation of auxiliary hypotheses (provided they were not *ad hoc*) and by allowing changes in the explicit definitions of theoretical terms in the theory. In 1948 he saw that it is never a theory alone from which we deduce putative states of affairs in the world, but a theory along with accounts of the initial conditions pertaining. 'Testing proceeds by taking the theory to be tested and combining it with all possible sorts of initial conditions as well as with our theories, and then comparing the resulting predictions with reality'.[20] We cannot make predictions about the future position of a moving body simply on the basis of Newton's second law, $F = ma$. We need to have knowledge of the initial velocity of the body, of its mass, of its position. Thus schematically Popper's original falsificationism becomes:

$$T \cdot I \rightarrow O \qquad (T \text{ and } I \text{ together imply } O)$$
$$\frac{\sim O}{\therefore \sim T \text{ v } \sim I} \qquad \begin{array}{l}(O \text{ is not the case}) \\ (\therefore \text{ either } T \text{ or } I \text{ is not the case})\end{array}$$

where T = theory under test; O = predicted observation; I = initial conditions.

The history of science provides innumerable instances where the theory under test has been preserved and assumptions about initial conditions checked and then altered. Galileo had more confidence in his heliocentric theory of the solar system and the inertial circular motion of the planets than he had in astronomical observations with which they conflicted. Newtonians, when confronted with falsifications of their laws of motion, rightly preserve the laws and claim that the statement of initial conditions must be faulty. In 1846 the perturbations of Uranus were ascribed to a hitherto unknown planet and its position and mass were calculated. Its subsequent discovery was a striking confirmation of Newtonianism.

This account is not quite qualified enough, as we need to consider our measuring instruments, the theories behind them and our computational formulae. If all these are designated by 'C' then schematically the situation is:

$$T.I.C. \rightarrow O$$
$$\frac{\sim O}{\therefore \sim T \text{ v } \sim I \text{ v } \sim C}$$

Again, the history of science is replete with instances where computational and instrumental assumptions were found to be faulty, rather than the theory under test. Say we predict micro-organisms in a tissue slide and fail to see them. It is quite reasonable to suspect the resolving power of the microscope. The Aristotelian answer to Galileo's observations of the irregular surface of the moon (an observation in conflict with Aristotelian predictions based on the doctrine of heavenly bodies being perfect and immutable) was to doubt the utility of his telescope. This was quite justified, given their view of the primacy of the senses in observations and the primitive, untried nature of the instrument. Recall how Newton himself put aside Flamsteed's observations by claiming that he had made inadequate allowance for refraction of light by the earth's atmosphere. It is perhaps Heisenberg's Uncertainty Principle which brings these issues into sharpest relief. The common account of this principle maintains that the act of observing an electron necessarily alters the state of affairs being observed because it introduces energy to it.

These computational issues provide much of the ongoing debate in social sciences. Should we use parametric or non-parametric statistics in analysis of the data? Are surveys an adequate data collection device for particular issues? Have we set reasonable alpha and beta error rates for testing the null-hypothesis? What are the problems with participant observation as a research method? In education research, how much does the presence of the researcher affect the classroom behaviour?

In the final analysis the observation itself can be denied. It can with reason be claimed that there was human error or stupidity or cupidity which made people 'see' something which was not there. An undergraduate who enthusiastically comes up with a falsification of the law that 'acids turn litmus red' is himself more likely to be failed.

The foregoing considerations have led the American logician W. V. Quine to propose a very modified version of falsification-ism. Knowledge is a seamless web which only here and there makes direct contact with reality. He takes the whole of science as being up for investigation in experimental situations. There are many possible readjustments in the interior of science when it meets with recalcitrant experience on the edge. This is because the content of science (laws, concepts, theories) is underdeter-mined by its boundary condition, experience. Quine says: 'there is much latitude of choice as to what statements to re-evaluate in the light of any single contrary experience'.[21] Thus we have the much written-on Duhem–Quine Thesis.[22]

In 1934 Popper was aware of these possible reactions to an observational disproof of a theoretical conjecture. In his *Logic of Scientific Discovery* he says that 'no conclusive disproof of a theory can ever be produced'.[23] His response to this, however, is to say that 'strict disproof' is too unrealistic a demand in physical sciences. For Popper, the critical, rational attitude is one where the theory alone is pushed forward for sentence at the earliest possible moment in the proceedings. Thus he wrote that a proper methodology in empirical science is one whose rules 'must be designed in such a way that they do not protect any statement in science against falsification'.[24] In 1948 this was reaffirmed: 'The proper reaction to falsification is to search for new theories which seem likely to offer us a better grasp of the facts'.[25] At the same time Popper was speaking of the history of science being propelled by a method which is revolutionary, which 'destroys, changes and alters the whole thing'.[26]

There is an unresolved tension in Popper's work at this point between what he would like to believe and what it seems he has to believe. In his later years he accepts a form of reformism rather than revolutionary overthrow of theories. The schema he uses to illustrate this is:

$$P_1 \rightarrow TT \rightarrow EE \rightarrow P_2 \text{ [27]}$$

where P_1 is some problem we start with, largely deriving from the current state of theory in a domain. For instance, once we accept the Continental Drift theory then a legitimate problem is: Did North and South America detach from Africa and Europe at the same time? We then propose some Tentative Theory (TT) such as a simultaneous rupture of the Americas. The business of science is then to Eliminate Errors in this view (EE). This leaves us with an altered theory (TT^1—Popper doesn't include this). In this case it might be a form of modified simultaneity, North America preceding South America. In turn we then have new problems created (P_2) which we attempt to solve in the same style as previously. This whole procedure has obvious affinities with Quine's image of repairing a boat at sea—it cannot be done by taking up all the boards at once; it can be done only in a piecemeal fashion, one board at a time.[28]

Cognitive Dissonance Theory has been one of the more rigorous theories of twentieth-century social science. Its history has recently been written and it illustrates well the process of theory adjustment, and the interaction of problems and evidence of which Popper speaks.

The theory of cognitive dissonance is much more complicated than we thought it was ten years ago. A good deal of research has been done since 1957. Many of the problems which were specified early have been solved. Hopefully, future research will lead to the emergence of still newer problems, which will lead to still more research, which will continue to yield an increased understanding of human behaviour. I guess that's what we mean by science.[29]

Subjectivity and Facts in Science

Popper is an empiricist in that it is individuals' experiences and observations which are going to count as evidence in science; not evidence *for* theories, but evidence *against* theories. These experiences and observations give rise to the corpus of 'basic statements' which we have in science; they are the 'potential falsifiers' of our conjectures and theories; they are the empirical basis of the science—the facts. Popper says they are 'statements of a singular fact which can serve as a premise in an empirical falsification'.[30] Among the corpus of basic statements, we find statements such as 'the current is 10 amps' (or better 'the ammeter reads 10 amps'); 'the temperature rose 25°c'; 'the star did not exhibit parallax'. It is important to see how Popper differs from the positivist tradition in respect of these basic statements. For the latter, they are the result of eyeball-to-eyeball confrontation with the world; the bedrock, foundation stones of science; the assertions that we cannot reasonably doubt. The quest for indubitable foundations has led some positivists to give a *phenomenological* rendering of these basic statements—'I have a red patch before my eyes'. Others settle for an object rendering of these basic statements—'I have a tomato in my sight'. The positivist programme demands that the theoretical component of basic statements be zero (they maintain a rigid observation language/theoretical language distinction which goes back to Hume's impression/idea distinction). It also demands that the conventional component of basic statements be zero (if the foundations were a matter of taste or decision then the solidity goes). In contrast to positivism, Popper says of the basic statements of science that:

(i) *Facts are theory-laden.* As soon as we describe any state of affairs we are involved in the use of universal names, concepts and symbols which gain their currency from the theoretical structures in which they are formulated. This is obvious in such cases as 'look at that person's super-ego struggling to repress the libidinous desires of his id'. It is perhaps less obvious in such cases as 'look at the inhibition of the person's response to the stimulus'. Popper correctly maintains that even the simplest account will embody theoretical commitments which overreach experience. In 1934 he was saying that simple statements such as 'here is a glass of water' are deceptively simple. 'By the word "glass", for example, we denote physical bodies which exhibit a certain law-like behaviour, and the same holds for the word "water". Universals cannot be reduced to classes of experience; they cannot be constituted'.[31] It is worth nothing that it is *statements*, not observations, that figure in science. This is important. Observations or experiences do not confirm or falsify anything; only statements do that. Science deals with reports, accounts, experimental findings. All of these are statements in a language, the kernel of which is some theoretical discourse or other (psychoanalysis, behaviourism, Newtonianism). Popper is aware that observation itself is something in which the observer plays a very active part. We don't just observe, we observe something. He notes that an observation is always preceded by a particular interest, a question, or a problem—'in short by something theoretical'[32]—again, a point lost on the authors of many school texts and curricula material.[33] Inasmuch as observation underlies basic statements, it is *propositional observation*, not object observation. It is a matter of seeing things 'as something'; it is not just seeing things in the sense of having undescribed and unconceptualised stimulation of the senses by external objects. We see 'that the tomato is on the table' or 'that the king is checkmated'; we don't just have undifferentiated brute stimulation—or, at least, the latter is of no concern to science. This is why two observers placed before the same object can be said to be seeing different things depending on what is already in their heads. They have the same object perception (pattern of stimulation) but different propositional perceptions. If we know the rules of chess we see that the king is in danger; if we don't know the rules we merely see that there are black and white pieces arranged on the board. Issues concerned with the theory dependence of observation have received close attention by philosophers of science such as Hanson, Kuhn and Feyerabend. This theory is very interesting, and a sobering draught for empiricism. In the end, though, it does not have much effect on epistemology—at least on non-subject-centred epistemologies such as will be developed here. It only reinforces the view that the distinction between 'observational' and 'theoretical' terms is mistaken. Popper concurs with this.

(ii) *Facts are partly conventional.* Popper admits freely that the basic statements embody elements of convention, agreement and decision among scientists. The world doesn't impose itself unambiguously on our basic statements, instead we face the world and decide to use some descriptions rather than others. We agree on the limits of reference of certain terms. The fact that we say of something that it is an 'acid', or a 'tree', or 'water' is not determined by what is out there in the world, but it is partly a matter of how the relevant scientific community elects to use particular words. Again as early as 1934 Popper says: 'Basic statements are accepted as the result of a decision or agreement, and to that extent they are conventions'.[34] For him a certain amount of conventionalism was a bitter pill that science just had to swallow. It was too much for the positivists and not enough for conventionalists. Popper certainly opposed the full-blooded conventionalism of Henri Poincaré who extended conventionalism to the appraisal of theories themselves. Poincaré regarded Newton's Laws as being true by convention. That is, it is decided in advance that nothing will count against them.[35] This was anathema to Popper because it opened wide the door to his *bete noir*, namely Relativism. It also ran contrary to his over-arching concern to have 'theories put their neck out'.

Knowledge as An Objective Creation

One of the main contributions of Popper to epistemology is his insistence that knowledge is an objective matter. It is something created and produced by human intellectual endeavour, but it has an objective existence independently of the process of its creation and of its creators. 'Objective' is meant in the sense that tables and chairs are objective in contrast to subjective dreams, wishes, hopes. 'Objective' does not mean true or beyond doubt.

He makes the distinction between the *first* world of material things, events and processes; the *second* world of human experiences, perceptions, thoughts, beliefs, hopes; and the *third* world of theories, the contents of belief, assertions, propositions and problem situations. Considerations of personal knowledge —'I know that x'—are items in the second world, the subjective world. Considerations of scientific knowledge—'$F = ma$'—are items in the third world, the objective world. Epistemology he correctly takes to be the theory of scientific knowledge, and consequently concerned with the nature and growth of the third world. Thus most traditional subjectivist or belief epistemologies —Hume, Locke, Descartes, Russell and most contemporary Anglo-Saxon epistemology—are by and large irrelevant to Popper's concerns because they are preoccupied with second-world items. These are the preoccupations of strengths of beliefs, of clarity of beliefs, of degrees of conviction, of foundations of belief. These are the same reasons why we have said that much of the currently fashionable (and interesting) discussion of perceptual oddities, preconditions for observation and factors influencing different perceptions of similar objects (*pace* Hanson *et al.*) are not really central to epistemology.

For Popper the structure and properties of the third world can shed light upon second world events, but *not* the other way around. Hence his anti-psychologism and anti-sociologism in the history and philosophy of science. When theories are proposed they are enmeshed in larger suppositions of a meta-physical kind (Newtonianism is enmeshed in deterministic, corpuscularian metaphysics). The ensemble has within it its own problems and methodologies; these exist objectively and independently of whether individual scientists recognise them or not. The determination of what numerically the Gravitational Constant is in the Newtonian formula

$$F = \frac{G\ M_1\ M_2}{r^2}$$

is an objective problem generated by the theory. It is a problem 'out there' waiting for a solution. This then generates the second-world events of scientists scratching their heads, thinking up hypotheses, organising research teams and having beliefs. It further generates first-world materials in the way of instruments and laboratories. The scope of the application of theories is a characteristically objective problem which puts in train second and first world events: 'Is Darwinian theory applicable to human evolution and to cultural evolution?' 'Is Marx's theory applicable to pre-capitalist societies?'. To use the terms of an alternative tradition, we have in Popper a thesis about the 'Relative Autonomy of the Theoretical'.

CONCLUSION

Both inductivism and falsificationism as accounts of rationality have the suicidal consequence that science is irrational. This indicates that something is wrong with the accounts. The accounts of rationality are not just about how some individual mind should process information on a page, or solve a puzzle, or decide on a course of action. Rationality is about the search for truth, about the intellectual appropriation of the world. It is concerned with sorting out and evaluating intellectual systems that contend with each other on the public stage—cognitive versus behaviourist psychologies; idealist versus materialist philosophies; theistic versus atheistic world views; liberal versus socialist politics; abortion on demand versus anti-abortion legislation. People generally, but school-teachers especially, are inevitably involved in appraisals of, and decisions concerning, such matters. They do this knowingly or unknowingly; whether they like it or not.

The argument of this book is that we should first get our accounts of rationality and methodology correct for science before rushing out and applying them elsewhere. Positivist onslaughts against religion and morality demonstrate how Pyrrhic such victories are—the weapon that renders religion irrational also renders science irrational! In the argument between Marxist and liberal-rationalist theories of schooling, it is of no benefit to anyone to use simplistic and inadequate evaluation criteria.

Popper's epistemology has many strengths—it takes the history of science seriously; it recognises the 'human factor' in intellectual systems; it is non-foundationalist and it sees knowledge as a determinate, independent, objective product in human history. It is a great pity that Peters and Hirst did not incorporate two central Popperian tenets in their approach to philosophy of education—make epistemology square with science and ignore the analysis of concepts and the search for meaning.

In the following chapter I shall examine Imre Lakatos' attempt to sophisticate falsificationism and thereby provide an adequate account of rationality and of the methodology of science.

NOTES

1. W. Whewell, *History of the Inductive Sciences*, London, J. W. Parker, 1837, Vol. I, p. 8. Example from J. Krige's Sussex Ph.D. thesis, 1978.
2. E. H. Carr, *What is History?* Harmondsworth, Penguin, 1964, Ch. 1. G. S. Jones, 'History: The Poverty of Empiricism' in R. Blackburn (ed.) *Ideology in Social Science*, London, Collins, 1972.
3. See David Dickson, 'Science and Political Hegemony in the 17th Century', *Radical Science Journal*, 8, 1979.
4. *ibid.*, p. 12.
5. P. B. Medawar, *Induction and Intuition in Scientific Thought*, London, Methuen, 1969.
6. Mary Horton, 'In Defence of Francis Bacon', *Stud. Hist. Philos. Sc.*, 1973, 4, (3).
7. *A System of Logic*, Longmans, Green & Co., 1965, p. 431. His italics.
8. Claude Bernard, in a book on experimental medicine, writes: 'Now to find truth, men of science need only to stand face to face with nature and . . . question her with the help of more and more perfect means of investigation'. Quoted in S. Amsterdamski, *Between Experience and Metaphysics*, Boston, Reidel, 1975.
9. One classic attempt at preserving the reasonableness of inductive arguments is Wesley C. Salmon, *The Foundations of Scientific Inference*, Pittsburgh, University of Pittsburgh Press, 1966. The central literature and a bibliography are in R. Swinburne (ed.) *The Justification of Induction*, London, Oxford University Press, 1974.
10. *Against Method*, London, New Left Books, 1975.
11. Peter Medawar in Bryan Magee, *Popper*, Glasgow, Fontana, 1973, p. 9.
12. John Eccles in above.
13. *Conjectures and Refutations*, London, Routledge & Kegan Paul, 1963, p. 256.
14. *The Aim and Structure of Physical Theories*, Princeton, University Press, 1954 (Orig. 1906), p. 21.
15. Correspondence, quoted in *Faith and Culture*, Catholic Institute of Sydney. Vol. I, 1978.

16. See E. A. Burtt, *The Metaphysical Foundations of Modern Science*, London, Routledge & Kegan Paul, 1924. Also Marx W. Wartofsky, 'Metaphysics as Heuristic for Science', *Boston Studies in the Philosophy of Science*, Vol. III. Gerd Buchdahl, *Metaphysics and the Philosophy of Science*, Oxford, Blackwell, 1969.
17. *Conjectures and Refutations*, p. 261.
18. Boris Podolsky, 'What is Science?', *The Physics Teacher, 3*. The American Biological Sciences Curriculum Study established in 1959 developed a school biology course—*The Web of Life*—on explicitly Popperian grounds. In the foreword to its much-used textbook it says scientists must 'give up any hypothesis, however much beloved, as soon as facts are shown to be opposed to it'.
19. First English Publication: London, Hutchinson, 1959.
20. *Objective Knowledge*, Oxford, Clarendon, 1972, p. 360.
21. *From a Logical Point of View*, N.Y., Harper, 1953, p. 42.
22. For a recent extensive discussion of the Duhem-Quine thesis see S. G. Harding (ed.) *Can Theories Be Refuted?*, Boston, Reidel, 1978.
23. *Logic of Scientific Discovery*, p. 50.
24. *ibid*. p. 54.
25. *Objective Knowledge*, p. 360.
26. *Conjectures and Refutations*, p. 127.
27. *Objective Knowledge*, pp. 285 ff.
28. *Word and Object*, Cambridge, M.I.T. Press, 1960, p. 3.
29. E. Aronson, 'Dissonance Theory: Progress and Problems', in R. P. Abelson *et al.* (eds.) *Cognitive Consistency Theories*, Chicago, Rand McNally, 1968.
30. *Logic of Scientific Discovery*, p. 43.
31. *ibid*. p. 94. In 1948 he says: 'I grant, of course, that science is impossible without experience . . . (but) perceptions do not constitute anything like the raw material . . . out of which we construct either "experience" or "science"'. *Objective Knowledge*, p. 342.
32. *ibid*. p. 342.
33. The *Australian Junior Secondary Science Project* (Cheshire Press, 1968) says: 'Experiments in astronomy involve gathering information by patient and careful observation, frequently over long periods of time, and then working out theories or models to fit these observations'.
34. *Logic of Scientific Discovery*, p. 106. A few pages later, he says: 'Basic statements are not justifiable by our immediate experiences, but are, from the logical point of view, accepted by an act, a free decision'.
35. Henri Poincaré, *Science and Hypothesis*, New York, Science Press, 1905. To be fair, Poincaré does stress that, having made the initial decisions to place the laws or theories out of court, they are then judged on the research they generate.

CHAPTER 5

THE METHODOLOGY OF SCIENTIFIC RESEARCH PROGRAMMES

Teachers are supposedly concerned with extending the domain of reasonable thinking in society and contracting the domain of unreasonable, stupid and bigoted thinking. An increasingly large number of life's concerns are being brought into the classroom. Sex, politics, counselling, ecology and unemployment are just some of the matters about which teachers are charged with developing reasonable opinions and thinking, over and above the more standard curriculum areas. The previous chapter has shown that we need an adequate account of rationality, an account which both inductivism and falsificationism fail to provide. Glib and easy accounts of rationality sell at discount prices. One recent writer on autonomy as an educational aim says that the autonomous person is one who makes decisions on the basis of 'his world as evidence'. A deceptively simple basis indeed! In psychotherapy, Albert Ellis speaks about a 'rational–emotive' approach to life's problems as being the criterion of mental health. Very nice, but hardly informative. The IQ argument rages around schools: some say nature, some say nurture, some say nature/nurture, others say 'a pox on all your houses'. Can we make reasonable decisions between the contenders, or is any opinion as good as any other? In history lessons it is compulsory to say that Galileo's belief in Copernicus' heliocentric theory of the solar system was rational, while the cardinals' belief in Ptolemy's geocentric theory was irrational, stupid and bigoted. What are the criteria of rationality on which we base this judgment? Behaviourist psychologists tell teachers to do it their way; cognitive psychologists tell teachers to do it their way. Can we ascertain which way is *the* way? This book will argue for an historical materialist epistemology and a Marxist theory of schooling. It will further contend that such views are better than their rivals. These tasks presuppose some criteria of what makes one theory 'better' than another. The criteria should not be naive. This chapter will examine the most sophisticated account yet provided of rationality; the most sophisticated set of criteria for the appraisal of competing beliefs. It is Imre Lakatos' *Methodology of Scientific Research Programmes* (or MSRP). It promises to be of great assistance to teachers, to researchers, to curriculum planners and to scientists.

Imre Lakatos went to London from Hungary in 1956 and became a student-disciple of Popper, whom he succeeded in the Chair of Logic and Scientific Method at the London School of Economics in 1966.[1] He was concerned to develop the Popperian position so as to accommodate justified criticism of the type that has been outlined. He was a defender of rationality against the many attacks that had been made upon it. For Lakatos, the history of science was to be our guide in the quest for rationality. He was dismayed by philosophers of science such as Paul Feyerabend saying that 'anything goes' in the choice between scientific theories; and by Thomas Kuhn's apparent suggestion that the history of science was a matter of mob psychology. Talk of magic and science being equivalent left him speechless. What then is his MSRP?

TEN THESES OF LAKATOS

1. *No belief is an island.* Beliefs (meaning the articulated content of beliefs, propositions) cannot be appraised in isolation. Beliefs are given intelligibility within a larger supporting framework; judgments concerning them will usually turn out to be judgments concerning that larger framework. A proposition is the tip of a theoretical iceberg. Consider some random statements in nuclear physics, theology and psychology.

An electron in an s-state always has a spherically symmetrical electron cloud with $(n-1)$ spherical nodes, where n is the principal quantum number.

Jesus Christ is to be confessed as one and the same Son . . . perfect in Godhead, the same perfect in Manhood, of one nature with the Father.

The development of personality proceeds, in large measure, by a series of energy displacements or object substitutions. The source and aim of the instinct remain the same when energy is displaced; it is only the goal object that varies.

It is obviously myopic to consider the rationality of belief in these propositions without appraising the theories in which they are embedded. In common discourse a person who says: 'a woman's place is in the home' is correct to insist that such a belief be appraised with cognisance of his larger beliefs about women, the home and the family.

2. *Not everyone is equal.* Scientific theories are not all of a piece, they are not undifferentiated wholes. Some propositions within them are epistemically privileged. Theories contain a *hard core* of

ontological, methodological and metaphysical commitments which are taken as being fundamentally important. These are not up for revision when the theory is put to the test. The hard core generates the *negative heuristic* of the theory. This tells us where not to look when conducting experiments and isolating variables. Part of the hard core of Newton's theory is the proposition that a body will accelerate only when a force is applied to it. If a billiard ball suddenly begins to accelerate, the negative heuristic of Newton's theory tells us not to look for what day it is, what colour the ball is, or consult our Tarot cards. Theories contain a *protective belt* of propositions which are alterable in the face of recalcitrant experience. These will consist of auxiliary hypotheses, statements about initial conditions obtaining for the experiment, computational formulae and technical assumptions. Both generate the *positive heuristic* of the programme. It tells us what factors and variables to investigate in our research and where to adjust our theories.

A dogmatic interpretation of any theory is one that expands the hard core; a liberal interpretation is one that contracts the hard core. To say that medicine, education and social service should all be bought and sold in the market place is to hold a dogmatic version of *laissez-faire* liberalism. To say that one can believe what one wishes about Jesus' divinity and the existence of God is to hold a very liberal interpretation of Christianity.

3. *In praise of continuity.* It is not just propositions, or theories, but connected series of theories which constitute the unit of appraisal in science. Theories are modified, not jettisoned in the light of recalcitrant experience. The inviolable hard core preserves an identity beneath the changing appearances of the protective belt. Where this obtains, the series is called a *research programme* (RP). The existence of research programmes is a necessary condition for any intellectual appropriation of the world to be scientific. For Lakatos, to 'apply the term "scientific" to one single theory is a category mistake'.[2] He represents the reformist wing of falsificationism. Popper, in his most revolutionary moods, advocated complete overthrow of theories and new beginnings. Even in his less extreme moods he insisted that modified theories were new theories. The history of science was a discrete history, not a continuous one. Lakatos extolled the virtues of continuity. The avoidance behaviour of rats presented a problem for Pavlovian classical conditioning theory. It appeared that a non-event (the absence of shock) was motivating rat behaviour (pressing a bar to avoid shock). How can non-

events figure in a science whose hard-core commitment was to stimulus-response analysis of behaviour? One could eschew the theory and speak in cognitive and teleological modes about the rat 'wanting' to avoid shock. On the other hand we could search for modifications of the theory consistent with our hard core. This was indeed done by many researchers. The result was a research programme in avoidance behaviour.[3] The previous chapter outlined a similar circumstance in the study of cognitive dissonance.

4. *Examine the track-record.* RPS have a history, they have a track-record. A *theoretically progressive* RP is one which makes novel predictions about the course of nature; it is *empirically progressive* if these predictions are confirmed. Mendel's theory of gene segregation has been a progressive RP. There were anomalies and recalcitrant results but these were either ignored, or modifications were made to the original formulation—sex-linkage, cross-over, mutations were introduced as auxiliary hypotheses. In contrast we have theoretically and empirically *degenerating* RPS. These make no novel predictions and have nothing confirmed. Characteristically they run alongside progressive RPS saying 'me too, me too'. Oxygen theory predicted that heated materials would not burn in a vacuum. This prediction was confirmed. Phlogiston theory could be modified to accommodate the fact—phlogiston needed a medium to travel on—but only after the event. The appraisal of RPS involves the identification of them as progressive or degenerating. Analytic philosophy of education is a degenerating RP; it has run into the sand.[4]

5. *Old research programmes never die, they just fade away.* Degenerating RPS go out with a whimper, not with a bang. Popper's much-acclaimed crucial experiments are figments of the philosopher's mind. Where there are crucial experiments they can be identified as such only in retrospect. Albert Einstein was wrong when he said that frequently in science, tests occurred which would pronounce sentences of life or death on a theory.[5] Capital punishment is rare in the court of theory appraisal. For Lakatos there is no such thing as 'instant rationality'. It can be quite reasonable to stick to degenerating RPS, as they occasionally make spectacular comebacks. The early history of an RP is often a time when difficulties and anomalies abound. Lakatos agrees with Feyerabend that new RPS require 'breathing-space'. The MSRP has no place for Popper's decisive falsification or

Kuhn's dramatic *gestalt* switches. Rationality tends to work more slowly than people think, and even then fallibly. 'There can be no instant—let alone mechanical—rationality. Neither the logician's proof of inconsistency nor the experimental scientist's verdict of anomaly can defeat a research programme in one blow. One can be "wise" only after the event'.[6] Feyerabend makes much of this admission, coming as it does from one whom he regards as the most sophisticated defender of Rationality. He takes it as tantamount to an admission of defeat—one cannot rationally criticise scientists who stick to a degenerating RP.[7] He also notes that the MSRP is not a method for the conduct of science; it has no practical advice on how scientists should pursue the truth.

6. *Three is not a crowd*. Tests in science are three-way contests between rival theories and nature. They are not, as is commonly believed, two-way contests between a theory and nature. When a clash occurs, a theory is not given up unless there is another around which can be adopted. A weak emaciated bird in the hand is worth none in the bush! The classic example is Galileo's evaluation of the two rival world systems of Ptolemy and Copernicus. The participants in the *Dialogues* were expected at the end of the day to judge one theory as better than another, not just to reject a theory. In the absence of the heliocentric hypothesis the geocentric hypothesis of Ptolemy was not abandoned but was merely modified and further modified. The triadic, rather than dyadic nature of scientific testing was a point argued convincingly by Kuhn against Popper.[8]

The question emerges of how the experimental results bear upon the rival theories. Where there are alternative theories within an RP the problem is not grave—say one-factor and two-factor theories within the classical conditioning RP of Pavlov. Where the theories are in different RPs the problem is acute. Lakatos does depend upon the Relative Autonomy of Facts principle. The experiment, E, has to impinge on both T_1 and T_2. Feyerabend denies that this circumstance can always be realised. 'Facts and theories are much more intimately connected than is admitted by the autonomy principle . . . the description of every single fact is dependent on *some* theory (which may of course be different from the theory to be tested.)'[9] There are two ways in which rival theories can fail to face the facts:

(i) T_1 can deny that E is relevant to it. Information about prices is relevant to some theories of value and not to others. This manoeuvre is made respectable if T_1 can demonstrate that the terms of E violate its ontology or are outside the domain of its applicability as specified by its state variables. RPS have ontological commitments as to what kinds of things exist in the world of their domain. A behaviourist is not going to accept an E whose terms are 'that person's libidinous desires were repressed by his superego'. State variables specify the domain over which T_1 is applicable. Theories of biochemistry have to account for the chemistry of eating cake, but they do not have to account for the outbreak of the French Revolution. For Aristotle place was a state variable so that change of place had to be explained; for Newton velocity is a state variable so only changes in velocity (i.e. accelerations) need to be explained. Specification of state variables is an important preliminary for appraising theories of schooling. The political economy of schools is inside the domain for Marxist theories, whilst the personal interactions among staff are outside the domain. For phenomenological theories of schooling, the former are outside and the latter inside.

(ii) What constitutes an explanation in T_1 can be different from what constitutes an explanation in T_2. Thus whether E is explained by both Ts is not just a matter of E alone. Aristotelian physics allowed teleological explanation; Galilean physics allowed only mechanical explanations.

Critics of Feyerabend's Incommensurability Thesis have responded to manoeuvre (i) by recourse to Ramsay reduction sentences to force the rival theories to face up to each other on the same domain, against the same phenomena.[10]

7. *We cannot avoid being conventional.* Conventions and agreements play an important role in scientific theory. The empiricist ideal was to eliminate conventions altogether in the cause of complete and utter objectivity—theory is to be determined entirely by the facts of nature. H. Poincaré was on the other extreme, allowing the truths of the highest laws in science to be determined not by nature but by agreement among scientists. 'Simplicity' has been a long-established criterion for choice among rival theories. Galileo said that 'Nature does not act by means of many things when it can do so by means of a few'.[11] Poincaré said that the choice between rival theories can be guided only by 'considerations of simplicity'.[12] These

sentiments were shared by Duhem, who, in commenting on nineteenth-century English mechanical models of electricity— with their weights, tubes, pumps—disdainfully said: 'We thought we were entering upon the tranquil and neatly ordered abode of reason, but we find ourselves in a factory'.[13] How much is simplicity in nature and how much is it something that we choose to bring to nature?

The MSRP recognises and allows the following elements of a RP to be conventional:

(i)   Conventions about relevant techniques for checking scientific assertions.

(ii) Conventions about the separation of basic statements from the rest of science. By agreement we take blips on a radar screen to be basic statements expressing the location of aircraft. All the electronic and radar theory which goes into this intepretation of the blip is by convention taken as established, corroborated background knowledge.

(iii) Conventions which set limits for the falsification of hypotheses. Standardly this is the setting of error rates— alpha and beta errors—in experimental design.

(iv) Conventions as to when experimental refutations are to be taken as refutation of the theory under examination and when they are to be taken as refutation of the accompanying *ceteris paribus* ('other things being equal') clause. When faced with seeming miracles, mechanical scientists can reasonably retort that 'other things were not equal'.

(v)   Conventions concerning what statements will be excluded from science on the basis of their syntactical structure. For example, the hypothesis 'There exists a solvent for all metals' is taken by agreement not to figure in a science—we cannot possibly falsify it.

(vi) Conventions determining which propositions will be in the never-to-be-given-up hard core of an RP and which ones are in the protective belt. For Engels the proposition 'dialectical laws apply in nature' was in the hard core of Marxism; for Lukács it was the protective belt, and was indeed rejected.

Lakatos acknowledged all these conventional elements in science whilst maintaining, correctly, that they did not undermine objectivity. There are reasons of a non-conventional kind which can be advanced for holding the conventions we hold. He refers to this feature of the MSRP as 'rationalised conventionalism'.[14] It is what Poincaré was implying when he said of geometry that it was 'conventional yes; arbitrary no!'. Once the conventions are made, our theory can be forced to put its neck out.

8. *Truth is at a discount*. Truth is a consideration for Lakatos, but it is pushed off the centre of the scientific stage. Progressive RPS can be specified independently of their truth content. We like to have truth, but apart from being a contentious entity in itself (see discussion in the following chapter), it is not something sought for in the first instance. He does say that the succession of progressive research programmes each superseding the other is likely to have increasing 'verisimilitude' in a strictly technical sense. He is doubtful whether we can speak of *better* correspondence or *degrees* of truth.[15] Truth lurks in the background. There is a fine difference between him and Kuhn, for whom truth is a concept altogether superfluous for the conduct of science.[16]

9. *By their fruits ye shall know them*. The Popperian, and ultimately Kantian, distinction between the context of discovery and the context of justification is maintained by Lakatos. In his words: 'The problem of appraisal is completely different from the problem of why and how new theories emerge'.[17] This distinction has had a chequered career through twentieth-century philosophy of science. The empiricist tradition of Russell, Carnap, Nagel and Hempel filleted the history and sociology of science out of the philosophy of science. They concentrated upon the finished products of scientific production: the laws, formulae, classifications. Their philosophical questions were about the interpretation and justification of these products. So Newtonianism becomes equated with the formula:

$$F = \frac{G \, m_1 \, m_2}{r_2}$$

and we ask questions about whether 'force' is a concept completely reducible to statements about masses and accelerations (as Ernst Mach argued it was). This ahistorical approach to the philosophy of science has been detrimental to understanding science. The cognitive claims of science cannot be appraised if the historical dimension is excluded; if the context of discovery is excluded. Of course the history of science was not totally ignored by advocates of the distinction. The empiricist Mach paid considerable attention to the history of science[18] but the same cannot be said of all others in the tradition. These are the people who, in Feyerabend's words, made 'the history of science duller, simpler, more uniform, more "objective" and more easily accessible to treatment by strict and unchanging rules'.[19] By the time this empiricist history trickles down to school texts and programmes it is often a complete travesty.

Consider, for instance, a widely-used Australian science text —New Senior Physics.[20] The opening chapter is on, predictably, the Scientific Method. It is an inductivist account. Facts are 'gained by direct, systematic observation'. A 'law' is a 'generalised statement of organised facts'. A theory is an explanation of the laws, and is to be discarded or modified if new facts are discovered with which it does not agree. The chapter on Newton provides the standard interpretation of Kepler's laws being induced from Tycho Brahe's data. Kepler's laws are then shown to be a deduction from Newton's Gravitational Law and hence confirmation of it. In contrast to this tidy picture, Duhem had long ago pointed out that 'If Newton's theory is correct, Kepler's laws are necessarily false'.[21] Popper concurs in this judgment.[22] In other texts we can read about how Galileo leaned over the Tower of Pisa and, by dropping two stones, established the new science. No one denies that the interests of pedagogy demand certain simplifications. But where students are expected, in one paragraph, to grasp the intricacy of the calculus and complex formulae, then it seems not unreasonable to expect that a modicum of historical complexity can be conveyed; more so if its absence gives a completely distorted picture of science.

To his credit, Popper brought the history of science into discussions of the philosophy of science. He shared, however, his empiricist adversaries' view that history should not touch questions of justification. There was complete agreement between Herbert Feigl and Karl Popper on this point.[23] Popper's recognition of history was not enough for Lakatos. Indeed, Popper was accused of not really writing history at all: what he wrote, said Lakatos, was 'drily abstract and highly ahistorical'.[24] The MSRP depends upon history for the evaluation of RPS, and Lakatos' elaborate case studies are directed precisely to this end. But it is the history of finished products which is taken into account, not the history of the production of these products. The argument of this book is that history is important for evaluation of theories, but it has to be a broader history than that envisaged by Lakatos. It has to be a history that will capture the ideologies and social interests involved in the production of science. It has also to capture the changing norms of scientific rationality.

10. *Reasons guide, causes push.* The MSRP distinguishes sharply between internal factors affecting the growth of science and external factors. It thus gives rise to a demarcation between 'internal' history of science and 'external' history of science. The former deals with the emergence of new theories, the uncovering of problems and anomalies. The latter deals with the socio-political-cultural influences and determinants of the internal history. There is then the crucial question of how the external history relates to the internal history.

Kuhn warranted the charge of being the 'enemy of rationalism' by asserting that the internal history of science is not *sui generis*; it is causally dependent upon the external history of science. The explanation of the growth of knowledge is in the end a psychological or sociological matter. It must be 'a description of a value system, an ideology, together with an analysis of the institution through which that system is transmitted and enforced'.[25] To be fair, Kuhn is somewhat ambiguous and may perhaps best be described as holding a form of modified externalism. A necessary condition for the overthrow of a paradigm is the build-up of a host of embarrassing anomalies, but it is not a sufficient condition. *Reasons* do not tip an old paradigm over the edge; they bring it to the edge and then *causes* push it over.

The externalist position in historiography of science came into prominence in the '30s, and then it was associated with Marxism. If one sees scientific activity and ideas as part of the superstructure of society then, on certain Marxist models, it is simply a reflection of changes in the economic base of the society. A classic externalist history of science is Hessen's account of The 'Social and Economic Roots of Newton's *Principia*'. Needham continued this line of analysis in England. His guiding principle for writing a history of science was that 'We cannot dissociate scientific advances from the technical needs and processes of the time, and the economic structure in which all are embedded'.[26] J. D. Bernal's *Science in History*[27] is informed by just such a principle. Although by no means Marxist, the sociology of science in the US following Robert Merton is clearly externalist in its programme. There is, of course, much grist for the externalist mill. William Smith, the 'father' of British geology, regarded his discipline as merely a service for manufacturing and engineering interests. In 1916 the President of Columbia University opened a new research centre saying: 'Manufacturers throughout the country could bring to the university, with such a laboratory, their great chemical, mechanical, or other engineering problems for solution at the hands of experts who will devote their entire time to such work'. On the other coast of America, at the same time, the famous California Institute of Technology was being established as an 'institution for the advancement of chemistry and other sciences as aids to industry'.[28]

The internalist position maintains that the growth of science is explicable entirely from within; at its extreme it is idealism. The historian of science A. R. Hall says that external factors can be looked to in surveying the rise and meanderings of particular sciences, but as a matter of fact they have only an occasional and then minimum impact. For him, science, even experimental science, must be treated as 'intellectual history'.[29] Popper's form of objectivism, science as 'third-world' activity, is in the internalist tradition.

Lakatos is a sophisticated, or rather complicated, internalist. He correctly recognises that there can be no history of science without a philosophy of science, or a theory of science. All study presupposes theory. Paraphrasing Kant, he writes: 'Philosophy of science without history of science is empty; history of science without philosophy of science is blind'.[30] There is no 'innocent reading', to use Althusser's phrase. He further sees that one's methodology of science will dictate where the boundary between internal and external questions lies. For a falsificationist the persistent refusal to give up a theory in the face of overwhelming contrary evidence is a fact to be explained by external considerations—psychological obsession and political pressure. Indeed Lakatos claims that what an historian regards as an external problem 'is often an excellent guide to his implicit methodology'.[31] Now there is an obvious tension here. For, on the one hand, Lakatos wants to derive the correct account of science, to derive a methodology of science, from reflections upon the history of science (philosophy of science without history of science is empty); yet, on the other hand, we also know that any history of science will reflect prior methodological commitments (do we include magic in it? Do we include the role of metaphysics?). Lakatos is aware of the tension but unfortunately does not adequately resolve it.

Lakatos' writings are replete with historical analyses and case studies, and he uses these to argue against contending method-ologies—falsificationism, conventionalism, inductivism—saying that they do not square with the facts of scientific history. His claim is that it is only the MSRP which does square with the facts. More accurately here, Lakatos says that the MSRP legitimises its own alteration and change in the light of recalcitrant facts in the history of science. That is, it is self-referring. It allows theories to alter in the face of facts (changes in protective belt propositions) and then it allows theories about theories (i.e. methodologies) to alter in the light of recalcitrant theories. Falsificationism as a methodology has itself to be falsified and abandoned because of its obvious inconsistency with facts in the history of science (Newton's theory was not abandoned despite anomalies; Lyell's Gradualism in geology was not abandoned despite obvious gaps in the stratigraphic record). The MSRP legitimates the modifica-tion of falsificationism and indeed represents just such a modifi-cation and elaboration.

When we look closer at the history to which Lakatos appeals in order to do all these things, we see that it is a very peculiar history. It is internal history; it is a 'history of events which are selected and interpreted in a normative way'.[32] His historical evidence is 'rationally reconstructed' evidence. His *modus vivendi* is first, to give a rational reconstruction of the history of a scientific research programme; second, to compare this with the actual history of events; third, to have recourse to external history to account for any failure of match between reconstructed and actual history.[33] This procedure is potentially self-destructive. The MSRP sets out trying to take history seriously, yet in the end it can ignore history altogether. These potentials are the more likely to be realised if one adopts, as Lakatos does, the discovery/ justification distinction, and rules all external questions out of the purview of philosophy of science. Consider one of Lakatos' central and most documented cases, that of Prout's theory about the atomic weights of all pure elements being whole numbers. He says at one stage that Prout knew well that anomalies abounded, but dismissed these as the result of impurities in his samples and the deficiencies of contemporary experimental techniques. This sounds fine and is remarkably in keeping with the methodology of the MSRP. But then, a few pages on in the text, Lakatos announces: 'Alas, all this is rational reconstruction rather than actual history. Prout denied the existence of any anomalies'. Similarly, he has Bohr entertaining the notion of electron spin when he had no conception of such a construct. These types of 'creative' moves in Lakatos' rationally re-created history have led

Kuhn to charge that 'what Lakatos conceives as history is not history at all but philosophy fabricating examples'.[34] Another astute commentator, Ernan McMullin, has said of it that it has very little to do with history. It is merely the exploitation of history to illustrate how the MSRP functions.[35]

Before joining this chorus of aghast critics we do need to appreciate that it is knowledge considered objectively (*à la* Popper) of which Lakatos is writing a history and with which he is centrally concerned. For objectivists, what is important is whether Bohr's theory allowed the possibility of electron spin; whether or not Bohr actually recognised the possibility is largely immaterial. The force of Kuhn's and McMullin's criticism comes from empiricist assumptions about history which Lakatos could well deny. Now this defence of Lakatos' procedures is not without a certain cost. The MSRP is clearly describing the situation (*qua* theory) in which the scientist finds himself, it is *not* giving an account of situations as seen or experienced by the scientist; furthermore, it is *not* giving advice to the scientist on how he should go about his business. Feyerabend recognises the dilemma here.[36] Once more we come up against the issue raised in the Introduction to this work: how does an objectivist epistemology relate to the actual doings and thinkings of individual subjects? For epistemology to have educational consequences, for it to guide practice, this gulf has to be bridged. Moreover, the bridge cannot be a figment of imaginations and hopes; it has to be demonstrably anchored at both eneds, or else we simply face up to the fact that there is no bridge—a theory of knowledge and the acquisition of knowledge and development of mind have nothing to do with each other. My claim is that a broadly Marxist epistemology of knowledge as the product of theoretical production provides the means for understanding the relationship of individual 'experiences' to objective knowledge.

We shall return now to the issue of externalist versus internalist accounts of science. For Lakatos, the positive and negative heuristics of a research programme explain and dictate its history. By definition, where this is not the case, there is an anomaly to be explained by external history. He believes that the number of anomalies is small and that we can always 'reconstruct more of actual great science as rational'. Now Lakatos is not precluded from explaining the original rise and formulation of the research programme in external terms. Minimally, this is what an externalist would seek. It is certainly what a Marxist would seek. Roughly, thought and cognition arise from practices which in turn are based in human and social needs. Ancient

Egyptians had a material need for food; they engaged in agricultural practices in the Nile delta. Euclidean geometry arose as a means of facilitating the reclamation of the periodically flooded land; subsequent development of Euclidean geometry, drawing out the theorems contained embryonically in the original programme, was much further removed from needs and practices. Development did presuppose a social division of labour (someone had to feed, house and clothe the mathematicians), but the theoretical development was basically autonomous. How autonomous the theoretical development is remains a *contingent* matter. To argue either pure externalism or pure internalism *in the abstract* is a fruitless exercise. Some research programmes will contain the seeds of special interests and deformations within them, so that even the internalist dynamic will actually reflect external factors. It will later be argued that the Gradualist Doctrine in Darwin's evolutionary theory is such a case. Skinner's Behaviourism is another such example; Taylorism in management theory is another. We also expect that the direction and tempo of the history of a research programme is not just an internal matter. The Spirit seldom 'moves where it willeth'. The University of California has recently been given half a million dollars to research the production of tomatoes suitable for mechanical harvesting. Once given this research problem, its solution will largely be an internal matter concerning biochemistry, plant genetics and agricultural science. The fact that this problem is worked on rather than one concerning how to develop a strain of tomatoes capable of surviving in down-town window-boxes is, however, a matter to be explained in terms of the power of Californian agribusiness and the University's co-option into ruling-class industrial concerns. All of these are issues that need to be discussed under the rubric of Ideology and Science, but this rubric is ruled out of court by Lakatos' internalism and his acceptance of the discovery/justification distinction. This point is well illustrated, as we shall see in Chapter 8, when Lakatos' student Peter Urbach surveys and reconstructs the IQ debate according to the MSRP. This is meant to be a vindication of the methodology, but in the whole of two long articles[37] there is no mention of politics, of ideology, of class control—in other words, no mention of the external factors which are demonstrably so important in this particular bit of pseudo-scientific debate.

SCIENCE AND METAPHYSICS

The MSRP does not give a satisfactory account of the place of metaphysical commitments in science, nor of their intellectual functioning in the maintenance or overthrow of research programmes. For a programme so concerned with the reasonableness of intellectual commitments and of the rationality of scientific development, this absence is significant. The issue will bear upon what is internal to science and what is external. It will bear upon the important question of how we appraise or argue for the boundary conditions of science; for those ultimate commitments regarding ontology, processes, permissible interactions which govern and regulate the theories and laws proposed by science. It will also allow us to understand better the intellectual complexity of the Scientific Revolution and the other major upheavals in the history of science.

Lakatos characterises the hard core of Newtonianism as the three laws of dynamics and the law of gravitation.[38] Now as far as epistemic privilege is concerned, these are the penultimate, not the ultimate, propositions. The ultimate commitments are those of the metaphysics in which Newtonianism is born; they are the propositions of the Mechanical World View or Newton's version of Corpuscularian Philosophy. These metaphysical boundary principles constitute the *General Conceptual Scheme* (GCS) of the science. They are propositions such as:

(i)   The world is independent of thought and is atomic in its basic constituents.
(ii) The real or mechanically efficacious properties of bodies are bulk, figure, texture, motion.
(iii) Time and Space are absolute, real entities; the latter is Euclidean in its properties.
(iv) Mass is inert; rest or uniform motion are equally 'natural'.
(v)   Gravitational attraction exists between all masses.
(vi) Energy is conserved in interactions.[39]

Now, it is easy to see that understanding the status of these fundamental propositions is crucial for understanding science. There is no obvious inductive procedure for establishing them; nor is there any obvious simple experimental disproof of them. Yet they constitute the backbone of one of the most powerful research programmes in the history of science. These regulative principles of a science, the propositions of a science's GCS, are as much metaphysics as they are physics. Questions emerge then as to:

(i) How can we appraise alterations in the GCS?
(ii) What will count as evidence for or against the propositions of the GCS?
(iii) What are the legitimate ways in which the metaphysical commitments can support the less ultimate scientific propositions when they clash with experience or are swamped with anomalies?

Any adequate account of scientific history will have to acknowledge that metaphysics has always been an indispensable part of science. This thesis is well attested to in the work of Gerd Buchdahl. Alexander Koyré, E. A. Burtt, R. Harré, Marx Wartofsky and others.[40] Lakatos is strangely silent on the matter.

The debate between Newton and Leibniz over the lynch-pin of Newtonianism—the supposition of action at a distance—was a metaphysical dispute. The latter flatly rejected it. It was an absurd notion, an 'occult notion', a notion which ran counter to the mechanical world view that the New Science was supposedly founded upon. It was the scientific work of Newton, Boyle and others that established the metaphysics of the Newtonian GCS.

The mechanical world view encountered serious problems in the nineteenth-century. These problems for its *philosophy* were generated by *scientific* developments in electricity and optics. In the first, the field of electrostatics opened up a whole array of non-mechanical and non-gravitational forces and entities. The GCS was stretched to accommodate these but with great reluctance, difficulty and lack of elegance. We now had repulsive as well as attractive forces; forces were perpendicular to, and not in the line of, the charges; weightless substances were introduced. The classical conception of matter was fast being eroded. In the second field of optics the work of Young and Fresnel on diffraction and refraction sealed the fate of Newton's particle theory of light and called for a non-particle wave theory. It was Einstein's Field Theory and its associated General Conceptual Scheme which provided the framework for science to overcome its crippling problems and launch new research programmes.

Historically, the most significant example of the overthrow of one physics by another, necessitating the overthrow of the metaphysics within which the first was embedded, was Galileo's establishment of the Copernican heliocentric system. It was by no means a matter of establishing one physical hypothesis over another. What physics was, what theories were, what adequate explanations were, what appropriate techniques for the investigation of nature were, had all to be overhauled before Galileo could establish his new mechanics. The geocentric system of Ptolemy was firmly embedded in the majestic, architectonic system of Aristotelian metaphysics.

Aristotelianism was the intellectual cement which held the religious, social, cultural and scientific worlds together. As Brecht notes in his play *Galileo*, the system of the earth at the centre, surrounded by the planets and further out the fixed stars, was seen to be paralleled by the Pope being surrounded by his cardinals, lesser bishops and, on the outskirts, the laity. Consider Aristotle's explanation of falling bodies in terms of the bodies seeking out their natural place in the element earth; and rising smoke being in terms of the smoke seeking its natural place in the realm of the element, air. Now, to reject the concept of natural places was not just to reject something in physics. It was, for instance, integral to the church's teaching on sexual morality. The great Thomas Aquinas spelled out and argued his account of vice, and sins against nature, in terms of the 'natural places' for the sexual organs and for semen. Anal intercourse, oral intercourse, coitus interruptus were all regarded as vices against nature because the fit and natural place for the deposition of semen was the vagina. Similarly, Aristotle's metaphysical concepts of substance and accidents with which he explained change were also pressed into service to account for the mystery of the Eucharist, this being in terms of the doctrine of transubstantiation. If Galileo's Earth moved, it was clear to many that other things were going to move as well. The question arises of how, rationally, commitment to the relevant metaphysics can sustain the associated physics, particularly in the face of experimental evidences. There should be no need to stress that I am *not* implying that the decision to accept or reject a metaphysics is a simple matter. In metaphysics, life is not meant to be easy. Faraday agreed that Newtonianism was good and adequate science, but he rejected it because it clashed with his metaphysical commitments to corpuscularianism. Einstein agreed that the Quantum Theory was adequate science, but he rejected it on account of his metaphysical commitments to determinacy. In these specific cases it seems a pointless exercise to set up a court to determine if their actions were rational or not. Their positions are, of course, identical with those of at least some of Galileo's opponents. Osiander, in his 1543 preface to Copernicus' *De Revolutionibus*, set the tone by agreeing that the heliocentric hypothesis 'saved the appearances', that is, was adequate as science, but was to be rejected on metaphysical grounds. Bellarmine repeated this against Galileo in 1615. They were in effect advocating an Instrumentalist account of science, where adequacy was one thing and truth was another.

CONCLUSION

The MSRP has been surveyed at some length, as it is the best and most sophisticated account of the rationality of science. In many places science clashes with *a priori* accounts of rationality—this indicates not that science is irrational, but that we have to change our account of rationality. The *MSRP* endorses this response. Although it is a methodology worked out in the natural sciences, my conviction is that it can, with benefit, be applied to the appraisal of research programmes in the social sciences. With a little stretching, it can be applied to rival programmes in philosophy, theology and the like. In the terms of the MSRP I shall later argue that analytic philosophy of education is a degenerating research programme, whilst the Marxist research programme in education is progressive.

NOTES

1. The chief publications of Lakatos are:
   'Changes in the Problem of Inductive Logic', in I. Lakatos (ed.), *The Problem of Inductive Logic*, Amsterdam, North-Holland Publishing Co., 1968. (*Collected Works*, Vol. II).
   'Falsification and the Methodology of Scientific Research Programmes', in I. Lakatos and A. Musgrave (eds.), *Criticism and the Growth of Knowledge*, Cambridge, C.U.P., 1970. (*Collected Works*, Vol. I).
   'History of Science and its Rational Reconstructions', in *Boston Studies in the Philosophy of Science, 8*, 1970. (*Collected Works*, Vol. I).
   'Popper on Demarcation and Induction', in P. A. Schilpp (ed.), *The Philosophy of Karl Popper*, La Salle, Open Court, 1974. (*Collected Works*, Vol. I).
   Proofs and Refutations (J. Worrall and E. Zahar (eds.)), Cambridge, C.U.P., 1976.
   Collected Works, Vols. I and II, J. Worrall & G. Currie (eds.), Cambridge, University Press, 1978.
2. 'Falsification and Methodology . . .', p. 118.
3. R. J. Herrnstein, 'Method and Theory in the Study of Avoidance', *Psychology Review*, 1969, 76.
4. Some of its recent publications witness to this. See particularly D. I. Lloyd (ed.), *Philosophy and the Teacher*, London, Routledge & Kegan Paul, 1976.
5. *The Evolution of Physics*, New York, Simon & Schuster, 1966, p. 41.
6. 'History of Science . . .', p. 101.
7. *Against Method*, London, New Left Books, 1975, p. 185.

8. Thomas Kuhn, *The Structure of Scientific Revolutions*, Chicago, University of Chicago Press, 1970, p. 77.
9. *Against Method*, p. 27. Elsewhere he says: 'The meaning of observation sentences is determined by the theories with which they are connected. Theories are meaningful, independent of observations; observational statements are not meaningful unless they have been connected with theories'. In 'Problems of Empiricism', in R. G. Colodny (ed.), *Beyond the Edge of Certainty*, New York, Prentice Hall, 1965, p. 213.
10. See J. W. N. Watkins, 'Metaphysics and the Advancement of Science', *British Journal for the Philosophy of Science*, 1975, 26, pp. 97 ff. Also J. Giedymin, 'Logical Comparability and Conceptual Disparity Between Newtonian and Relativistic Mechanics', *British Journal for the Philosophy of Science*, 1973, 24.
11. *Dialogue Concerning the Two Chief World Systems*, Stillman Drake (trans.), Berkeley, University of California Press, 1967, p. 117.
12. H. Poincaré, *Science and Hypothesis*, London, 1902, p. 146.
13. *The Aim and Structure of Physical Theory*, Princeton, Princeton University Press, 1954, p. 70. Quoted in Marx Wartofsky, 'Metaphysics as a Heuristic for Science', *Boston Studies in the Philosophy of Science*, 3, p. 134.
14. 'Falsification and Methodology . . .', p. 134.
15. *ibid.* p. 188.
16. *The Structure of Scientific Revolutions*, pp. 170 ff.
17. I. Lakatos and E. Zahar, 'Why did Copernicus' Research Program Supersede Ptolemy's?', in R. S. Westman (ed.), *The Copernican Achievement*, Berkeley, University of California Press, 1975, p. 355.
18. See material in R. S. Cohen and R. J. Seeger (eds.), *Ernst Mach: Physicist and Philosopher*, New York, Humanities Press, 1970.
19. *Against Method*, p. 19.
20. F. T. Barrell, *New Senior Physics*, Sydney, Jacaranda Press, 1967.
21. *The Aim and Structure of Physical Theory*, p. 193.
22. *Conjectures and Refutations*, p. 62.
23. Feigl's remarks in R. M. Chisholm *et al.* (eds.), *Philosophy*, Englewood Cliffs, Prentice Hall, 1965, on the absolute distribution of questions of discovery and justification (p. 472), are almost identical with those of Popper in his *Logic of Scientific Discovery* (p. 31).
24. 'History of Science and its Rational Reconstructions', p. 113.
25. *Criticism and the Growth of Knowledge*, p. 21.
26. *Time: The Refreshing River*, London, Allen & Unwin, 1943, p. 144. Quoted in R. Johnston, *Australia & New Zealand Journal of Sociology*, 1976, Vol. 12, No. 3.
27. London, Watts, 1954.
28. See an excellent book, David F. Noble, *America by Design: Science, Technology and the Rise of Corporate Capitalism*, New York, Knopf, 1979. The foregoing quotations are from p. 145.
29. 'Merton Revisited or Science and Society: The Seventeenth Century', *History of Science*, 1963, 2, p. 14.
30. 'History of Science and its Rational Reconstructions', p. 91.
31. *ibid.* p. 107.
32. *ibid.* p. 108.
33. 'Falsification and Methodology . . .', p. 138.
34. 'Notes on Lakatos', *Boston Studies in Philosophy of Science*, 8, p. 143.
35. 'History and Philosophy of Science: A Marriage of Convenience?', *Boston Studies in the Philosophy of Science*, 32, 1974, p. 215.
36. 'Consolations for the Specialist', in *Criticism and the Growth of Knowledge*, p. 215.

37. 'Progress and Degeneration in the IQ Debate' Pts. I, II, *British Journal for Philosophy of Science*, 1974, 25, 26.
38. 'Falsification and Methodology . . .', p. 133.
39. See G. Weigel and A. Madden, *Knowledge: its Values and Limits*, Englewood Cliffs, Prentice Hall, 1961, p. 73.
40. *Metaphysics and the Philosophy of Science*, Oxford, Blackwells, 1969; *Metaphysics and Measurement*, Cambridge, Harvard Univ. Press, 1968; *The Metaphysical Foundations of Modern Physical Science*, London, Routledge & Kegan Paul, 1924; *Matter and Method*, London, Macmillan, 1964; 'Metaphysics as Heuristic for Science', *Boston Studies in the Philosophy of Science, 3*, p. 142; J. W. N. Watkins, 'Metaphysics and the Advancement of Science, *Brit. J. Phil. Sc.*, 1975, 26; Stefan Amsterdamski, *Between Experience and Metaphysics*, Boston, Reidel, 1975.

CHAPTER 6

MARXIST EPISTEMOLOGY

Marx observed that 'Men make their own history, but they do not make it as they please; they do not make it under circumstances chosen by themselves, but under circumstances directly found, given and transmitted from the past'.[1] This is obviously true of the knowledge people produce, and also of the theories of knowledge or epistemology they produce. Indeed, this very *historicity* of thought is one of the key elements of historical materialism. In order to understand Marx's epistemology, we have to situate it in the context of its own problems and debates. To ignore the historical context is like trying to understand Antony's speeches independently of Cleopatra's replies: one person's contribution to a dialogue cannot be understood as if it were a soliloquy. Marx was not a systematic philosopher of knowledge; he was involved in creating knowledge and, incidentally, in providing intimations of a theory of knowledge. His work contains the outlines of an epistemological research programme which has been subsequently developed, a development contributed to by sources outside Marxism.

Marxist epistemology is important to education. In practical terms, the widely-read works of Paulo Freire are basically the epistemology of the early Marx writ large and translated into pedagogical practice. In theoretical terms, an epistemology is required in order to ground and criticise much of the current radical critiques of schooling.

This chapter will give a glimpse of the epistemological situation in which Marx wrote. The theory of knowledge held by the early Marx will be outlined by way of a select commentary on his *1844 Manuscripts* and his *Theses on Feuerbach*. Here, the importance of practice for knowledge is highlighted. These writings contain the seeds of an epistemology which give promise of overcoming many of the conundrums facing orthodox empiricist and rationalist epistemologies. His later writings, particularly the *Grundrisse* and *Capital*, contain the model of knowledge as the product of particular processes of theoretical production and consequently introduce into epistemology the all-important distinction between the real and theoretical objects of knowledge. We construct knowledge, and such constructions are the theoretical objects of science. They are tested not by correspondence with real objects, but by their instrumentality, by their ability to guide efficacious action and intervention in the world.

THE SITUATION OF MARX

With some notable exceptions (Spinoza and Hegel) both British empiricism and Continental rationalism were individualist and foundationalist in their epistemology. The standard epistemological question was posed in terms of what is required in order for an individual to lay claim to knowledge of the world. There were two terms and two relations in the question. The terms and relations were shared by both epistemological traditions. The terms were a Subject (beliefs of an individual, propositions of a science) and an Object (the external world). The relations were, first, one between the Subject and the Object; and, second, one between certain states of the Subject and other states of the Subject. The first relation was the truth relation; the second was the evidence or guarantee relation. In the empiricist tradition, what emerged was certainty about knowledge, but scepticism about a world independent of thought (Berkeley); or certainty about the world, but scepticism about knowledge of it (Hume). Kant's theory of knowledge was one which united elements of the empiricist and rationalist traditions: 'Our empirical knowledge is made up of what we receive through impressions and of what our own faculty of knowledge . . . supplies from itself'.[2] The mind was to have an active role in the acquisition of knowledge, in contrast to Locke's *tabula rasa* upon which sense impressions etched out their marks. It was not for nothing that Kant referred to his epistemology as being a Copernican Revolution. Copernicus asserted that the movement we see the heavenly bodies undergoing is in reality a combination of two movements, their real movement and our real movement. What we see of reality is a function of what is 'out there' in the world, and what is 'in here' in our minds. With his distinction between the *noumenal* world (the things in themselves, of which we do not have knowledge) and the *phenomenal* world (of which we do have knowledge) Kant introduced a basic tension in his system between materialism and idealism, between objectivism and subjectivism. Lenin, in his commentary on Kant, recognises this, and says that materialist and idealist solutions to the tension have dominated post-Kantian European philosophy.[3]

Hegel criticised the Kantian scheme as being a refined

version of scepticism—if knowledge is to be confined to appearances, then it should not rightly be called knowledge.[4] He eliminates the thing-in-itself as something which is a 'mere abstraction void of truth and content'.[5] Hegel dominated early nineteenth-century European philosophy. All significant intellectuals, Marx included, defined themselves in relation to him. His central thesis concerning how subjects objectify and externalise themselves in material artefacts which stand independently of them, and through which the subjects are both known and also through which they create and transform themselves, is crucial for comprehending Marxism. It gives systematisation to the doctrine of Alienation contained in the early Marx and also provides for a coherence between this writing and Marx's economic analyses in *Capital*.

THE 1844 MANUSCRIPTS

These early philosophical writings[6] of Marx have been much commented upon. An observation of Leszek Kolakowski is noteworthy: 'The epistemological content seems to me as important as the general theory of man's alienation that most historians concentrate on'.[7] The epistemologically significant theses are:

(i) Consciousness arises from practical activity (p. 113).

(ii) The foundations of human practical activities are to be found in human needs. *Problems* necessarily arise for us, and we seek their *solutions*.

(iii) Consciousness is essentially and necessarily social. Marx says that above all we must avoid postulating 'Society' as an abstraction *vis-à-vis* the individual. The individual is the social being. Consciousness is from the very beginning a social product (p. 139).

(iv) The senses themselves are transformed through labour. The eye has become a *human* eye, just as its object has become a social, human object. The senses have therefore become, directly in their practice, *theoreticians* (p. 140). Marx believes in neither the Immaculate Conception nor the Immaculate Perception.

(v) Sense perception is the basis of all science; but it is perception considered actively. True practice is the condition of a real and positive theory (p. 144, p. 191).

(vi) Nature (or the object of perception) is itself partly humanised. Raw nature is overlaid by humanised nature:

the realm of things, of artefacts, of commodities, of ordered nature. This is the realm inhabited by most people most of the time.
(vii) There is *one* science, not a division between natural and social sciences (p. 148).

There are two central themes here which will be built upon in his subsequent work: first, the stressing of *practice* as a determinant and judge of consciousness; second, the stressing of the essentially *social* dimension of consciousness and theoretical activity.

THE THESES ON FEUERBACH
The *Theses on Feuerbach*[8] represent the quintessence of the early Marx's epistemology. Here we have his break with Feuerbach, whose influence on him in the young Hegelian circle was so strong; we have his cryptic criticism of Hegel; and we have the germinal formulation of Marx's own theory of Historical Materialism. They form indeed, as Engels remarked, 'the first document in which the brilliant germ of the new world view is deposited'.[9] A full and elaborate commentary would contribute much to a system of Marxist anthropology and epistemology.[10] What follows will be a selective commentary whose aim is twofold: first, to lay a foundation for Marxist epistemology, to indicate the shape of some of the central commitments; second, to develop their educational implications.

The *first* thesis rejects the mechanical, deterministic materialism of Helvetius, d'Holbach, Feuerbach and the other French materialists, epitomised by Laplace. To predict the future course of world history on the basis of the present velocity and position of its molecules is to leave out the reality of human agency and transforming praxis. To Marx, such a project is arrant nonsense. He commends the idealist tradition for recognising the place of human beings in the construction of history and knowledge, but criticises it for being basically contemplative and not seeing activity as being practical, sensuous activity. This activity is itself an objective constituent of the world. It transforms nature and creates a real, existing humanised nature. Both material and cognitive appropriation of the world is anchored in needs— originally natural, given needs, then social and constructed needs.[11] Human activity and labour not only transform the senses, making them human senses, but they create the instruments and technologies through which we view the world.

From spectacles to seismographs, our relationship to the world is mediated by labour and its creations.

From the time of his D.Phil. thesis, when he supported the 'soft' determinism of Epicurus against the 'hard' determinism of Democritus, Marx attempted to balance the real, material limitations on human freedom with his championing of self-transforming, revolutionary praxis. This thesis is just one instance of his life-long battle to avoid the fatalism of one camp and the idealism of the other.

The *second* thesis is Marx's so-called 'pragmatic' account of truth. 'Truth is not a question of theory, but is a *practical* question'. Bertrand Russell and Sidney Hook have both taken a simple reading of this, and have ascribed a fairly crude version of pragmatism to Marx—to say a statement is true is to say it works.[12] In equally simple terms, Marx has to be read as saying that if a statement is true, it will work. That is, efficaciousness is a criterion, not a definition, of truth. We can elaborate this important point.

(i) Truth was defined classically as the adequacy of thought to reality. It was a correspondence theory which captured much of common sense and common usage. In Aristotle's terms: 'It is true to say of that which is that it is, and it is false to say of that which is not that it is'. In more contemporary terms, we say that '*p*' is true if and only if *p*. That is, the sentence 'the cat is on the mat' is true if and only if the cat is actually on the mat. Note immediately that this is an account of the *meaning* of truth, it has nothing to do with the *determination* of truth. As such it is not inconsistent with the second thesis, provided that the thesis is not read as a definition. The correspondence theory is, in many respects, vacuous. It is somewhat like the injunction: 'do good'. Even if we all agreed with it, the question is how we do good, and what is the good we are to do.

(ii) The correspondence theory was bound up with a reflective and passive account of human thinking. There was a thinking subject, having thoughts and making judgments about an external world, and posing the question as to which thoughts were true. Marx rejects this account of human thought.

(iii) There are many well-known problems for those holding the correspondence theory. It sounds nice, but what have we actually been told which we didn't already know? In brief, how can there be 'correspondence' between reality and a sentence?

What do adverbs correspond to? What do theoretical terms correspond to?

(iv) Tarski's semantic theory of truth is developed in order to rescue the correspondence theory from its difficulties, but in so doing we must recognise that it has dropped altogether any reference to 'correspondence' or 'reality'.[13] Truth is a statement about sentences in a formalised language and sentences in its metalanguage. 'True' is always 'true in L'. Concerning the 'meaning' of truth, Tarski has perhaps said all that needs to be said.

(v) Thought *begins* as a practical matter. How do we catch fish? Where will crops yield the most? In Rylean terms, 'knowing how' precedes 'knowing that'; skills, competencies, crafts, practical attainments are sought after and mastered. Contrary to what Aristotle says, we do not (phylogenetically or onto-genetically) desire to know the truth prior to desiring food, clothes, lovers and shelter.

Science, or propositional knowledge, arises out of this practical matrix; truth becomes the goal of science. It still, however, retains the imprint of its origins. There are many truths in the world, most of which no one cares about noting, let alone pursuing. Utility enters into the selection process. Bacon was correct in saying that knowledge was power. We know in order to work on, master and manipulate nature; to turn it to our own ends. 'Human knowledge and human power meet in one; for where the cause is not known the effect cannot be produced. Nature, to be commanded, must be obeyed'.[14]

(v) Science, or the search for truth, is itself practical. We identify problems, design experiments, conduct research, make choices, manipulate materials and instruments. A scientific experiment is a highly constrained, and in many ways artificial, situation. Nature is invariably 'tortured' in order to expose its secrets.[15]

In the *third* thesis, Marx asserts the coincidence of the transformation of people and consciousness with their transformation of their material circumstances. Just before writing the *Theses*, Marx noted in *The Holy Family* that there is a connection between materialism and communism in that 'if man is shaped by his surroundings, his surroundings must be made human'. This is in contradiction to idealisms and spiritualisms of all varieties, which were saying that personal transformation is just a matter of 'changing one's heart' or developing a 'new consciousness'. Marx knew, as did Paulo Freire, that to try to change hearts without changing structures which prevent good hearts is pointless. Having defended materialism against idealism in this regard, Marx in the third thesis criticises a mechanical materialism, specifically the environmental humanism of Robert Owen and the other Utopian socialists. In the present day, this thesis is in contradiction, on the one hand, to the spiritualism of Billy Graham and the cosmic counter-culture (salvation is in one's head), and, on the other, to the mechanical impersonalism of B. F. Skinner's behaviourism.

The theologian Reinhold Niebuhr clearly saw that when collective power, whether in the form of imperialism or class domination, exploits weakness, it can never be dislodged unless power is raised against it.[16] Appeals to conscience and morals are just ineffective, and resort to better education is basically idealist daydreaming. Idealist educators and religious moralists customarily overlook practice, struggle and politics as the mechanics of social transformation. Marx refers to these mechanisms as 'revolutionising practice' or 'praxis'.

These issues were raised nearly fifty years ago when George S. Counts threw down the gauntlet to educational idealism in his address to the Progressive Education Association of America.[17] He asserted that it was utter foolishness on the part of the PEA to pin its hopes for a humane American society on the schools of the middle class. He recognised that a capitalism which debased everything it touched, and convulsed the world into a Great War and the Depression, was not going to change its character at the wave of a piece of chalk. Counts formed the breakaway Reconstructionist Movement, which has been much analysed in recent writing.[18]

The *sixth* thesis rejects internalist and individualist accounts of 'human essences'; there is nothing 'essential' about humans which is *within* them (e.g. souls). Rather, the human essence is the 'ensemble of the social relations'. The former position is one favoured by conservatives of all shades who have recourse to arguments such as 'the proposal runs against the datum of human nature'. Marx asserts that if sense can be made of 'human nature' talk, it will have to regard human nature as changeable, historically specific and created by social intercourse. Once more the starting point for Marxist analysis is the society, the network of social relations, rather than the individual. This is repeated in the *ninth* and *tenth* theses. There he rejects the notion of society being a collection of isolated, atomistic individuals, each having their own private interests to pursue. This is the model of 'Civil Society' so common in Liberalism. In his *Grundrisse* Marx asserts, against this view, that 'Private interest is already itself a socially determined interest'. Thus the problematic of Mill's *On Liberty* is rejected; as also would have been the problematic of Stanley Milgram's *Obedience to Authority*, which poses the question of obedience in terms of individuals resisting social pressures. But of course the 'individuals' are themselves formed by other social pressures. This consideration has sobering implications for ethical theories and opinions which promote private conscience to the position of final arbiter of the good. 'Private' conscience is an illusion; it is always a socially formed conscience.

The *eighth* thesis asserts that social life is essentially practical and that mysteries have their rational solution in practice. Societies do not maintain themselves in existence by thinking, but by doing—making bread, building houses, ploughing. Answerable mysteries are solved by practice. We ascertain the tensile strength of a metal by performing the relevant operations on it; we discover whether there is gold in those hills by going and looking and digging; we find out whether we like Greek cuisine by ordering and eating taramosalata, moussaka and the like. As Mao said, in the end, to know a pear we have to bite it. Unanswerable mysteries are *dissolved* by practice. Running and exercise are good dissolvers of the incapacitating, florid, mental life of psychotics. The efficiency of much psychotherapy is traceable to the cathartic effect of just discussing and revealing problems.

Engels, in discussing scepticism, says: 'The most telling refutation of this, as of all other philosophical crotchets, is practice, namely experiment and industry. If we are able to prove the correctness of our conception of a natural process by making it ourselves . . . then there is the end to the Kantian ungraspable "thing-in-itself"'.[19] If we can synthesise uric acid in a laboratory, or make artificial esters in our test tubes, then we no longer have to ponder over whether there is an unbridgeable gulf between organic compounds and inorganic compounds. Practice has bridged the putative gulf. We answer questions about whether schools can be organised democratically by organising them democratically. The question of whether a society can continue to function without a king is answered not in the abstract, but in the concrete—do away with the king and establish an alternative form of government. The 'power' of

correct thinking is exhibited in its ability to intervene successfully in the causal mechanisms of the world and to create or
embody its own conceptions.

The famous *eleventh* thesis is perhaps the most quoted remark
of Marx: 'The philosophers have only *interpreted* the world in
different ways, the point is, to *change* it'. This gives scandal to
contemporary philosophers nurtured at the breast of positivism
or analysis. Surely, they say, philosophy leaves the world as it
is. As many have said, philosophy is talk about talk; it is at one
remove from the world and far removed from changing the
world. In the light of what we have already said, this cryptic
sentence of Marx's is neither as simple as it has been taken to be,
nor, however, is it as scandalous.

Marx believes that, as a matter of fact, there is a propensity for
certain intellectual errors to be generated by certain practices
and social arrangements. Thus, inasmuch as philosophers are
concerned with promoting truth and minimising error, they
have to be concerned with the practical transformations of the
world. Bernard Lonergan speaks of the flight from understanding being a communal flight which springs from the very fabric
of a society.[20] In such a situation the fabric needs to be altered.
Education systems are places where battles are waged for the
'hearts and minds' of each generation. The major forces are
capital on the one hand and labour on the other; those who
appropriate surplus value and those who create it; those who
control the raw materials and means of production in a society,
and those who control only their labour power. Schools do, and
always have, systematically reflected the interests of capital.
Their primary function is the creation of suitable labour power.
If this clashes with the pursuit of truth, so much the worse for
truth. If philosophers are concerned with truth they cannot
stand aside from this struggle.

We are now in a position to appreciate what the 'germ' of
Marx's new world is: it is *practice*. Marx offered a new version of
materialism. Specifically, it was *historical* materialism; a materialism which saw practice or conscious human activity as
mediating between mind and matter; between subject and
object. It was something which by its mediation altered both
society and nature. Consciousness arises out of and is shaped by
practice, and in turn is judged in and by practice. There is the
seed of a Marxist epistemology and of a theory of science.

These early and cryptic epistemological theses of Marx were
developed and systematised in what is known as the 'Praxis'
tradition in Marxism. We can see this in the work of Georg

Lukács, Antonio Gramsci, Henri Lefebvre, Paulo Freire and others. But there is also a non-Marxist tradition that we can, with profit, look to in order to see what the elaborated value of the epistemological 'germs' are. This is the tradition of the American pragmatists, in particular Charles Sanders Pierce and John Dewey. The discussion of Pierce belongs to a separate work. I agree with a commentator on his work that 'The shift of orientation from the foundation paradigm to that of inquiry as a continuous self-corrective process requires us to rethink almost every fundamental issue in philosophy'.[21] Chiefly on account of their educational importance, Dewey and Freire will be discussed here.

JOHN DEWEY

John Dewey, who was taught by Pierce and influenced profoundly by Hegel, is a source in pragmatism for the explication of the early Marx's notes on the interrelationship of experience, activity and cognition.[22] Dewey was of course one of the foremost educational theorists of the century and so attention to him is doubly rewarding, as we have the chance not just to explicate the epistemology of the early Marx but also what may be taken to be some of its educational and curricula consequences.

Dewey saw himself as an empiricist who took science seriously and who stressed the primacy of activity for all cognition: '. . . there is no such thing as genuine knowledge and fruitful understanding except as the offspring of doing . . . Men have to *do* something to the things when they wish to find out something . . . The laboratory is a discovery of the condition under which *labor* may become intellectually fruitful and not merely externally productive'.[23] Elsewhere Dewey refers to experience as being an active, vital thing, not just the passive registration of an already given reality, but tied up with efforts to transform the given. The 'salient trait' of experience is its 'connection with a future'.[24] A consequence of this is the acknowledgment of connections and causal mechanisms having a *real* existence in nature. In contrast to passive empiricists such as Hume, who believed: 'upon the whole, necessity is something which exists in the mind, not in objects', Dewey's engagement in the transforming of nature led him to a very realist and Marxist account of the reality of causal mechanisms.

Marx's criticism of the 'sensationalism' of Feuerbach is something with which Dewey would concur. Sensations had no more epistemological status for Dewey than a 'shower or a fever'.[25] Experience is sensation reflected upon; it is full of 'inference' in Dewey's terms. He is another who denied the empiricist myth of the 'virgin perception'. He also denied the *Robinson Crusoe* myth of the isolated individual much loved by liberal political theory and empiricist epistemology. Clearly it was only in association with others that intellectual, practical, spiritual talents of people could be developed. The individual was a socialised individual.

Dewey aligns himself with the fallibilist tradition of Hegel, Marx and Pierce. For him, 'even the best established theories retain a hypothetical status'. He shared Marx's suspicion of high-flown abstractions and utopian ideals. Marx's trenchant criticism of religion is echoed in Dewey's remark: 'There is a danger in the reiteration of eternal verities and ultimate spiritualities. Our sense of the actual is dulled, and we are led to think that in dwelling upon ideal goals we have somehow transcended existing evils'.[26] Dewey had deep aspirations concerning the power of reason in the transformation of the world. This is reflected in occasional remarks about 'moth-eaten slogans' standing in the way of a planned economy and comments about 'sin being ignorance'. However these protestations of rationalism belied an increasing sense of the *material* impediments to the betterment of society. Specifically in America he saw the class system of capitalism as the enemy of reason. Indeed, echoing Marx's eleventh thesis, he said that the class system had to be 'abolished' in order to allow the exercise of intelligence to be effective.[27] That is, philosophers had to transform the world in order to create the conditions for interpretation. The *politics* of how this was to be done is another story. He certainly opposed the economic determinism of the American Communist Party and what he saw as its Stalinism. He was involved in university industrial action, but there was little appreciation of how any large-scale assault on capitalism might be organised. The question of what we do when arguments fail to convince was not in the end faced by Dewey.

PAULO FREIRE

Freire is a one-time professor of Education, who was banished from Brazil at the time of the 1964 coup. His synthesis of Catholicism, Marxist Humanism and practical educational and political involvement has won his work a very wide audience.[28] Freire's epistemology is central to all his writings. It is the most 'worked out' and elaborated part of his educational and social theory. For Freire, knowledge is derived from experience and is gained and tested in practice, in the active engagement of human subjects in the transformation of the natural and social world. He uses the same term which both Aristotle and Marx use to denote this essential unity between action and reflection in the process of knowledge acquisition—'Praxis'. Although Freire's epistemology is the most philosophically rigorous part of his work, it still requires amplification and further argument. It is nowhere 'got together', presented in full. The texts present us with scattered comments, appeals, assertions, truncated reflections. There is an epistemological 'surface' which is dotted with features and various amounts of subsoil, but not a complete profile exposing all the roots and interconnections. His epistemology is basically that of the young Marx; indeed it can be boiled down to Marx's famous 1845 *Theses on Feuerbach*. Viewed in this light, the profile becomes clear and the interconnections obvious. As well as giving us the intellectual heritage, this also indicates some of the deficiencies of Freire, the lacunae, the areas which require further analysis and reworking.

In the following paragraphs I will isolate the features of Freire's theory of knowledge; elaborate them where necessary; show the connections with Marx; contrast them with alternative traditions and suggest, where appropriate, educational implications.

(i) **Realism.** We are subjects who exist in a real world, a world of material objects and of nature which exists independently of people. As Marx does in the first thesis on Feuerbach, Freire maintains a real distinction between knower and known. In Idealism, the latter is merged with the former. For Berkeley, Leibniz and Kant the world does not exist apart from the subject. In Materialism, the former is merged with the latter. For Bergson and others the subject or mind does not exist apart from the world. On this point Freire quotes Sartre: 'There are two ways to fall into idealism: the one consists of dissolving the real in subjectivity; the other in denying all real subjectivity in the interests of objectivity'.[29]

(ii) **Subjectivism.** Although there is a world of nature independent of people, when people experience that world and each other they begin to create a social or human or cultural world which is itself a reality. 'Reality is never just simply the objective datum, the concrete fact, but it is also men's perception of it'.[30] That is what Popper calls the second world and Berger and Luckman the 'symbolic universe'. For Freire it is vital that this cultural realm 'becomes the object of men's knowledge so that they can perceive its conditioning power'.[31] We need to challenge the assumptions we bring with us, as formed individuals in society, to any study of society. The knower is neither Robinson Crusoe nor a feral child who confronts the world without assumptions. Do we accept assumptions such as: 'it is individuals who know'; 'the poor are poor because they are lazy'; 'metropolitan culture is superior to native culture'; 'learning cannot occur unless there is a teacher'? This point is important for the theory of ideology.

(iii) **Abstraction.** Knowledge involves abstraction from experience; in the process of reflection upon experience we abstract and thus create intellectual categories for comprehending the world and our experience of it. Freire is not a naive empiricist or a sensualist. Knowledge does not come from people simply having sense stimulation. Marx, in his *Grundrisse*, speaks about 'thought appropriating the concrete . . . in terms of the abstract'. The world, as it is conveyed and verbalised in people's knowledge, is a world composed of abstractions and is demarcated by concepts. What Freire and others are stressing here is the *active* part the mind plays in knowledge acquisition. It is a point overlooked by nearly all advocates of Discovery Learning. People never just see, just experience, just discover; they always see and discover particular things, depending upon what is already in their heads. To ask children to observe is pointless; they have to be directed to observe particular classes or types of things. Once again the quality or worthwhileness of observations will depend upon the quality of the abstractions or theories or world views which people bring to bear on their researches. Freire discusses this under the heading of 'codification'.

(iv) **Codification.** The process of abstraction depends upon and creates images, symbols, ideas, concepts and words. We try to create 'representations' of concrete reality. This procedure is vital to Freire's pedagogy and his literacy programmes. It is hierarchical: there are, and he quotes Chomsky on this, 'surface structures and deep structures'. There are naive and sophisticated ways of representing phenomena; immediate and theoretical ways. The surface ways are usually ideological; they represent the interests of the powerful classes. We 'immediately' see the sun as going around the earth; 'terrorism' as desperate actions of isolated individuals; 'theft' as breaking and entering. In his literacy programme the codification initially takes the form of a photograph or sketch which represents a real existent, or an existent constructed by the learners. The learners' original words and descriptions are gradually replaced by less immediate and more theoretical ones such as 'power', 'profit', 'production'. 'In the process of decodifying representations of their existential situations and perceiving former perceptions, the learners gradually, hesitatingly and timorously place in doubt the opinion they held of reality and replace it with a more and more critical knowledge'.[32] Shades of Plato and Galileo! Importantly for epistemology, we do not codify in a vacuum but in a particular historical, cultural, linguistic and class situation. Some codifications are helpful, others unhelpful; some accurate, others inaccurate; some reveal, others mystify.

(v) **Distancing.** Freire maintains that an 'operation basic to the act of knowing is the gaining of distance from the knowable object'.[33] This is part of the reflection side of praxis. He opposes a total immersion in activity—a mindless activism—on the grounds that it does not provide for the critical distancing in the act of knowing. Similarly (and for reasons already given) he opposes any view which would maintain that people are the best judges of their own situations. They need to stand back and reflect on their situation as an object of knowledge. This is why peasants immersed in a culture of silence, without the experience of being reflective and active subjects, face such an enormous epistemological obstacle. Likewise schools, with their constant round of bells, periods, assemblies, are not conducive to intellectual and cognitive development. In Western, urban situations, the pressures against distancing or reflection are as great. Where time is divided between travel, work, rent and health worries, TV and families, reflection and distancing are discounted.

(vi) **Agency.** There are constant references throughout Freire to agency or activity as a necessary condition for knowledge. If we wish to know we must do, we must act. 'Knowing is the task of subjects, not of objects. It is as a subject, and only as such, that a man or woman can really know'.[34] This connects Freire with the experimentalist tradition in philosophy and opposes him to forms of intellectualism and rationalism. Dewey agrees with

Freire on this matter—if we want children to know about soil then they should do something with soil; if we want them to know about democracy then engage them in democratic experiences. The necessity of agency to change of consciousness is something testified to by liberation movements and consciousness-raising groups. In the novel *Burn*, by Norman Gant, William, who had cultivated a black slave to lead a revolution, provides a clear example of this point. He says to José Dolores: 'If I had told you to make a revolution you wouldn't have understood. But to rob a bank? Yes. That was possible. Then you had to kill to defend yourself. Then you killed to defend others. The rest came by itself.'

(vii) **Problematising.** Knowledge acquisition begins with problems, with puzzles, with tasks. Pedagogy must be problematic: 'To be an act of knowing then, the adult literacy process must engage the learners in the constant problematising of their existential situations'.[35] Hence Freire will pose to urban workers questions such as: 'Why is it that you build high-rise office blocks and yet live in shanties?', or his account of asking rural workers what the enemies of cotton are. Replies begin at ground level and work up: poor soil, insects, lack of rain, transportation, marketing, imperialism. Once more, Freire is at one with the most enlightened education theorists. Learning will proceed better if it is based on problems, and problems that are relevant to the immediate situation—in jargonese, if there is motivation to learn. This is why Freire castigates the use of Readers in peasant education which talk of 'Jack and Jill going up the hill'. Little wonder such programmes fail.

In science teaching, one can teach electricity in terms of formulae and equations and textbook exercises, that is, teach in the normal accepted manner, or one can problematise the situation. Who doesn't have a power point in the bedroom? Who would like a light in the toilet? Who might want a water service installed? Once the real problems and needs are uncovered, the teaching of electricity, circuitry and load capacities and earthing can proceed in an efficient and engaging manner.

Freire extends this point by saying that we should not dichotomise the manner in which scientific knowledges are initially acquired and the manner in which they are transmitted. 'If the development of scientific knowledge . . . cannot be separated from a problematic approach . . . neither can the apprehension of this knowledge'.[36] Again, if people wish to develop knowledge of poetry, literature, painting, history and science, Freire is saying, as many others do, that they ought to compose poetry, write literature, try painting, create history and be scientific. The dichotomy of discovery and transmission has had a particularly debilitating effect in the sciences. Similarly, in mathematics, the end point of mathematical science might well be a set of formulae. But to teach the end point instead of the procedures results in a minimum of understanding and comprehension and a maximum of ignorance of what mathematics and mathematical reasoning is. Consider a series of numbers that we might wish to find the sum of: 1, 2, 3, 4, . . . 97, 98, 99, 100. One way to teach (the standard way) is to give the formulae for the sum of an Arithmetic Progression (AP) which is: $AP = an + \frac{1}{2}n\ (n-1)d$, and fill in the variables. Another way is to problematise the matter: Is there a way of solving it without formulae? What do $1+100$ add up to?, $2+99$, $3+98$? Do you see a pattern emerging?

(viii) **Causality.** This is the touchstone of knowledge claims, at least about social processes. 'The more accurately men grasp true causality, the more critical their understanding of reality will be. Their understanding will be magical to the degree that they fail to grasp causality'. Marx maintains also that causality is a critical element in knowledge claims. Ideology typically inverts the causal relation so that effects become causes. For example: 'People are dole scroungers, therefore they will not work', rather than: 'People cannot work therefore they are dole scroungers'. Or: 'People do not pass exams therefore they are poor', rather than: 'People are poor therefore they do not pass exams'.

(ix) **Holism.** To know things is to know things in relation; to know a part is to know how it connects with the whole. In the process of codification, different impressions of the same object or process are utilised so that interrelations might be recognised. It is the total vision which we call knowledge. Again, Freire is at one with the best classical and contemporary thought in this stress on context, background or framework for a knowledge of something. Although it is a slightly different matter for Plato, he insisted that we can never know particulars, only universals. To know a piece of music is not just to hear sounds, but to hear notes, and notes as articulated and patterned in specific ways. For Plato, to know a particular is to know it as an instance of a universal. To know something as a good deed is to know what good as a universal is; to know something as a white object is to know what the universal whiteness is. An analogy which is often used to portray this holist position is that of a group of blindfolded people around an elephant. One holds its tail and says he is holding a snake; another its leg and says he is holding a tree; another its trunk and says he is holding a lizard, etc. Then the blindfolds are removed and they all see that they were holding different parts of the same whole. Many forms of curricula organisation militate against such grasping of the whole.

It is usually the case that development of theoretical understanding enables unlike and dissimilar things to be seen as interrelated. Take for instance a rotating compass needle, a configuration of iron filings, a current induced in a wire, a wire moving in a particular area. At an immediate, sensory, empirical level these events are disparate and disjointed. A theory of electromagnetism, however, enables them to be seen and known as different instances of the same thing. Without the theory they are not seen as related, much like the rotation of celestial bodies and the falling of terrestrial bodies prior to Newton's theory of universal gravitation. This example points to a critical weakness of empiricism, particularly any covering law model tied to empiricism—it is simply not the case that related events are experienced or seen as similar or related.

One of the great strengths of Marxist theory is that it is a holist theory. Coups in Chile, wars in Vietnam, inflation in Australia, *Donald Duck* comics in the New Hebrides may not appear to be related, but with a sufficiently developed theory of capitalism a case can be presented for their being so. This has enormous importance for the teaching of social sciences and history.

An important part of a genuinely holist approach to knowledge is the historical dimension. Things simply cannot be understood if looked at as a time slice of history. This is why sociology even of a structural variety, let alone a functionalist aberration, is hard put to lay claim to knowledge. It is concerned only with the contours of the present and lacks the wherewithal to understand the present as the material outcome of an interplay of tendencies in history. An ahistorical understanding tends to see situations and social realities as necessary or immutable when they are in fact contingent and changeable. Thus ahistoricism is conducive to ideological misunderstanding. Typical examples are the role of women, forms of the family, functions of the State, educational curricula and practices, and forms of religious organisation. Naive consciousness sees not just particulars, but particulars without history. Ideological institutions can sanctify contingent circumstances and give them the appearance of permanent realities. Not long ago, suits were regarded as an immutable part of being a male school-teacher; the fact that professors run departments in universities currently seems immutable. Can we have a genuine knowledge of the 1975 coup in Australia without a knowledge of the history of class struggle in Australia, particularly the history of the ruling class's use of judicial and political instrumentalities to maintain its power over the working class?

(x) **Fallibilism.** One of the features on the terrain of Freire's epistemology is 'fallibilism'. Others might call it 'relativism', others 'subjectivism', others 'scepticism'. I refer to a position indicated by statements such as: 'Further critical consciousness always submits that causality to analysis; what is true today may not be so tomorrow. Naive consciousness sees causality as a static, established fact and thus is deceived in its perception';[37] and: 'If the act of knowing is a dynamic act—and no knowledge is ever complete—then in order to know, man not only 'ad-mires' the object, but must always be 're-ad-miring' his former ad-miration'.[38]

Minimally, what this is saying is that no knowledge is ever complete. This is not unduly controversial: as Paul said, and most would agree, 'we see as through a glass darkly'. I use the term 'fallible' to indicate just this—that our ideas can be improved upon and understandings deepened. But to say that knowledge is never complete is not to say that what is true today may be false tomorrow. If this is unqualified, then it must be a form of scepticism. Freire does have a developmentalist, dialectical, dynamic view of reality: a process ontology. If reality is changing, if it is a flux, if we never step into the same river twice, as Heraclitus said, then our knowledge may turn out to be out of date. In this sense, what was true may now be false, but the property of 'truth' no longer applies to the same reality-statement couple since the reality has changed. This is common-place. People grow up, they change, they may once have been chauvinists—they no longer are. This process ontology, coupled with a fallibilist epistemology, is a powerful aid to tolerance and an inhibitor of dogmatism. There are good outcomes. But a thorough-going scepticism or relativism is just dangerous and ideological. It leads to paralysis and failure to be committed. Witness the political sterility of extreme libertarianism. I take it that there is enough in Freire to indicate that he is not a relativist —one idea is not as good as another (the naive-critical consciousness distinction; the fragmented-whole vision distinction; the very culture-circle movement all suggest this). Likewise I take it that he is not a sceptic—knowledge is possible (otherwise why the pedagogy, why the scholarship and analysis, why the hope?).

(xi) **Social Dimension.** A most important aspect of Freire's epistemology is that it has a social dimension. There has been a long tradition in Western philosophy which poses the question of knowledge in terms of how an individual knows the world. There has been a sort of *Robinson Crusoe* model operating since Plato: an individual goes about the world thinking and/or having sense impressions and the epistemological question is: how does he know that his thoughts or impressions are veridical or true? The fact that man is part of a community has for so long been taken as irrelevant background noise for epistemology. Freire rejects this individualism: 'Just as there is no such thing as an isolated human being, there is also no such thing as isolated human thinking. In the act of thinking about the object s/he cannot think without the co-participation of another subject.[39] It is the "we think" which establishes the "I think" and not the contrary'. Thus the 'I think' is enhanced if the 'we think' is enhanced. That is, people tend to gain if they promote a better level of thought among their community of contacts. Taking education as an instance, co-operation rather than competitiveness ought to be the rule; in personal relationships dialogue, exchange and encouragement rather than secretiveness, intellectual hoarding and discouragement; in social affairs openness, debate and public discussion. I take it that it is something like this that makes intelligible Freire's claim that for one person to know requires that someone else knows.

To stress the social dimension of knowledge is also to draw attention to the lively possibility of ignorance. The community may lack the concepts and theories that enable correct understanding. If that is so, then individuals simply miss out; there is not much they can do. This is akin to what some Marxists speak of as an 'epistemological obstacle'. The American Jesuit Bernard Lonergan, in the Preface to his book *Insight*, wrote of this: 'No problem is at once more delicate and more profound, more practical and perhaps more pressing. How, indeed, is a mind to become conscious of its own bias when that bias springs from a communal flight from understanding and is supported by the whole texture of a civilization?'

One can restate this as the problem of ideology. In a class

society the ruling ideas are the ideas of the ruling class. These are consistent with their own material self-interest and will be maintained despite their clashing with reality or being against the interest of the majority. It is this climate of ideological ideas and practices into which one is born. Plato's ascent from ignorance to knowledge can be seen as the process of abstraction, or replacing ideology with science.

I have said that Freire is not a systematic philosopher. Even so, with respect to epistemology and education he is, as Paul Hirst has said, a person who has made one of the most significant contributions of recent decades. Features of his epistemological landscape are: realism, subjectivism, abstraction, codification, distancing, agency, problematising, causality, holism, fallibilism and social dimension. These features can be substantiated by seeing Freire in the context of a Marxist theory of knowledge. They can in parts be further substantiated by reference to recent philosophy of science. There are immediate consequences of his theory of knowledge for people and institutions concerned with the development and transmission of knowledge. The features have implications for curricula, ways of teaching, educational administration, community relationships. Above all, the theory underlines the point that education is a political activity, and those involved in teaching ought to be aware of this and act accordingly. 'Education, its content and its method, is not neutral', as Freire so often says.

THE LATER MARX AND A MODEL OF MARXIST EPISTEMOLOGY

I have prepared the ground for an account of Marx's epistemology. What the early Marx discussed as 'practice' is in the later Marx discussed as 'production'. *Capital* is a long, complex and scientific study of commodity production. Marx believes that the analysis is applicable to mental production, that is, the terms, concepts and schema of the first can be used to explicate production of ideas and theories in society. If this is successful then we have a new model for epistemological discussion; a model which will overcome many of the problems which plague standard epistemology.

Mao speaks of ideas not dropping out of the sky but rising out of practices; Popper speaks of the third world being a natural product of the human world; Lenin speaks about cognition being a 'reflection' of the real world, that is, of ideas being in some way produced by human engagement in the world;

Althusser speaks of knowledge as the effect of a process of theoretical production. All of these embody something of the epistemological programme of the later Marx, itself the development and articulation of the 'germs' relating cognition to practice. The later Marx contains the outlines of an epistemology which is both materialist and historical.

MANUAL AND INTELLECTUAL LABOUR

Aristotle analysed human work, intentional transforming activity, in terms of his fourfold division of causality. Marx adopted this for the simple case of artisan production. Consider, for instance, the activity of producing a statue. We can identify the following components or aspects of the process:

material cause — the substance worked upon (marble)
efficient cause — the energies and powers working on the substance (sculptor and his activities)
formal cause — the end product or result (statue of a particular kind)
final cause — the purpose of the activity; the intentions of the artist.

When expounded to large-scale commodity production, the schema becomes:

material cause — raw materials, objects of labour
efficient cause — technology, labour power
formal cause — commodities, use values
final cause — schemes, plans, designs.

The most general model for economic practice, that is for the activity of producing goods, is:

raw materials + labour and $\rightarrow$ products
productive forces

For example:

water, oranges + labour, machines $\rightarrow$ orange juice.

Of course, products are only 'provisionally' products; there is nothing in their nature that makes them products. A product of one process figures as raw material for another productive process. Juicing machines are the product of one process and part of the technology or productive forces for another; orange juice is a product here and a raw material there—as in the production of Cointreau.

Furthermore, any account of material production will need to incorporate details of the patterns of ownership and control which operate in the productive processes: who owns the raw materials and means of production and who controls the distribution of products will have to be taken into account in order to understand the process with which we are dealing.

The model as outlined is very abstract; we need to be aware that Marx was insistent that any scientific study of production had to treat production not as a general category, but in definite historical form. Marx is particularly insistent that the technologies and instruments of production available are the central determining forces for shaping the form of the productive process.

How does the analysis of commodity production relate to the analysis of mental production, to the process of theory construction, to epistemology? The relation is via the concepts of practice and of work. Scientists are like artisans in many respects. They work on certain raw materials; they use certain instruments and techniques for the analysis and transformation of their materials; they entertain certain goals as a result of a problem situation which they recognise or have thrust upon them; they create or manufacture certain products. We can speak of the *theoretical* work of the scientist and the *practical* work of the artisan. Jerome R. Ravetz[40] from outside the Marxist tradition, and Louis Althusser[41] from within the tradition, have developed this model of knowledge as production in interesting and informative ways.

Reverting to the simple case, and once more using Aristotle's scheme or analysis, how can we characterise the work of a scientist in the production of cognitive claims, of theory? We have a:

material cause — observations, experimental results, concepts, laws, problems.

efficient cause — technologies, instruments, methods, scientific labour—the problematic.

formal cause — higher laws, new concepts, theories

final cause — mastery of situations, fulfilment of needs, goals and plans of procedure.

REAL AND THEORETICAL OBJECTS
One vital difference in this analogy is that the scientist does not work upon real objects in the world; rather he works upon

theoretical objects, upon intellectually constructed raw materials. There is a *real object* of science (objects and events in the world) and there is a *theoretical object* of science (formulae, descriptions, observations). Knowledge construction *begins* with the latter and ends in the construction of a *new* theoretical object. In this context we can understand discussion about the theory dependence of observation and the process of abstraction and simplification in scientific work: both of these are constituents of the raw materials with which science works. The empiricist tradition conflates the real and theoretical objects of science; and where the distinction is dimly perceived, it asks the wrong kinds of questions about their relationship.

Galileo. Take, for instance, Galileo's achievements, which have been discussed in Chapter 3. There were real world objects and events—pendulums on chains, balls rolling on planes, objects sliding across surfaces. Galileo wanted, of course, to understand these, but in order to do so he abstracted from them, simplified them, symbolised them and quantified them. By so doing he generated and constructed the raw materials of his science, the intellectually created objects about which his science of mechanics was concerned. Take, again, his analysis of falling bodies. The real objects (stones, cannon balls) fell slantedly and unevenly. Galileo represented this state of affairs in terms of two components of motion—a horizontal component and a vertical component. These were theoretical abstractions. He used the parallelogram to find the resultant motion which was the theoretical object corresponding to the real object. Having constructed these theoretical objects he was then able to ask questions of them—was the horizontal component a constant? Was acceleration of the vertical component a constant? How can we measure both? His science of mechanics is produced as a result of his scientific work on the theoretical objects of knowledge he created. Aristotelian science and Galilean science shared the same real objects, but they had different theoretical objects. (Their respective *accounts* or *descriptions* of the real objects may differ of course—the 'sun rising' being the obvious example of descriptive disagreement. Further, as development of one science generates new experiments and tests, its class of real objects will begin to differ from the original shared class.)

Millikan's Oil Drop Experiment. This famous 1909 experiment to determine the charge of an electron can be used to illustrate the real/theoretical object distinction and also, in passing, to illustrate some problems for an empiricist account of science and some deficiencies of standard school science teaching. In simple terms, what Millikan did was to spray charged oil particles into a space between two electric plates. The force of gravity pulled the drops down and the voltage across the plates was adjusted to control the velocity of fall. If Q is the charge on the drop, then the electric force on it is given by: $F = VQ/d$, where V is the plate voltage and d the plate separation. Then the velocity of the drop is a function of F directed upwards and weight (mg) downwards. Thus: $f - mg = KV$, where K is a constant. At this stage the gas in the chamber was ionised (its molecules lost or gained electrons). Some of the charged oil particles absorbed these ions and consequently altered their charge and thus their velocity of fall. If Qn is the charge difference (the charge of the ionised molecules) then another set of equations can be derived: $Qn = dK (v_1 - v)/V$. If the first and second equations are solved (we assume that the mass increase of the oil drop when it accepts the ion is negligible) then Millikan found that Qn could always be represented by: $Qn = ne$, where n was a whole number and e the putative charge of the electron (1.6×10^{-19} coulombs).

In the original publication of these results, Millikan said that 2,000 drops were observed, yet 'in not one single instance has there been any change [of velocity] which did not represent the advent upon the drop of one definite invariable quantity of electricity, or a very small exact multiple of that quantity'.[42] A widely-used Australian school science text reproduces this paragraph and adds that 'it is an amazing fact that the proof of the discrete nature of electricity required no further measurements than those of the different velocities of an oil drop'.[43]

There are many aspects of this experiment to notice:

(i) It is not the observation of nature but the experimentation upon and manipulation of nature that Millikan was engaged upon.

(ii) It took place in a specific moment of physics. It depended upon the physics of electric fields being worked out; upon the concept of electrons being articulated; and upon the technology of observation, measurement and voltage manipulation being available. The experimental results in turn feed into other calculations in physics. Its proof of discreteness gave impetus to Bohr's model of the atom and its value of e enabled the mass of an electron to be calculated, since Thompson had already derived the proportion e/m.

(iii) While Millikan worked on and manipulated real objects with his left hand, he fashioned theoretical objects with his right. While oil drops were going up and down in the chamber, formulae and values were going on and off his notepaper. The question emerges as to how the theoretical objects relate to the real objects.

There are, however, some very important aspects of the experiment which, on the account thus far given, cannot be appreciated—Millikan's actual results were nothing like he claimed they were, and nothing like science texts describe them! In his laboratory notebooks we constantly see marginal comments such as: 'error do not use', 'very low something wrong', 'a mistake somewhere'; and then notes such as: 'publish', 'beautiful result', 'good finding'.[44] That is, discreteness was *not* given in his data but imposed upon it and abstracted from it. For those holding an inductivist account of science we have here a scandal—Millikan did not follow Gradgrind's admonition to be swayed 'just by the facts and nothing but the facts'. Those falsificationists who maintain that a conjecture has to be abandoned when confronted with a single recalcitrant observation must likewise be scandalised by Millikan's behaviour. On both counts his Nobel Prize would seem to be unwarranted. Our non-empiricist account of science is consistent with the Millikan episode, because of the distinction drawn between the theoretical and real objects of a science. Millikan fashioned theoretical objects using determinant raw materials and means of production; these theoretical objects are then the subject of knowledge claims in science and are assessed not by correspondence, but broadly by utility.

The episode also confirms Paul Feyerabend's frequent observation that standard science teaching makes 'the history of science duller, simpler, more uniform, more "objective" and more easily accessible to treatment by strict and unchangeable rules'.[45]

Avoidance Behaviour. Consider another illustration of this important epistemological point concerning the difference between real and theoretical objects of a science. In psychology there has been for many decades a flourishing science of 'Avoidance Behaviour'. As is the nature of the subject it begins with general concerns about why people avoid certain circumstances, and then drops down to rats pressing bars in cages with lights flashing on and shocks being given. The real object is nature in varying degrees of contortion and torture: a rat moving about a natural environment, then a rat in a contrived experimental situation, then a rat immobilised to varying degrees in a highly structured bar-press contraption. There are as many theoretical objects as there are sciences of avoidance behaviour. Teleological accounts will have objects such as 'anticipations' and 'strategies'. Thorough-going behaviourist accounts will speak of '*CS*' and '*CR*' and 'motivating effects of S^+ cues'. Then, of course, there are many species differences within the genus of behaviourist accounts. A thesis of mine on the subject was concerned with how a 'non-contingent S^- can reinforce behaviour'. This problem arose because of contradictions generated within the theoretical object of the paradigm I was working within: namely, that 'a contingent S^+ had to remain an S^+ even though the animal is consistently avoiding shock'. Now, the esoteric and highly sophisticated behaviourist science of avoidance—the theoretical object—has left the poor old rat pressing his bar a long way behind. It has to relate to it (as Galileo said, 'our science has to be about the world not words'), but the relationship is not one of reduction or simple correspondence. I will maintain that it is rather one of control, effectivity, manipulation. The truth of the theoretical object is its power and instrumentality.

Social Science. The distinction is an important one to recognise in social science. For instance, we speak of the Consumer Price Index (CPI) rising from 5.7 to 6.3. That sounds neat, and it articulates in defined ways with other elements of our theoretical discourse. But there is no sense in which it corresponds to any actual state of affairs among real objects. It is riddled with conventions—do we include newspapers in the calculation? Do we allow for seasonal fluctuations? What weighting is to be given to meat versus toiletries? What do we take as the average consuming unit? According to what we *choose* on these matters the CPI goes up or down, the real objects just keep on moving. Or, we hear that a multinational makes a profit of $X millions, and we use this fact in some social scientific calculation. The 'fact' is a theoretical fact; it is not in any neat sense a real world fact. Again, it is riddled with conventions—how much do we write off as depreciation? What value do we place on our fixed capital? What do we take as exchange rates and when do we take them? Does maintenance count as investment or payment? One standard objection to Marx's class analysis theory is that the concept of class is an abstraction. How odd and peculiar that it should be so! Of course it is an abstraction, it belongs to the theoretical discourse of a social science, just as 'CPI' or 'profit' do. Social science, as well as natural science, works on intellectually constructed objects. It proves itself in practice, not in observation.

Approximate Analogies. Theoretical objects are things in a theoretical discourse; they are developed, defined and refined within the discourse. A scientist constructs these with a pen in his right hand, whilst his left hand is manipulating real, material objects. With an absolutely vital qualification, we can think of this as the relationship of a recipe to a cake. The recipe exists, and is constructed on paper; it is materialised and proven in the cake, in the real object. The analogy does not work inasmuch as recipes are *ad hoc* creations and are altered in an arbitrary manner as a result of practice. The analogy works better if the recipe is developed within a science of foodstuffs and bio-chemistry; and alterations to it are made on the basis of knowledge of the reactions of carbonates and glutens and the like. A better analogy is the relationship of the plans for a bridge and the constructed bridge. A blueprint is prepared in conformity with principles of mechanics, and is then materialised in the real world.

In Act V of *A Midsummer Night's Dream* Shakespeare provides us with something of the essence of this distinction:

> The poet's eye, in a fine frenzy rolling
> Doth glance from heaven to earth, from earth to heaven,
> And, as imagination bodies forth
> The forms of things unknown, the poet's pen
> Turns them to shapes, and gives to airy nothing
> A local habitation and a name.

Some theoretical objects are scientific and others are ideological. The former characteristically break with common sense rather than canonise it; they are constructed within theory as a result of determinate rules and procedural principles and are not just *ad hoc*, for the occasion, constructions; they correctly 'latch' on to causal processes in the real and so can be materialised or actualised. The theoretical objects of an ideology characteristically take up, in an uncritical way, the conceptualisations of common sense; they are mostly constructed in an *ad hoc* manner, being largely determined by external interests; they often lack the capacity to be materialised. Aristotelian physics provides an example of extremely sophisticated ideology. Its theoretical objects were ideological in that they did not break with common sense, with everyday experience. The notions of 'natural place', of 'up and down' direction, of teleology, and others, are outgrowths of everyday, lived experience. Classical mechanics broke with the everyday as the determinant of science. The ideal types of some discourses are theoretical objects, but not necessarily scientific ones. Many ideal types are just purifications of everyday notions.

MARX ON METHOD

The real object/theoretical object distinction makes intelligible, and is in turn rendered intelligible by, the contentious 'Method of Political Economy' in the Introduction by Marx to his 1857 *Grundrisse*.[46] In the study of political economy, Marx says, it seems correct to begin with real and concrete objects, such as 'populations'. He points out, however, that on closer examination this proves false. The real objects turn out to be abstractions (theoretical objects in our terms). The 'population' designation covers a multitude of things: classes, wages, labour, capital and division of labour. This holds also for designations such as 'nation' and 'State'. He advocates abstracting a small number of determinant, general relations such as 'division of labour', 'money'. Once we have these (basic theoretical objects) we ascend to other such objects—'need', 'exchange value', 'world markets'. We then have connections with the worldly real objects. But now the obvious and transparent real objects are seen to be more complex than first appeared. This process, stated paradoxically by Marx as 'ascending from the abstract to the concrete', is claimed to be 'obviously the scientifically correct method'. There is good evidence for Marx in affirming this. A mathematical science requires analysis and abstraction; it requires clearly defined theoretical objects. Thus, Marx praises Adam Smith for being able to throw out every 'limiting specification of wealth-creating activity'—gardening, cooking, building, manufacturing—and reduce them all to the abstract category 'labour in general'. How reminiscent this is of Galileo's advice: 'The computer who wants his calculations to deal with sugar, silk, and wool must discount the boxes, bales, and other packings; so the mathematical scientist, when he wants to recognise in the concrete the effects which he has proved in the abstract, must deduct the material hindrances'.[47] Failure to follow this advice proved a millstone around the neck of Aristotelian mechanics. For Aristotle, physics was in one compartment and dealt with things as they were; mathematics was in another, and dealt with idealised and abstracted things. Descartes, although a renowned mathematician, held on to this same dichotomy: he was alarmed at the licence which Galileo exercised in bringing mathematics into the realm of physics. If in nature there were no vacuums, frictionless surfaces, weightless strings or point masses, then one was doing violence to reason to introduce them into science. This revulsion of Descartes is basically an empiricist revulsion, it stems from a failure to distinguish between the real and theoretical objects of a science. The theoretical objects do *not* have to mirror the real objects; the theoretical *system* has to be able to intervene and act effectively on the real.

It has been pointed out previously that the theory developed in *Capital* is not a descriptive account of the economy of any particular country; it is, rather, a generalised, theoretical system which relates to any particular real system only when a number of specified conditions are met. It establishes tendencies or potentials whose manifestation or actualisation is a contingent matter. In order to be scientific, the conditions for actualisation have to be specified; in order to be interesting and useful, they have occasionally to be met. Without the first, Marxism is open to Popper's charges of being an unfalsifiable religion; without the second, Marxism is open to liberal charges of being a daydream. These conditions include commodity production being dominant; a closed national economy; investment for profit and the existence of classes. To the extent that the system is not ideal, we have to modify predictions and prescriptions.[48] Thus Marx says that the abstraction 'labour in general' as the source of wealth finds its pure expression only in the economy of the United States, where labour has been deskilled and routinised; where the actuality is generalised labour. Thus, 'an immeasurably ancient relation, valid in all forms of society, nevertheless achieves practical truth as an abstraction only as a category of the most modern society'.[49]

The 'Method' section is explicit about scientific knowledge being the effect, or product, of intellectual production. The raw materials for it are 'observations and conceptions', and the products are new 'concepts'. The method by which science appropriates the world is different from the methods used in artistic, religious, practical appropriations of the world. The totality of science as it appears in the head is a 'product of a thinking head'. Science does not begin with real objects in the world but with intellectually constructed objects, with con-

ceptions. The empiricist confrontation between a knowing subject and a real object is absent in Marx. Kolakowski remarks on
this: 'Traditional empiricism, which presents cognition as the
creation of concepts abstracted from individual observations of
the properties of species, fails to take into account the basic fact
of consciousness: the indispensability of general knowledge to
the perception of the concrete.'[50]

It is worth noting, of course, that Marx is a realist and opposes
all idealisms which would eliminate the real object (Berkeley) or
make it dependent upon the theoretical object. We have first to
abstract in order to know the real, but 'this is by no means the
process by which the concrete itself comes into being'. He is
insistent that 'the real subject retains its autonomous existence
outside the head'. Surprisingly, there have been tendencies
towards idealism within the Marxist tradition.[51]

PROBLEMATIC

Just as economic production cannot occur in a free-floating
manner—we cannot produce what we want, where we want
and how we want—neither can theoretical production. We
require raw materials, circumstances for work, and above all we
need machinery for the creation of new or transformed concepts. For this machinery we choose to use the term *problematic*,
a term popularised by Louis Althusser. A problematic en-
compasses things such as:

— basic metaphysical and ontological commitments;
— what kind of relations hold between the basic entities;
— what constitutes an explanation;
— what general laws hold;
— directions about method and methodology.

As a result, it is the problematic which recognises and specifies
the problems that face a system and also recognises those that
do not. The problems of devils being red or green does not arise
for those whose ontology does not include devils. Marx does not
use the term 'problematic', but his writings suggest a strong
sense of it. In the *German Ideology*, when speaking of German
social criticism, he says: 'The whole body of its inquiries has
actually sprung from the soil of a definite philosophical system,
that of Hegel. Not only in their answers but in their very
questions there was a mystification'.

The problematic is objective in the sense that it predates the individual's thinking, and it determines and sets limits to such thinking—like a sewing-machine, which predates any particular worker and determines what kinds of productive activities the worker can engage in. This is the sense in which the 'we think' determines the 'I think'; or the way we can interpret Popper's saying that third-world properties determine the second-world events of scientists' thoughts and experiences. The problematic also determines what kinds of raw materials can be utilised; not any old raw materials can be processed—we cannot feed sheet-metal into a sewing-machine. 'Facts' about the uncon-scious, about libidinous urges and repression, cannot be operated upon by a behaviourist problematic. 'Facts' about divine intervention, reconciliation and grace cannot be operated upon in giving a materialist interpretation of Jewish history. Following the analogy through, we can also see that patterns of ownership, authority and control will enter into determination of what is processed, at what time and to what purpose. These are part of what Lakatos has labelled the 'external' influences on science. Industrial research laboratories and business-controlled universities will generate, obviously, knowledge which serves the interests of business. Where ignorance or ideology best serves those interests, then it also can be produced. We have mentioned previously the research for a harvestable tomato; we could add the myriad research programmes conducted by the military-industrial complex. Louis Althusser provides a succinct account of this view when he says that the production of knowledges 'is constituted by a structure which combines the type of object (raw material) on which it labours, the theoretical means of production available (its theory, its method and its technique, experimental or otherwise), and the historical re-lations (both theoretical, ideological and social) in which it produces'.[52]

With respect to method we need to make a number of distinctions, but before doing so we will raise some questions about commodity production which will then have their ana-logues in scientific production. Consider the case of a person sewing a coat. We can ask of this:

(i)   What is the method or technique for producing the coat?
(ii) What characteristic makes the coat a good coat?
(iii) How do we justify our choice of characteristic for good-ness?

The first question is one of *method*. In this case there would be broad guidelines that could be laid down, but only broad ones. Coat-making is to some extent a craft; there are many nuances and skills which need to be picked up in the course of an apprenticeship. It entails 'tacit knowledge' in Polanyi's sense. The second question is what we will call a *methodological* question. Here we argue about appearance, cut, lightness, fashion, function. When judging a tailoring contest, the criteria used for assessment are the outcome of methodological deliberations. The fact that there are such contests means that assessment is not an entirely subjective matter.

The third question is what I will call a *metamethodological* question. This is involved when we come to argue for, and justify, our chosen criteria for goodness. Why is it that a neat cut makes a good coat? Is cut a better indicator than durability?

We will turn now to the production of a scientific theory. The questions we can ask are of the same kind as the.above:

(i)   Is there a *method* by which the 'secrets of Nature' can be wrested from her? In the Baconian ideal there was such a routinised, mechanical method. This was the inductivist view of science and the one that has much currency in school textbooks. It is given contemporary expression in the procedures of the big research laboratories. Popper, Lakatos and others have undermined its simple faith. Einstein's dictum that science is the 'free creation of the human mind' is an anti-methodist position.

(ii) Of the product, we can ask whether it is good. Is the heliocentric theory a decent theory? Here we have *methodological* considerations. Some will say it is good because there is much evidence for it (Inductivism); others will say it is bad because there is some evidence against it (Dogmatic Falsificationism); others will say it is good because everyone says it is (Conventionalism); others will say it is good because it allows us to reform the calendar, traverse oceans, predict eclipses (Instrumentalism); and so on.

(iii) At the next level of argument we try to justify our putative methodologies; here we have *metamethodology*. A conventionalist will argue for his position, perhaps, as Poincaré did for his views in geometry—'conventional yes; arbitrary no'. Lakatos, as we have seen, claims that only his MSRP can be an answer to (ii) as only it can be reflexive at the level of (iii). That is, for instance, falsification as methodology falsifies itself.

TRUTH

We are now in a position to raise again the vexed question of truth. It might well be said that the knowledge as production model or metaphor has some merit and interest as far as the context of discovery is concerned, but it fails to shed light upon the crucial context of justification. This is a legitimate concern. Theoretical production works on the creations of intellectual labour and produces new and altered propositions, theories and concepts. How do these relate to the real objects and processes of the natural world? I have previously said that the second thesis on Feuerbach provides a clue to the Marxist account—'The question whether objective truth can be attributed to human thinking is not a question of theory but is a practical question'. My answer in brief is that correspondence is neat and simple, but useless as an account of truth—one cat may correspond to another or match another or look like another, but 'cat' cannot look like a cat. The test for correspondence cannot be any looking at a theoretical product, then a real object, and seeing if they match. This is blatantly absurd. In effect, what we do is see whether our theories work; we see whether they can enable us to intervene in the processes of the real world; at best we expect them to be able to materialise and externalise themselves in the real, to create real objects on the basis of directions and information that the theoretical object provides.

Engels illustrates this variant of *Instrumentalism* when he speaks about the artificial production of organic chemicals finally laying to rest disputes about their composition, and about whether they could be synthesised from inorganic chemicals. Likewise, for him the Copernican system was a hypothesis where *observational* evidence was not decisive. The hypothesis was only proved three hundred years later when the calculations of Leverrier led Galle to discover the planet Neptune.[53]

Consider a theory such as that of Mendelian inheritance. There were no direct observational grounds for checking on the separation and combination of the genetic 'factors'. The results of experimentally controlled plantings displayed at the phenotypic level the proportions that his 'factor' theory suggested. Here, of course, we have to idealise and abstract the real results. The total submersion of a recessive characteristic in the first generation, and then its reappearance in the second generation in the proportion of 1:3, is only approximated to in the real world. There are many conventional elements which underlie our final confident assertion that the ratio is 1:3.

Consider atomic theories. Werner Heisenberg told Albert Speer in 1942 that the *theory* of nuclear fission had been fully worked out, that is, that the process of theoretical production had gone its course; the raw materials had been worked over and new concepts, equations and formulae produced. At this stage there was nothing for the theoretical objects to correspond to; they remained suspended. They were materialised in the desert of New Mexico in 1945, and shortly after upon the city of Hiroshima. The process of theoretical production went on *within* theory; the checks and corrections were dictated by established procedures and conventions in the problematic. There was little in the way of checking each state against real objects—on the whole there weren't any. In one sense the theory was true in 1942, but it was proven true in 1945 when its power was realised and embodied; when it produced objects in the real to 'correspond' to its theoretical objects; when it was manifested. We use 'correspond' with hesitancy, as it would be rash to say that in the middle of the nuclear holocaust there was some neat and distinct process occurring captured precisely by our representation of:

$$^{235}_{92}U + ^{1}_{0}n \rightarrow ^{236}_{92}U \rightarrow ^{148}_{57}La + ^{85}_{35}Br + 3\,^{1}_{0}n$$

This approximates to the real; the bomb goes off only because it does so—'for nature to be commanded it must first be obeyed'. We *revise* and sophisticate our accounts, depending upon our purposes, interests and capabilities—do we want to know precisely the course of an unabsorbed neutron? Who wants nuclear bombs to go off as the price for the pursuit of truth? As Sir Mark Oliphant observed, 'When the bomb went off, that was the end of a beautiful subject'.

Realism about the external world and a separation of the real and theoretical objects of a science is tantamount to *fallibilism* in epistemology, and this openness is a condition for the growth of science. Galileo expressed this succinctly: 'It always seems to me extreme rashness on the part of some when they want to make human abilities the measure of what nature can do'.[54] Engels echoed this when he spoke of being conscious of the necessary limitations of all acquired knowledge, because of its being 'conditioned by the circumstances in which it was acquired'.[55]

EXPERIMENTATION

The model enables us to revise the place of experimentation in the production of knowledge. The result of an experiment is not just another observation among many we might have got by walking around with our eyes open. It is the controlled attempt to isolate and manipulate in the real the objects and processes which we have utilised and defined in our theoretical discourse —but not the theoretical objects in any exact sense (there are no point masses in the real). We are happy with saying that a chemical reaction can be represented as $HCl + NaOH \rightarrow NaCl + H_2O$, even though in the real all manner and means of impurities, side reactions and hydrolysis may be present.

The experiment tortures nature; it confines and restricts processes; we are dealing, in Roy Bhaskar's terms, with a 'closure'. Our instruments and measuring devices are *not* just to enable better observation, they are, rather, to connect with, 'plug into' processes in the real and be causally acted upon by these processes. Litmus paper does not simply allow us to see an acid; it is causally acted upon by the acid and consequently changes colour; an ammeter 'indicates' current by being one physical system which is causally interacting with another, and ultimately a needle moves on a graduated scale.

CONCLUSION

The epistemology I have outlined has many attractive features:[56]

— It provides an objective account of knowledge in the sense that beliefs in individual minds are not the focus of investigation.

— It situates knowledge in a Popper-like third world, but this world is not a detached one. The process of its generation and the process of its testing are accounted for.

— It is historical; to see theories as products is to invite the examination of the processes, techniques and raw materials by which, and out of which, they are constructed.

— It is fallibilist; products can always be reworked as raw material; our conceptions of nature are not frozen.

— It is practical, in that human action, praxis, is placed at the heart of the process; cognition is developed and tested in practice.

— It is catholic in that there is no single method prescribed for the production of all theoretical objects; it is a case of horses for courses, different problematics having their own rules and criteria, their own quality control.

— It allows a realistic conceptualisation of the internal/ external history discussion. Obviously, the distribution of products (the acceptance of theories) is going to be largely an external matter; the supply of raw materials will be a social and political decision; the processing will be largely an internal matter.

— It allows a place for productive relations in epistemology; how research is organised, and by whom, will figure in our theory.

NOTES

1. *18th Brumaire of Louis Napoleon*, in K. Marx and F. Engels, *Selected Works*, Moscow, Progress, 1969, Vol. I, p. 398.
2. *Critique of Pure Reason*, Norman Kemp Smith (trans.), London, Macmillan, 1964, p. 42.
3. *Materialism and Empiro-Criticism*, Moscow, Progress, 1947, p. 260. See discussion of these themes in David-Hillel Ruben, *Marxism and Materialism*, Hassocks, Harvester Press, 1977.
4. *Science of Logic*, London, George Allen & Unwin, 1966, Vol. I, p. 57.
5. *ibid.* p. 133.
6. *The Economic and Philosophic Manuscripts of 1844*, Dirk Struik (ed.), New York, International Publishers, 1964.
7. *Marxism and Beyond*, London, Paladin, 1971, p. 63.
8. The edition of the *Theses* used here will be that in Vol. I of the *Selected Works*. The *Theses* are more properly called 'notes'. They were literally scrawled on a piece of paper in 1845 with numerous erasures.
9. Preface to *Ludwig Feuerbach and the End of Classical German Philosophy* in *Selected Works*, Vol. III.
10. Ernst Bloch, 'Marx's *Theses on Feuerbach*', in *On Karl Marx*, New York, Herder & Herder, 1971.
    Nathan Rotenstreich, *Basic Problems of Marxist Philosophy*, New York, Bobbs-Merrill, 1965.
    Marx Wartofsky, *Ludwig Feuerbach*, London, Cambridge University Press, 1978.
    Wal Suchting, 'Marx's *Theses on Feuerbach*', in J. Mepham and D.-H. Ruben (eds.), *Issues in Marxist Philosophy*, Hassocks, Harvester Press, 1979, Vol. II.
11. Agnes Heller, *The Theory of Need in Marx*, London, Allison & Busby, 1976.
12. Bertrand Russell, 'Dewey's New Logic', in *The Philosophy of John Dewey*, P. A. Schilpp (ed.), Evanston, Northwestern University Press, 1939. Sidney Hook, *Towards the Understanding of Karl Marx*, London, 1933.
13. A. Tarski, 'The Concept of Truth in Formalised Languages', in J. H. Woodger (ed.), *Logic, Semantics, Metamathematics*, New York, Oxford University Press, 1956.
14. *Novum Organum*, Ch. III, J. M. Robertson (ed.), London, 1905, p. 259.
15. This theme is well dealt with by Roy Bhaskar in his *A Realist Theory of Science*, 2nd edit., Hassocks, Harvester Press, 1978.
16. *Moral Man and Immoral Society*, London, SCM, 1932.
17. 'Dare Progressive Education be Progressive?', *Progressive Education*, 1932, 9.
18. Walter Feinberg, *Reason and Rhetoric*, New York, Wiley, 1975, Ch. 6. Samuel

Bowles & Herbert Gintis, *Schooling in Capitalist America*, London, Routledge & Kegan Paul, 1976.

19. *Selected Works*, Vol. III, p. 347.
20. *Insight*, New York, Longmans, 1957, p. xi.
21. Richard Bernstein, *Praxis and Action*, London, Duckworth, 1972, p. 177. Pierce's chief epistemological works are in E. C. Moore (ed.), *Charles S. Pierce: The Essential Writings*, New York, Harper and Row, 1972.
22. The standard bibliography of Dewey's work itself exceeds 150 pages. Some of the more important items from our perspective are *Reconstruction in Philosophy*, New York, 1920; *Experience and Education*, New York, 1938; *Democracy in Education*, New York, 1916. The standard critical anthology on Dewey is P. A. Schilpp (ed.), *The Philosophy of John Dewey*, Chicago, 1939.
23. *Democracy and Education*, p. 275.
24. 'The Need for a Recovery of Philosophy', in *John Dewey: On Experience, Nature and Freedom*, R. Bernstein (ed.), New York, Liberal Arts Press, 1960, p. 23.
25. *Essays in Experimental Logic*, Chicago, University of Chicago Press, 1916, p. 253.
26. *A Common Faith*, New Haven, Yale University Press, 1934, p. 49.
27. *The Educational Frontier*, W. H. Kilpatrick (ed.), New York, Appleton-Century, 1933, p. 316.
28. *Education for Critical Consciousness*, London, Sheed & Ward, 1974.
   Pedagogy of the Oppressed, Harmondsworth, Penguin, 1972.
   Cultural Action for Freedom, Harmondsworth, Penguin, 1972.
   Pedagogy in Process, London, Writers & Readers Publishing Coop, 1979.
29. *Cultural Action . . .*, p. 31.
30. *ibid.* p. 31.
31. *ibid.* p. 35.
32. *ibid.* p. 34.
33. *ibid.* p. 33.
34. *Education for Critical . . .*, p. 99.
35. *Cultural Action . . .*, p. 51.
36. *Education for Critical . . .*, p. 126.
37. *ibid.* p. 44.
38. *Cultural Action . . .*, p. 34.
39. *Education for Critical . . .*, p. 136.
40. *Scientific Knowledge and its Social Problems*, Harmondsworth, Penguin, 1973.
41. *For Marx*, London, Allen Lane, 1969.
   Reading Capital (with E. Balibar), London, New Left Books, 1970.
42. Gerald Holton, *The Scientific Imagination*, London, Cambridge University Press, 1978, p. 60. I am dependent upon this source for the historical facts regarding Millikan's experiment. I am indebted to my colleague Colin Gould for bringing this work to my attention.
43. H. Messel (ed.), *Senior Science—Physics*, Sydney, N.S.W. Government Printer, 1966.
44. *The Scientific Imagination*, p. 64, p. 70.
45. *Against Method*, London, New Left Books, 1975, p. 19.
46. Martin Nicolaus (trans.), Harmondsworth, Penguin, 1973.
47. *Dialogue Concerning the Two Chief World Systems*, p. 207.
48. For an interpretation of Marx on these lines see Mihailo Markovic, *From Affluence to Praxis*, Ann Arbor, University of Michigan Press, 1974.
49. *Grundrisse*, p. 105.
50. *Marxism and Beyond*, p. 66.

51. Gramsci at one point describes belief in an objective external world as having a religious origin. Freire at one stage speaks about there being no world if people were to cease being. Nature as appropriated is always 'nature for man' in Marx's terms, but he is insistent that it have a real independent existence. In *The Holy Family*, he says: 'there is a world in which *consciousness* and being are distinct; a world which continues to exist when I do away with its existence in thought' (p. 255, Moscow).
52. *Reading Capital*, p. 41.
53. *Selected Works*, Vol. III, p. 347.
54. *Dialogue Concerning the Two Chief World Systems*, p. 101.
55. *Selected Works*, Vol. III, p. 363.
56. For further accounts of Marxist epistemology see:
J. Curthoys and W. Suchting, 'Feyerabend's Discourse against Method: A Marxist critique', *Inquiry*, 20, 1978.
Robert S. Cohen, 'Dialectical Materialism and Carnap's Logical Empiricism', in P. A. Schilpp (ed.), *The Philosophy of Rudolf Carnap*, La Salle, Open Court, 1963.
Keith Tribe, 'On the Production and Structuring of Scientific Knowledges', *Economy and Society*, 2, 1973.
Dominique Lecourt, *Marxism and Epistemology*, London, New Left Books, 1975.
Peter Binns, 'The Marxist Theory of Truth, *Radical Philosophy*, 1973, 4.
Milton Fisk, 'Idealism, Truth and Practice', *Monist*, 1976, 59, (3).
F. R. Dallmayr, 'Marxism and Truth', *Telos*, 1976, 29.
Mihailo Markovic, 'The Problem of Truth', *Boston Studies in the Philosophy of Science*, 5, 1966.
John Stachel, 'A Note on the Concept of Scientific Practice', *Boston Studies in the Philosophy of Science*, 17, 1974.
Marx W. Wartofsky, *Models: Representation and the Scientific Understanding*, Boston, Reidel, 1979.
Hilary Putnam, 'Explanation and Reference', in his *Mind, Language and Reality*, Vol. 2, Cambridge University Press, 1975.
Alfred Sohn-Rethel, *Mental and Manual Labour*, London, Macmillan, 1978.
Barry Hindess, *Philosophy and Methodology in Social Science*, Hassocks, Harvester, 1977.
Ted Benton, *Philosophical Foundations of Three Sociologies*, London, Routledge & Kegan Paul, 1977.
Paul Hirst, *Durkheim, Bernard and Epistemology*, London, Routledge & Kegan Paul, 1975.
Roy Bhaskar, *The Possibility of Naturalism*, Hassocks, Harvester, 1979.
John Mepham and D-H. Ruben (eds.), *Issues in Marxist Philosophy*, Vols. 2, 3, Brighton, Harvester, 1979.

CHAPTER 7

IDEOLOGY

The last decade has seen an upsurge of studies on ideology; studies contributed to by historians, political scientists, philosophers, psychologists, sociologists. There has been a plethora of books and articles on the place of education systems in the maintenance and transmission of ideology. As might be expected, while some of this scholarship is informative, much of it is dull and uninformative. Positivist sociology has tended to characterise ideology in very simplistic and empiricist terms, describing it as a mode of thinking thrown off its proper course, as something shady, something which should be banished from our minds. One writer refers to it as a 'dirty river muddied and polluted by the impurities that have flooded into it'. Proper thought, in contrast, is like a 'pure stream, crystal-clear and transparent'.[1] The early chapters of this book suggest that such a dichotomy is too simple to be useful. Some new-wave sociologists, perhaps under the influence of Kuhn and Feyerabend, collapse all thought into ideology. For them there is no longer any distinction between science and ideology. This view must be rejected.

Some analytic philosophers of education have approached the subject via the conceptual analysis of sentences containing the word 'ideology'. Richard Pratte, in a very recent work,[2] chooses, among others, the sentence, 'The rank-and-file Puerto Rican living in New York City rejects ideology. He is more interested in better pay and improved living conditions'. By a process of conceptual analysis he concludes that an ideological belief is one that 'no amount of positive evidence can establish as true' and further that it is 'not capable of being refuted by any evidence'. The use of metaphor is advanced as an indicator for the presence of ideology. It should be clear that none of these features is going to distinguish science from ideology. Hume and Popper knew that no amount of positive evidence can establish a universal statement as true; Quine, Lakatos, Kuhn and Feyerabend have all established that scientific theories are not straightforwardly falsifiable; Toulmin, Wartofsky and Harré have shown how influential and important metaphor is in the growth of science. Pratte's methodology is bankrupt, serving mainly as an illustration of the limitations of analysis in philosophy, and of the importance of an appreciation of the philosophy of science for carrying on intelligent investigation of subjects. The account of ideology developed in this chapter will complement the account of knowledge previously given. It sees ideology as arising out of, and being sustained by, certain practices. Because work and production are so important to human society, conceptualisation of these is taken as a test-case for the separation of science and ideology. People are born into, and formed by, an intellectual milieu. There is a public knowledge and a public culture in which we live and work and have our being. Schools are pivotal in the creation and transmission of this milieu. Consequently there is an onus on teachers to be self-critical and reflective about how they participate in the transmission of understanding versus ignorance, competence versus incompetence, liberating ideas versus repressive ideas.

'IDEOLOGY'—ORIGINS OF THE TERM

The term 'ideology' was coined at the time of the French Revolution by Antoine Destutt de Tracy, a member of the newly-founded 'Institut de France' (1795). It was to apply literally to his 'science of ideas', a new discipline developed in his *Eléments d'Idéologie* (1801–1815). The group with whom he worked were empiricists and rationalists, concerned with establishing a new order in the intellectual realm to supplement the bourgeois revolution in the social and political realms. They wanted to eradicate the influence of superstition, prejudice and magic on the minds of individuals; to understand the operation of the mind, the growth and association of ideas, in order to detect and prevent the spread of faulty consciousness. They were clearly in that noble English tradition of Bacon, Locke and Hume. Their project was reminiscent of Bacon's attempts to isolate and banish the 'idols' from the mind and reflected Hume's efforts to introduce methods of the 'experimental sciences into the moral sciences'. The group saw universal education as the solution to the reform of consciousness, and consequently to strife and disorder in the affairs of people. At this stage 'ideology' was a neutral term; 'ideologues' were the progressive, radical, liberal, scientific scholars. Napoleon Bonaparte, originally a supporter of the group, turned on them after his defeat in Russia, and in 1812 referred to them contemptuously as 'ideologues' and blamed their liberal and anti-authoritarian beliefs for his ignominy. Thus arose the *pejorative* sense of the term 'ideology', a usage which Marx variously picks up, and which has subsequently become the standard interpretation.[3]

SIGNPOSTS TO IDEOLOGY

In the early work of Marx, and in various letters of Engels, there are scattered depictions of ideology and hints towards an account of it. Marx and Engels were concerned with the criticism of religion—'the premise of all criticism'—and, more generally, with the criticism of German post-Hegelian thinking. This is what was referred to as the 'German Ideology'. For Marx, thought does not descend from the heavens but rather it is born of the soil; it is anchored in social practices. The point of departure for his critique of the German ideologists, and part of the reason why they were indeed ideologists, was that it had 'not occurred to any one of these philosophers to inquire into the connection of German philosophy with German reality, the relation of their criticism to their own material surroundings'.[4] In various places we are told that ideology belongs to the super-structure of society;[5] that it is something generated from the class structure of society;[6] that it typically inverts the causal mechanisms of the social world, religious consciousness being for Marx the paradigm of this;[7] that it is false consciousness.[8] The recurrent theme is that ideology is thought which refuses to understand itself as historical—this is why so much meta-physics and essentialism is rejected as ideology. Marx says of the classical economists: 'The same men who establish social relations in conformity with their material productivity also produce principles, ideas and categories conforming to their social relations. Hence these ideas, these categories are no more eternal than the relations which they express'.[9] Lack of historical sense is endemic in much *theological discourse*. This is something of which at least some practitioners of theology are now aware. Jürgen Moltmann has observed of Bultmann's theology: 'The simple distinction between religion and politics which Bultmann introduces when he speaks of Jesus' activity "being miscon-strued as political activity" is nothing but the projection back of the separation of religion and politics—"religion is a private matter"—from the bourgeois world of the 19th century'.[10]

Political theory is another field rich in ahistorical conceptualis-ations, particularly in relation to the State. An American Hegelian, Washington Gladden, took leave of all terrestrial and historical considerations when he said of the State: 'It springs out of an impulse divinely implanted in the human soul'.[11] When questions are then asked about obligations to the State, it is 24-carat ideology with which we are dealing. Locke's *'tabula rasa'* model of mind is a prime example of ahistoricism in *epistemology*. In *science*, Ernst Mach correctly observes that 'the historical investigation of the development of a science is most needful, lest the principles treasured up in it become a system of half-understood precepts, or worse, a system of *prejudices* . . . it shows that which exists to be in great measure *conventional* and *accidental*'.[12] Thomas Kuhn testifies to the revolutionary effect that historical researches had on his comfortable empiricist understanding of science.[13] In *ethics* and *metaphysics* ahistoricism abounds. Sören Kierkegaard generalises from the inner doubts and loneliness of small-town, Protestant Danish life to the crisis of mankind. What should be seen as historically specific is seen as a function of universal and transcendent features of the soul's relation to God. *Education* also provides many examples of essentialism and of the conduct of thought without regard to history. The great French Thomist, Jacques Maritain, prescinds altogether from the actual history of schooling to say: 'Thus the prime goal of education is the conquest of internal and spiritual freedom to be achieved by the individual person, or, in other words, his liberation through knowledge and wisdom, good will and love'.[14] This is nice, but soporific; it lulls people into a dream-world and away from the hard work of concrete analyses and political programmes based upon them.

PROCEDURAL CONSIDERATIONS

Remember, of course, that our concern is with *objective consciousness*, with the 'we think' rather than with subjective consciousness, private thoughts and the lonely 'I' thinking. I have argued that the latter is parasitic upon the former; the 'we think' determines the 'I think'. There is a pre-existing stock of raw materials, products and instruments which the individual confronts and which limits and orchestrates his own thinking. It is the features of that stock which we are interested in analysing. One of the major weaknesses of mainstream accounts of ideology is the emphasis it places on *personal* factors in the explanation and aetiology of ideology—weak or suggestible minds; immoral pursuit of self-interest; lack of education, and the like.

Remember also that we have struggled with varying success to avoid *empiricism* in epistemology and moreover to avoid discussion of epistemology in empiricist terms, on the terrain laid down and charted by the empiricist problematic. I shall endeavour to avoid falling back into empiricism in our account of ideology. Mainstream discussion about 'muddy thinking' which 'distorts its object' and so on is classically empiricist discussion. The trademark of empiricism is the setting up of a subject-object couple, and then inquiring about how elements in the first relate to elements in the second; how the thought of an individual relates to a world outside the individual. It embarks on *justificationist* endeavours tracking thought (ideas) to experience (sensations); or complex ideas to simple ideas, and so on. It characteristically conceives theory as static; and indeed, with Hempel and Carnap, tries to axiomatise it. The role of theory is to explain 'observed facts' and we accept or replace theories and models depending on their capacity to do so. Scientific experimentation and manipulation—the use of geiger counters, electron microscopes, cyclotrons—is conceived as, and assimilated into, everyday experience. All of this comes about by confusing the theoretical object of science with the real object of science. In contrast, we have proposed an epistemology which sees science and theory as the theoretical product of certain theoretical practices. Scientific knowledge *is* knowledge of that theoretical object; it is something created, generated, produced by the working of a problematic upon *conceptual* raw materials of a scientific, commonsensical or ideological kind. There is *no* knowledge of a real object against which our theoretical object can be assessed; to know a real object is to construct a theoretical object. 'Observation' of the real is not the way to verify theoretical claims in quantum physics; it might seem attractive, but it cannot deliver the goods. Verification of theory involves, first, proof within a theory (showing that correct procedures have been adhered to; for example, conventions about counting and statistical error rates have been followed); second, the creation in the real of the theoretical object (Bowen's reaction series for crystallisation of magma is verified by laboratory creation of molten magma and observation of the order of crystallisation of its minerals); third, the choice, where necessary, between competing theoretical objects and concomitantly competing productive processes.

CONSCIOUSNESS AND PRACTICE

So far in this discussion I have not given a theory of ideology; I have characterised it in certain ways, pointed to certain tell-tale signs of ideological consciousness, and have made allusions to some factors which generate ideology. In the previous chapter I laid down a model for knowledge as the effect of a productive process; this is applicable to ideology. Consciousness is the consequence of certain productive processes; processes which are characterised by the alteration of raw materials into products using determinate means of production and occurring within specific patterns of productive relations. The question concerning a theory of ideology can be phrased in terms of the features of the productive process which results in ideological consciousness and how they are different from that which results in scientific consciousness. We are concerned with *practices*; consciousness is the product or result of engagement in certain practices and activities, or more generally, as I have characterised it, of production processes. The isolation of ideology will be the isolation of *ideological practices*; a theory of ideology will be a theory of the creation and maintenance of those practices; the overthrow of ideology will be in large measure a practical matter; it will be the overthrow or abandonment of entrenched practices. Wilhelm Reich was correct when he observed in the '20s that bourgeois ideology was enshrined in the hundred and one little daily practices the working class as well as the bourgeois class engaged in. At one level this is known as *etiquette*, the conventional code of good manners which governs social life and which at the same time cements class hegemony—women shall not pour their own drinks at a dinner party and then will have only one glass; men will retire for cigars and port while women withdraw for chatter; politics and religion will not be discussed in social gatherings; orders of precedence will be observed in table setting; and women will wait for men to open doors for them. At another level this is known as *civics* and is taught as such in schools—how we are to behave on ceremonial occasions; what the established parliamentary customs are; what the procedures are for participation in rituals and celebrations of important cultural myths and legends; how we stand for 'God Save the Queen' or come together for Thanksgiving Day. At another level it is *law*—we will *not* walk on the grass; swim naked at the beach; obtain abortions in humane and hygienic hospitals; enter into hire-purchase without the consent of our husband; disobey conscription notices; burn the flag or disfigure images of the Queen; stay away from school. The procedural principle of historical materialism leads us to an examination of this kaleidoscopic array of criss-crossing practices in order to comprehend social consciousness. They all contribute to the 'common sense' of a society; a common sense which Gramsci aptly called 'the practical ideology of the ruling class'.

WORK AND CONSCIOUSNESS

Karl Mannheim, John Dewey and Erik Erikson[15] all agree that people's work life, their productive life, is of the utmost consequence for their personality, consciousness and emotional life. (Work is a significant absentee in the 'science' of psychology.)[16] Marx of course concurs in this judgment. People's nature 'coincides with their production, both with *what* they produce and with *how* they produce'.[17] For Marx, it is ultimately in work, in the economy, that the foundations of ideology are to be located. *Capital* presents us with an account of ideology by a case-study approach. The object of the work is expressed in its subtitle: 'A Critique of Political Economy'. It intends to lay bare the laws of capitalist production and to uncover the sources of error and ideology in the attempts of others, notably Smith and Ricardo, to do the same. Following Hegel, human labour, productive activity, objectification and externalisation are of supreme importance for Marx's metaphysics, his epistemology and his anthropology. Subjects express themselves in labour. Self-consciousness is dependent upon this creative process; we know ourselves in our creations. For Hegel, God had to create the world; it is in his creative act that he knows himself. In labour we have:

(i)   The creation or transformation of things (Marx's 'human-ised nature'), including, of course, cultural and intellectual things.

(ii) The creation or transformation of consciousness, both of individual belief and of social, objective consciousness.

The question that the early Marx addresses is whether objectification of a subject can occur without *alienation*. Alienation of the subject is a consequence of the alienation of the object, that is, the removal of a subject's creative endeavours from him. The concern of the later Marx is the same, namely the productive life of people, here considered in a specific form, the Capitalist Mode of Production (CMP). We have an economic analysis coming into focus and a philosophical analysis going out of focus, but the former is still permeated by the latter. The continuity in Marx is that he sees production as being of central material *and* philosophical importance. The spectacle of Marx's thought growing out of its Hegelian origins is indeed a vindication of Marx's own claim, to which we have repeatedly alluded, namely that people make their own history but they do not make it as they please.

The classical economists were no fools; Marx continually praises them for their 'scientific merit' and 'ruthless scientific honesty'. Nevertheless they misunderstood social production. The understanding of this misunderstanding about a matter so vital is the clue to understanding ideological consciousness. Insight into outsight on such a topic is informative. Peter Hamilton correctly observes that, for Marx, 'Both proletariat and bourgeois alike, ruled and ruler, are subject to ideological conceptions and accept them as true because of their mutual existence in a system of social relations. Ideology is not produced to "cover-up" reality in a conspiratorial fashion, but is systematically generated by the structure of social relationships'.[18]

WORK, EXCHANGE, VALUE
Aristotle dissected the elements involved in the simplest instance of work, namely those involved in artisan activity. This was *praxis* or intentional human activity expressing itself in a material product, an artefact. His analysis was in terms of the fourfold division of causality we outlined in the previous chapter, where we have:

material cause — substance worked upon
efficient cause — labour and instruments
formal cause — determinate end product
final cause — plans, design, purposes.

He recognised the difference between productive activities engaged in for their own sake and those engaged in for external reasons. Corresponding to this, we can analyse artefacts in terms of their *use value* (ability to satisfy human needs) and their *exchange value* (ability to be exchanged for other artefacts).

Aristotle also dissected simple exchange. Consider person *A* who makes artefact α and person *B* who makes artefact β. They meet and exchange products, but the exchange is not capricious or arbitrary. A certain number of αs exchange for a certain number of βs. To explain this balance is the central problem of political economy. Marx writes of Aristotle that the brilliance of his genius 'is shown by this alone, that he discovered, in the expression of the value of commodities, a relation of equality'.[19] As Marx in *Capital* has it:

$$x \text{ commodity } \alpha = y \text{ commodity } \beta$$

But even with his brilliance, Aristotle could not discover what brought the equivalence about or what constituted that equivalence. There was a social obstacle to knowledge. 'The peculiar conditions of the society in which he lived alone prevented him from discovering what "in truth" was at the bottom of this equality'.[20] The 'peculiar conditions' were that exchange had not taken on a universal form and it was still largely simple and private; furthermore the *inequalities* in the slave society of Athens prevented the thinking of the concept of equal labour.

For Marx there was a property of α and β in virtue of which they exchanged as equal. This was their *value*: '. . . the common substance that manifests itself in the exchange value of commodities, whenever they are exchanged, is their value'.[21]

Value is the amount of abstract labour involved in the production of the commodity; commodities are 'congealed labour'; value is measured as *labour time*. Marx has a *labour theory of value*. But for Marx, it is *not* concrete, individual, specific labour which is congealed in the commodity; it is, rather, the amount of socially necessary labour that is required. Thus the value of A's α (say a shoe) is not a reflection of the amount of A's labour that has gone into α, but rather the average amount of labour that all shoemakers of average skill would expend in producing an α. Thus if A has relatively poor techniques, or inefficient machinery, then the labour actually expended on α is more than its value (and conversely, of course).

It is of vital importance in this account of value to keep firmly in mind the distinction between the theoretical and real objects of a science. If we feel uneasy with Marx's *abstraction* from a specific, concrete shoemaker and his shoe, to saying that the value of the shoe is a calculation based on the *average* time of making shoes of that sort, then our unease is very likely the result of confusing the real and theoretical objects of economics. Value is not a natural or sensible property, it is the property of a theoretical object.

When A and B meet and exchange their products or artefacts, α and β, there is something going on behind their backs: 'by an exchange, we equate as values our different products, and by that very act, we also equate, as human labour, the different kinds of labour expended upon them. We are not aware of this, nevertheless we do it. Value therefore does not stalk about with a label describing what it is'.[22] By exchange they also convert α and β as use values into exchange values. The exchange value of α is realised in the use value of β and vice versa. For instance, the shoemaker exchanges his shoe for the oranges of the farmer.

In exchange, *A* and *B* are concerned only with how much of β and α respectively they will finally receive. In simple exchange, when the properties of α and β have been stabilised by custom, then the 'proportions appear to result from the nature of the products'. To *A* and *B* their own social action, brought about by exchanging, 'takes the form of the action of objects, which rule the producers instead of being ruled by them'.[23] Here, at the point of exchange, we have the *Fetishism of Commodities*; it is this fetishism which for Marx is the key, the secret of understanding ideological consciousness in general. Certain practices produce causally their corresponding consciousness, in this case ideological and mystificatory consciousness. When we fetishise, we take as independent, external and self-sustaining things that are the reflections and outcomes of particular, definite forms of social relations or personal features. Thus, in fetishism, underwear or shoes can become the sexual object. For Marx the fetishism of commodities is something over which we have no control, it is a consciousness generated by the pattern of productive relations. To find an analogy we have to go to the 'mist-enveloped regions of the religious world', a world where the productions of the human brain appear as independent beings, endowed with life and entering into relation both with one another, and with the human race.[24]

CAPITALIST PRODUCTION

We have dealt so far with elementary production and exchange. The capitalist mode of production, however, is not simple; it also generates a very significant illusion. In simple exchange and circulation, the value of α equals the value of β, and, as Marx observes, 'circulation begets no value'. The commodity owner can, by his labour, create value, but not self-expanding value. He can increase the value of his commodity by adding fresh labour; he can for instance convert leather into boots and ordinary boots into dress boots. But, 'twist and turn as we may, the fact remains unaltered. If equivalents are exchanged, no surplus-value results'.[25] Within the sphere of circulation the only way capital can accumulate is by following the cardinal rule of the petit-bourgeois manipulator, 'buy cheap and sell dear'. This gives rise to *merchant's capital*; in Benjamin Franklin's observation, 'War is robbery, commerce is generally cheating'. But this form of accumulation cannot be universal—it is impossible that everybody should follow the adage. It can account for the early primitive accumulation of capital, the initial conversion of money into capital, but it simply cannot account for the standard, regular process of capital accumulation and capital expansion characteristic of capitalism. There can be no explanation of this if we restrict ourselves to the sphere of circulation.

What is the answer to this riddle? We seem to be facing the economic parallel to the theological 'creation *ex nihilo*', or the violation of the economic equivalent of the second law of thermodynamics. The answer is in brief that to become a full-blown capitalist, Moneybags has to buy a very special commodity, human labour power. It is when labour power becomes a commodity among other commodities, to be bought and sold on the market, that we have the precondition for the generation of surplus value, that we have the beginning of capitalism as an economic system, as a mode of production.

In the CMP the capitalist, A, goes out and buys the wherewithal for production. This includes raw materials, technology or means of production and, most importantly, the labour time of worker B. Now A exchanges his α (wages) for B's β (labour power). At the point of exchange there is *no* exploitation; equivalents are exchanged. B's labour power is bought at its value. The capitalist does not, and has no need to, cheat at the point of exchange. But A gets richer and richer, he accumulates more and more capital. Why does this happen? Marx's incisive conceptual and theoretical contribution was to this question. From it comes his *Theory of Surplus Value*. The answer to this question, in brief, is that one of the commodities A buys, labour power, has the unique property of itself generating value. Although A buys it at its value, it generates more value for him than he paid for it. It creates surplus value which, because A has ownership of the means of production, accrues to him.

That *labour* is the source of value and exploitation of labour the source of profit is intuitively known to both employees and employers, if not to economists. Exploitation is heightened by either lengthening the working day or increasing productivity. The former generated the prolonged and bitter class struggles over the eight-hour day and the ideological struggle surrounding it. The latter generated the science of 'Time and Motion' studies and industrial psychology. It also generated automation, mechanisation and the conveyor-belt. A Ford employee in the 1970s said: 'Mr Ford's given credit for inventing this . . . There is no let-up, the line is always running . . . You hear the slogan: "Ford has a better idea". They have better ideas of getting all the work possible out of your worn body for eight hours'.[26]

METHOD OF ANALYSIS

The foregoing is a guide to Marx's account of the CMP. What is important for our purposes is to appreciate the form of analysis utilised by Marx, as this then provides the account of ideology we are searching for. The *categories* which Marx uses are:

(i)   real inner connections
(ii) phenomenal forms of (i)
(iii) illusions generated by (ii).

So, with respect to profit, Marx says: 'It is a converted form of surplus value, a form in which its origin and secret of its existence are obscured and extinguished. In effect, profit is the form in which surplus value presents itself to the view, and must initially be stripped by analysis to disclose the latter'.[27]

Likewise in the CMP, the wage form is a systematic illusion. Wages appear to be paid for labour (we get paid at the end of the working week) but they are paid for labour power. They appear fair as they are the value of labour power (the cost of producing and reproducing labour power), but this obliterates the reality that labour power creates surplus value. The development of money as a universal equivalent for exchange of commodities 'actually conceals, rather than disclosing the social character of private labour and the social relations between the individual producers'.[28] In this passage Marx attributes part of the illusion to the fact that people seek to understand forms of their social life 'not in their historical character, for in his eyes they are immutable, but in their meaning'.

Compare this with Galileo's analysis of planetary motion where we have:

(i)   the real motion of the planets
(ii) the apparent motion, which is the reverse of (i)
(iii) the illusions and delusions generated by (ii).

The business of science is to explicate the causal connections between each of these levels. Marx, like Galileo, rejects simple empiricism as a method for comprehending the relationships— 'Value . . . does not stalk about with a label describing what it is'. Galileo knew that the appearances of the planetary motion (ii) were a consequence of (i) and (iii). What we can see is a product of:

(i)   what is out there in the world
(iii) what we bring in our heads to the observation.

Or, as Hanson said, 'there is more to seeing than meets the eyeball'. The way Marx expressed this was to say: 'The apparent motions of the heavenly bodies are intelligible only to someone who is acquainted with their real motions, which are not perceptible to the senses'.[29] Both Marx and Galileo appreciated that the components of (iii) were things resistant to rational argument; they were not going to fall over and die at the sight of a syllogism. Galileo says: 'Aristotle's error and Ptolemy's, and Tycho's and yours, and that of all the rest, is rooted in a fixed and inveterate impression that the earth stands still, this you cannot or do not know how to cast off, even when you wish to philosophise about what would follow from assuming that the earth moved'.[30]

COMPARISON WITH CLASSICAL ECONOMISTS

Our claim has been that ideological consciousness has its origin in the productive life of a society; it is generated out of features of that productive life—commodity production, division of labour, formation of classes. We have also said that examination of mistaken attempts scientifically to understand that productive base would be a clue to the interpretation of theoretical ideologies more generally. To this end we have noted Marx's account of the social obstacles hindering Aristotle. What can we point to as the reasons why Marx was able to formulate his analysis of the CMP while Smith and Ricardo were not?[31]

   (i)   Economic conditions—the CMP was fully established as the dominant mode of production.
   (ii) Social/Ideological conditions—the idea of human equality had become fixed in popular opinion and so prepared the way for the notion of equality of human labour.
   (iii) Theoretical conditions—the work of classical economists was available for use and criticism; Hegel's philosophical corpus was extant; the French socialists had produced their treatises.
   (iv) Historical/Political conditions—there had been an upsurge in class struggle in the mid-nineteenth century; the periodic crises of capitalism had already appeared; the proletarian uprisings of 1848 had occurred.

SCIENCE AND IDEOLOGY

We can isolate three phases of scientific knowledge:
   1. The processes of its creation.
   2. The science itself.
   3. The applications and uses of the science.
That specific interests and social forces impinge on and determine (1) is not controversial. The path was set by Archimedes,

who formulated his Principle, and more generally opened the door of mathematical physics, as a direct consequence of an order from Hiero, the tyrant king of Syracuse, to determine whether his crown was solid gold or not. It is *unlikely* that a Roman Catholic scientific community is going to create the scientific knowledges necessary for artificial contraception. It is *likely* that a medical community dominated by men is going to produce knowledges necessary for a female contraceptive pill, long before it does so for a male one. Undoubtedly particular interests and values, particular ideologies, do affect to varying degrees the direction and tempo of scientific research; which problems are in focus and which are out of focus. Background ideology can affect which truths among many possible truths science discovers. Science often does find out things about the world, the question is *which* things it finds out.

That special interests impinge on and determine (3)—the application of science—is not controversial either. Indeed, this is to be expected. Furthermore, we might expect as a working hypothesis that science will be utilised to further the interests of the more powerful groups in society rather than the less powerful. The technology of *Concorde* does not serve the interests of the Parisian or New York worker. Scientific psychology began as a handmaiden of industrial bosses. In America, Taylorism and management theory were overtly developed for, and applied in the interests of, the captains of industry. Industrial chemistry, applied mathematics, economic geology are all witness to the obvious fact that scientific knowledges have practical applications and these applications themselves stimulate and direct the formation of the knowledge. The contemporary revolution in production made possible by the physics and mathematics of the micro-processor is a clear case of struggle over what applications science will have. Importantly, it is often the case that in the course of the development and application of a scientific programme, transformations and alterations occur which change it from a science to a theoretical ideology. This was indeed the fate of Darwin's theory in its development as Social Darwinism.

The most controversial questions are concerned with (2)—the body of scientific theories themselves. Do interests and ideology deform not the search for, and applications of, science, but science itself? The issue is whether the claims of science, its cognitive content, is affected by ideology. Science purports to give us correct accounts of the natural world; it is an enterprise whose products have cognitive significance—its claims are either true or false. It might be acknowledged that science is *not just* the search for truth in some detached, otherworldly sense, but it is possible to insist that it is *at least* partly the search for truth and that it has to be appraised on its cognitive standing, not its genealogy or progeny. For instance, the question of whether Archimedes was commanded by a tyrant who then used his Principle for ill-gotten ends does not affect the cognitive standing of Archimedes' Principle. It is truth about the world. Thus, when we are discussing the cognitive claims of the corpus of science, it might be alleged that considerations of ideology do not impinge. To say that ideology does not impinge on (2), however, is too simple a matter. It does.

CONCLUDING COMMENTS

(i) The explication of particular ideologies will be a matter for specific study. Their history will be accounted for partly by internal reasons and partly by external causes. Calvinism arises out of the transfer from Feudal to Capitalist production, but then in many respects leads a life of its own. London Institute philosophy of education arises partly because of internal reasons (moribund state of philosophy of education) and partly from external causes (professionalisation of education). It then has a certain dynamic of its own. Legal ideologies arise fairly directly out of the need to protect ill-gotten gains; the State arises as the vehicle for cementing class control—indeed in many places it is still only property owners who are allowed to vote. State reports and 'studies' further the extension of theoretical ideology. The huge report *Work in America* is supposedly concerned with worker alienation and job dissatisfaction and the political and economic means of overcoming this blight. Not surprisingly, the index contains *no* entries for 'Communism', 'Socialism', 'Worker Control'.[32] There is systematic exclusion here. The concepts necessary for a scientific account of work are not available. It is akin to pre-Galileans doing mechanics without the concept of 'acceleration'. The report is ideology in that it (a) ignores the relationship of job dissatisfaction to the class structure of America; (b) accepts the given economic arrangement and operates within it; (c) advances the interests of those who benefit from the status quo (that 10% of Americans who control about 70% of the nation's wealth, and consequently its politics).

(ii) There still remains the questions of how ideology gets a grip on people, of what the mechanisms are for its inculcation and, further, of what facilitates its incorporation. This is the transition from objective social consciousness to subjective private consciousness. The beginnings of an answer are, as I have said, in the *practices* in which people are engaged from childhood. This, however, is only the beginning. Once consciousness develops it does achieve a semi-independence. We have to inquire as to what makes the *intellectual* component of an ideology believable, reasonable, palatable. Some such features are:

(a) Being characteristically empty, general and indeterminate. Concepts such as 'Freedom', 'Progress', 'Dignity', can cover a multitude of sins. The Church in the Philippines can preach about 'Liberation', 'Redemption', 'Better Life', but as soon as peasants organise themselves and take over estates, the Church recoils, crying 'Reds', 'Communism'. A Republican candidate in Idaho ran on the positively vacant platform of 'Backward Never, Forward Ever', and presumably people voted for him.

(b) Being reified. Thus we have 'Liberty drives us on' or 'America declares war on Spain'. This should be translated as: 'the American ruling class's interests conflict with those of the Spanish ruling class and so it sends its working class to war'. The soldier who deserted, saying: 'it was a rich man's war and a poor man's fight', knew that the reifications were just that.

(c) Being selectively applied. Russian troops in Cuba constitute a threat and an affront, while American troops in Turkey are just part of the scene. Britain fights World War One so that 'small nations can exercise self-determination' whilst at the same time it sends troops to Ireland to crush the independence movement. 'Violence' is a West Bank Arab shooting an Israeli; Israelis driving Arabs from their land and starving them to death is 'securing our homeland'. The Nazi move east is 'Expansionism'; the American move west is 'Opening the Frontier'—a point not lost on Hitler who, before his attack on Russia, told his generals to treat the population like 'redskins'.

NOTES

1. For an excellent review of orthodox sociology on the topic of ideology see Nigel Harris, *Beliefs in Society*, Harmondsworth, Penguin, 1971, ch. 1.
2. *Ideology and Education*, New York, David McKay, 1977.
3. The early history of the term 'ideology' has been much written upon. See: J. S. Roucek, 'A History of the Concept of Ideology', *Journ. Hist. Ideas*, 1944, V.

132   *The Marxist Theory of Schooling*

George Lichtheim, *The Concept of Ideology*, New York, Vintage Books, 1967.
M. Seliger, *The Marxist Conception of Ideology*, Cambridge, University Press, 1977, ch. 1.

4. *Selected Works*, Vol. I, p. 19.
5. *ibid.* p. 25.
6. *ibid.* p. 47.
7. *ibid.* p. 25.
8. Engels' 1893 letter to Mehring in *Selected Works*, Vol. III, p. 496.
9. *The Poverty of Philosophy*, Moscow, Progress, 1955, p. 95.
10. *Crucified God*, New York, Harper & Row, 1974, p. 36.
11. For an account of such views see Anthony Skillen, *Ruling Illusions*, Hassocks, Harvester Press, 1977, ch. 1: 'Philosophical Statism'.
12. *The Science of Mechanics*, p. 316. Quoted in A. Janik and S. Toulmin, *Wittgenstein's Vienna*, New York, Simon & Schuster, 1973, p. 137.
13. *The Structure of Scientific Revolutions*, Chicago, University Press, 1970. Introduction.
14. *Education at the Crossroads*, New Haven, Yale University Press, 1943, p. 11.
15. In *Young Man Luther* (London, Faber & Faber, 1959, p. 15) Erikson says: 'Probably the most neglected problem in psycho-analysis is the problem of work, in theory as well as in practice: as if the dialectic of the history of ideas had ordered a system of psychological thought which would as resolutely ignore the way in which the individual and his group make a living as Marxism ignores introspective psychology'.
16. In the *1844 Manuscripts*, Marx had written how 'the history of industry was an open book of man's essential powers' and that 'a psychology for which this, the part of history most contemporary and accessible to sense, remains a closed book, cannot become a genuine, comprehensive and *real* science'.
17. *Collected Works*, Moscow, Progress, 5, p. 31.
18. *Knowledge and Social Structure*, London, Routledge & Kegan Paul, 1974, p. 29.
19. *Capital*, Moscow, n.d., Vol. I, p. 66.
20. *ibid.*
21. *ibid.* p. 66.
22. *ibid.* p. 78.
23. *ibid.* p. 79.
24. Speaking of devoted Aristotelians, Galileo says: 'Such people remind me of that sculptor who, having transformed a huge block of marble into the image of a Hercules or a thundering Jove . . . and with consummate art made it so lifelike and fierce that it moved everyone with terror who beheld it, he himself began to be afraid, though all its vivacity and power were the work of his own hands; and his terror was such that he no longer dared affront it with his mallet and chisel'. *Dialogue Concerning the Two Chief World Systems*, p. 111.
25. *Capital*,
26. Studs Terkel, *Working*, New York, Avon, 1972, p. 228.
27. *Capital*, Vol. III, p. 48.
28. *ibid.* Vol. I, p. 80.
29. *ibid.* p. 433.
30. *Dialogue . . .*, p. 171.
31. This account is dependent upon an unpublished Ph.D. thesis by Liz Jacka of the N.S.W. Institute of Technology.
32. See Roger S. Gottlieb, 'A Marxian Concept of Ideology', *The Philosophical Forum*, 6, (4).

CHAPTER 8

THE IQ CONTROVERSY

In 1969 Arthur Jensen published a long article in the *Harvard Educational Review*: 'How Much Can We Boost IQ and Scholastic Achievement?'[1] His opening sentence was: 'Compensatory education has been tried and apparently it has failed'. The article elaborates why it failed in terms of scholastic achievement being a function of intelligence, and intelligence being for the most part a genetically determined ability. Thus 'Headstart' programmes, differential financing of ghetto schools, open admissions policies were beating their heads against the solid wall of nature. Richard Hernnstein echoed Jensen but focused upon class and intelligence.[2] His assertion was that social classes were distinguished by intelligence as well as money. In California William Shockley advocated a policy of rewarding low-intelligence people who submitted to sterilisation ($100 for each IQ point below 100!).[3] Across the Atlantic, Hans Eysenck claimed Jensen and Hernnstein as the clearest popular exponents of his long-held position on race and intelligence. The *New York Times* coined the word 'Jensenism' in 1969; *Newsweek* introduced these views to the world in an article titled 'Born Dumb'; a Southern Congressman read the entire 123-page article into the *Congressional Record*; Daniel Moynihan observed that the 'winds of Jensenism' were blowing strongly around Capitol Hill. All these things heralded the most recent revival of the 'IQ controversy'. The examination of this controversy enables us to concretise and illustrate some of our central motifs. These are as follows:

(i) The importance of an historical perspective for the appraisal of theories.
(ii) The interpenetration of science and ideology; the presence of ethical and political commitments *within* research programmes.
(iii) The importance of seeing theories as being embedded in research programmes which then become the unit for appraisal.
(iv) The importance of the internal *and* external criticism of research programmes.

All of these considerations come together when we see intellectual constructions generally as the result of a process of intellectual production. We can identify the raw materials of the IQ theorists; the means of production; the composite nature of their products and the utilisation of these. Intellectual production does not occur in a vacuum. IQ theory has been produced out of, and for, the school system. Marx spoke of ideas being material forces when they gripped the masses. Given the number of teachers, school administrators, teacher-educators and politicians who have been gripped by IQ theory, it certainly counts as a material force to be reckoned with.

THE IQ ARGUMENT

Following Norman Daniel,[4] we can summarise the IQ argument as:

(1) IQ tests measure intelligence.
(2) Intelligence is an important determinant of success in school life.
(3) Intelligence is highly heritable (80%).
(4) Mean black/white and social class differences in intelligence are large (15 points for the former).
(5) It therefore follows that:
    (a) Intelligence is resistant to change.
    (b) Inequalities in intelligence are not eliminable.
    (c) Race and class differences in intelligence are probably genetic in origin.
    (d) Attempts to achieve greater equality in areas where intelligence is important (education, social position) are unrealistic.

There are certain simplifications here. Following Imre Lakatos' system, which we outlined in Chapter 5, we can regard premises (1)–(4) as part of the *hard core* of the IQ research programme. There is additionally a *protective belt* of auxiliary commitments concerning the validity and reliability of particular tests; whether the form of inheritance of intelligence is Mendelian or non-Mendelian and whether intelligence is a unitary entity (Spearman's *g* factor) or a pluralistic entity (Guilford's factors). This will generate a *positive heuristic* for the programme. It will suggest research on culture-fair tests and the investigation of IQs of people with varying degrees of genetic similarity. It will also generate a *negative heuristic*, directing research away from particular areas: from non-quantifiable research, and from class and political analysis.

THE BACKGROUND
Intellectual endeavour which is not cognisant of history is likely to be ideological endeavour, conversely a sense of the historicity of the objects of thought and modes of thinking about those objects tilts the scales in favour of scientific thought. What Marx said about the classical economists is applicable to proponents of the IQ argument—'their categories are historical and transitory products'.

Eugenics
The IQ argument has its intellectual origins in the mid-nineteenth century with Charles Darwin. His book *The Origin of Species* not only contained the germ of a brilliant new world view, but also the germ of eugenic ideology. In the final paragraphs of the book he advocates limiting marriage among the poor so as to control the amount of 'inferior stock' in society. He believed that the superior families of England had been naturally selected on account of their superior traits, intelligence included. Darwin's cousin, Francis Galton, can be regarded as the father of IQ testing and the science of intelligence. His famous book *Hereditary genius* was published in 1869, ten years after *The Origin*. He thought it desirable to help nature along by determining who the intelligent and unintelligent were, and by promoting the breeding of the former and the infertility of the latter. To these ends he founded the British Eugenics Society in 1908. His original tests were of sensory-motor skills, this based on an assumption that such skills were an indicator of intelligence. Unfortunately the Irish, blacks and other foreigners outscored the English. The first attempt to deal with this embarrassing anomaly was by characteristically *ad hoc* manoeuvres. R. Meade Bocke, in 1905, suggested that the whites' 'reactions were slower because they belonged to a more deliberate and reflective race'.[5]

Thorndike, who was to become one of the giants of twentieth-century psychology, suggested in 1903 that 'the apparent mental attainments of children of inferior races may be due to lack of inhibition, and so witness precisely to a deficiency in mental growth'.[6] Subsequently the anomaly was dealt with by dropping reaction time as a measure of intelligence. Recall Imre Lakatos' story of the reaction of Newtonian scientists to the imaginary case of planetary misbehaviour: 'Either another ingenious auxiliary hypothesis is proposed or . . . the whole story is buried in the dusty volumes of periodicals and the story never mentioned again'.[7] This little intellectual dance at the very beginning of the IQ story does illustrate some important general themes which are persistent throughout its subsequent history (perhaps suggesting a certain genetic weakness in the programme!):

(i) All intelligence tests begin with the identification *in advance* of groups that are *accepted* as intelligent and unintelligent. These then become the reference groups against which the tests are validated.

(ii) The raw material of the 'science' is an abstraction from the real world; it is a socially produced, theoretical object —the IQ score.

(iii) Judgments of intelligence are comparative and relative rather than absolute.

(iv) External factors rather than internal ones determine, for the most part, moves in the research programme.

Binet in 1895 in Paris and Stern in 1912 in Germany developed non-sensory, verbal tests using teacher-selected reference groups. Their ink was hardly dry when, across the Atlantic in the shadow of the Statue of Liberty, Henry Goddard was using the tests to screen the hundreds of thousands of European immigrants arriving on Ellis Island. His conclusions were that the majority of Jews, Hungarians, Italians and Russians were feeble-minded. L. M. Terman updated the test using white middle-class Americans as norms. This became the Stanford-Binet Intelligence Test, a test which was to become the prototype and validator of nearly all subsequent IQ tests. He had quite definite goals in mind: 'If we would preserve our state for a class of people worthy to possess it, we must prevent as far as possible the propagation of mental degenerates . . . the increasing spawn of degeneracy'.[8] The first revision of this test was prompted by finding that girls were constantly outscoring boys. This, of course, would never do, and items were changed and juggled to bring about an equality. One wonders what would have happened if it were found that boys were consistently outscoring girls! One also wonders why such juggling was not done when it was found that whites were outscoring blacks!!

In 1904 the Carnegie Foundation and Union Pacific Railway funded Charles Davenport to establish a Eugenics Laboratory and Records Office. This was the start of the American Eugenics Movement, which numerous prominent biologists and psychologists joined. At the height of the Depression three-quarters of all colleges were teaching Eugenics courses; some thirty States had passed miscegenation laws prohibiting interracial marriages. IQ tests were an integral part of this movement. Studies showed correlations between low IQ and criminality, sexual promiscuity and degeneracy. One simple long-term solution to these ills was the sterilisation of those with low IQs. By 1930, 60,000 people had been sterilised.

Character Education

Historically, another important component of this IQ-Eugenics movement was the Character Education Movement,[9] founded in 1908 by educators and clergy who were members of the National Education Association. The first chairperson of the movement declared that it was the purpose of the school to 'transform children by educational surgery'. The great L. M. Terman, in what was to become a canonical work in IQ literature, said: 'moral judgment, like business judgment, social judgment or any other kind of higher thought process, is a function of intelligence'.[10] E. L. Thorndike believed that 'To him that hath a superior intellect is given also on the average a superior character . . . The abler persons in the long run are the more clean, decent, just and kind'.[11] This movement and programme needed diagnostic tools; a need which the IQ testers filled. The 1921 Symposium on Intelligence Testing found a phalanx of testers committing themselves to extending their science into the measurement of character. Soon the results poured in.

H. Hartshorne and M. May demonstrated that children of northern European parents were more honest, co-operative and charitable than those of Irish or Italian descent.[12] Davenport showed that northern European children were highest-scoring in humour, frankness, sympathy and loyalty; while the Irish were lowest in all these traits and top only in one—suspiciousness.[13] His Centre's research committee showed that being a 'prostitute, a murderer, homeless, a tramp, a pauper and generally a ne'er-do-well' were all functions of intelligence and the nature of one's germ-plasm, this germ-plasm being differentially distributed among races and social classes. The *Downey Will Temperament Test*[14] was able to detect and chart the weaker personality structure of Blacks. The developer of the test interpreted the aggressiveness of the northern Blacks in terms of compensation for their 'inferiority complexes'. Koh's *Ethical Discrimination Test*[15] measured morality in terms of knowledge of proverbs—'a penny saved is a penny ——?'. For more in-depth analysis of the minds of children, the *Woodworth Cady*

Questionnaire was used. This was able to identify psychotic and neurotic tendencies in children. They were psychotic if they felt they were being treated unfairly by teachers, not getting a square deal in life, afraid of the dark, worried about their health or anxious to get away from school and get a job. Not surprisingly, children of Italian and Jewish parents were the ones to benefit from special therapy after administration of the test.[16] S. L. Pressey developed a *Paranoid Scale*[17] in which any concern for injustice, or belief that one was oppressed, enabled the respondent to score top marks.

Handmaidens of Industry
Industrial Psychology was taking wing at the same time as IQ testing; indeed there was a considerable mixture of flocks. E. L. Thorndike developed testing programmes for large insurance companies; L. J. Thurstone worked for Westinghouse and Carnegie Steel, trying to develop scientific management techniques—he used the science of testing to identify and overcome problems in the workplace. Hugo Munsterberg of Harvard was using Binet's procedures to assist large Boston firms with their labour turnover problems. All of this fitted in with Frederick Taylor's mushrooming time and motion studies, performance breakdown analyses and general prostitution of the Academy to the needs of industrial bosses. As an historian on the subject has related: 'scientific management not only conditioned the industrial climate for the psychologists, it determined to a large degree the direction, scope, and nature of psychological research'.[18]

This thumbnail sketch of the milieu out of which the IQ movement emerged has been given because the child is father to the man. We can see operating clearly in the formative period pressures and influences which later become less visible; this because, once set upon its course, the process of production of IQ science and testing can be sustained without direct intervention. In this early period, we have the psychological counterparts to the 'hired prize-fighters' of economics of whom Marx spoke. We also have yet another instance of the fact that 'those who posit are themselves posited'. This history has been well researched and written up by Clarence Karier and Walter Feinberg.[19]

WHAT IS INTELLIGENCE?
Many contributors to the IQ debate have taken the first premise of the argument for granted (IQ measures intelligence) and have

then argued about intelligence. This assumption is question-able, as there is considerable confusion within the literature on what 'intelligence' means; and it is obvious that numerous other factors affect performance on IQ tests.

The common account of intelligence is a *realist* one: the noun 'intelligence' refers to a real existing ability, which is a capacity to learn. Intelligent behaviour is possible because a person has intelligence. This realist view is carried over into much of the scientific work on intelligence. Spearman refers to intelligence as an 'amount of general mental energy'. Jenson refers to it as a 'biological reality' similar to 'atoms, genes and electromagnetic fields'. Eysenck claims that these real abilities are dependent upon 'genes for intelligence' which are varyingly distributed within a population and among populations. For realists, 'intel-ligence' is a *hypothetical construct* rather than an *intervening variable* in psychological theory.[20]

But there have, been others in the debate who take a non-commonsensical *fictionalist* account of intelligence. This is ex-plicitly the position of behaviourists. The best-known and most influential account of this sort has been that of Gilbert Ryle, whose book *The Concept of Mind*[21] was devoted to eradicating the myth of the 'Ghost in the Machine'. In the experimental literature, L. S. Cronbach echoes this account: 'Factor analysts often speak as if they were discovering natural dimensions that reflect the nature of the nervous system. Correlations and factors, however, merely express the way performances covary in the culture from which the sample is drawn'.[22] Fictionalists interpret 'intelligence' in psychological theories as an *intervening variable*. It is merely a shorthand way of saying that in certain circumstances people will regularly be found to act in certain ways; it expresses a relationship rather than referring to an entity. Fictionalists occur in two basic varieties:

Hard fictionalists, or ontological fictionalists—those who believe that intelligence simply does not exist.

Soft fictionalists, or methodological fictionalists—those who believe that psychological theory can proceed on the assump-tion that intelligence has no real existence over and above intelligent behaviour.

As we might expect, some contributions to the debate are just confused. Indeed, Jensen at one point performs the remarkable feat of encompassing at least three contradictions within two sentences. He says: 'We should not reify *g* as an entity of course, since it is only a hypothetical construct intended to explain covariation among tests. It is a hypothetical source of variance (individual differences) in test scores'.[23] Note there that:

(i)   If *g* is not reified it is an intervening variable, not a hypothetical construct.
(ii) If *g* is not reified it does not explain the observed covariation but merely names it.
(iii) Nothing can be the causal source of variance unless it has a real existence. That is, for *g* to be a source it has to be reified.
(iv) This confused fictionalism is in contradiction to the realist position he has elsewhere endorsed; a position in which intelligence is as real as atoms.

Unfortunately, there has been much more testing of intelligence than there has been a science of it. Hans Eysenck, himself one of the major proponents of the IQ argument, has remarked: 'Intelligence tests are not based on any very sound scientific principles, and there is not a great deal of agreement among experts regarding the nature of intelligence'.[24] The theoretical position of most IQ exponents and test constructors has been a particular version of fictionalism known as *operationalism*. Its classic statement was given in 1923 by E. G. Boring: 'Intelligence is what intelligence tests measure'.[25] This was a carry-over into psychology of the operationalism which P. W. Bridgmann had a little earlier advocated in physics. This in turn was an upshot of the *positivist* tradition in philosophy, the tradition which dealt with the surfaces of things and eschewed analysis of mechanisms underlying appearances. As Otto Neurath remarked: 'Physicalism knows no 'depth', everything is on the surface'.[26] Both Jensen and Hernnstein advocate forms of operationalism. The former says: 'If the measurements are reliable and reproducible, and the operations by which they are obtained can be objectively agreed upon, this is all that is needed for them to qualify as proper scientific data'.[27] Although operationalists might turn their backs on theory at one corner they meet it again at the next. It merely replaces the question: 'What is intelligence?', with the question: 'What is an intelligence test?'. To scoff at weightlifting or a chemistry examination as a putative measure of intelligence is to say that we do have some theory about intelligence by virtue of which we are able to demarcate the class of intelligence tests.

At the beginning of a science a certain amount of operation-alism is inevitable. Scientific concepts are usually opaque and ambiguous when first formulated. They are refined as work on them, and with them, continues. This truth has led some to draw analogies between the history of temperature measure-ment and the history of IQ measurement.[28] The *similarities* are that the first measures of temperature conflated tube variation, atmospheric pressure and variation in liquid expansion rates. Galileo's thermometer was simply a tube filled with water inverted over an open dish. The first measures of intelligence were likewise primitive, and compounded many variables. The *differences* are that there was a science of heat and temperature developed which interacted with the measurement technology and enabled more and more of the compounded variables to be isolated. There has been no comparable development in in-telligence theory, or at least none that has affected the ongoing production of tests.

These theoretical problems and confusions in intelligence theory are a subspecies of the general intellectual disorder and disarray in which psychology as a whole finds itself. There has been a tragic marriage between psychology and empiricism; the terms of the marriage contract being a point-by-point affirmation of positions which have been rejected by scientific practice and in philosophy of science. Thus, we have methodological pre-scriptions such as '. . . stimuli and responses are the raw data of psychology. Merely observing data is not enough, however, for the scientist also has to set down a record of his observations in a form which is not limited to the particular case and which he hopes will have some generality. This is where theorising comes into the picture'.[29] Here we have all the familiar shibboleths: the distinction between observational and theoretical terms; the Inductivist collapsing of theory into empirical generalisations; the commitment to theory-free observation; the view that the data of science are observations. These theoretical problems have been surveyed in order to show that the confident manner and the self-importance of the white-coated tester is perhaps not warranted. As far as metatheory is concerned, the science of intelligence is confused, chaotic and arbitrary.

WHAT DO INTELLIGENCE TESTS MEASURE?

Of any test, we can ask: 'Is it reliable?' and: 'Is it valid?'. The first question is concerned with whether the test regularly gives the same result in the same circumstances. A ruler which expanded and contracted with temperature change would not be a reliable measure of length. The second question takes two forms. We can ask whether the test is measuring what it is supposed to be measuring; this is known as 'construct validity'. We can also ask whether the particular test gives the same results as other tests which have been accepted as measures of some quality; this is known as 'concurrent validity'.[30] Operationalists wish to replace questions about an IQ test's construct validity with questions about its concurrent validity. But to do this requires a standard. The standard for all IQ tests this century has been the original Stanford-Binet test. This was itself concurrently validated against judgments of intelligence made by school-teachers; against years of schooling and against success in life. Now, an edifice is only as strong as its foundation. How valid in the construct sense was the Stanford-Binet? Was it a pure measure of intelligence? It would seem not.

For instance, a child aged nine was supposed to:
1. Know the date, day of week, day of month, month of year.
2. Recite the days of the week.
3. Calculate the change from 20 cents when 4 cents were taken out.
4. Read a passage and remember six items.
5. Arrange five equal-appearing cubes in order of weight.

It is not noteworthy that results on this correlated with teacher judgments of intelligence, years of schooling completed, and even success in life. That this performance is uniquely determined by intelligence is much more doubtful. In the 1960 Stanford-Binet, the vocabulary sub-set asks children to define the following words: 'shrewd, mosaic, piscatorial, casuistry, brunette, ambergris, incrustation'. The picture-identification sub-set gives pictures of two women, one a neat, tidy, typically Anglo-Saxon college girl, the other an unkempt Negro woman, and asks: 'Who is prettier?' No prizes for guessing the correct answer. The American Army used the Binet for its Alpha and Beta intelligence tests in World War One. One question was: 'Why should you not give money to beggars on the street?' The possible answers were: because it—
   (i)   breaks up families
   (ii) makes it hard for the beggar to get work
   (iii) takes away the work of organised charities
   (iv) encourages living off others.
Only the last is acceptable!

Other tests, of course, are not much better. The widely-used Wechsler Intelligence Scale (itself validated against the Stanford-

Binet) has a comprehension sub-set which asks: 'Why are criminals locked up?' and: 'Why do we elect (or need to have) senators and congressmen?' Correct answers include: 'Criminals need to be segregated from society for the protection of society' and: 'Electing senators makes government responsible to the people'.

Thus it is apparent that other things besides 'intelligence' are contributing to performance on IQ tests. They are testing what language you speak, what income your parents have, how good your teacher is and how much you have absorbed the dominant social ideology. That they are systematically racist and anti-working-class is to be expected—they were designed to be that way. L. M. Terman, even before he had data, was saying that the 'dullness of Indians, Mexicans and negroes was racial' and that it 'could not be wiped out by any scheme of mental-culture'.[31] J. M. Cattell, another landmark in the illustrious history of IQ testing, was saying that a 'savage brought up in a cultivated society will not only retain his dark skin, but is likely also to have the incoherent mind of his race'.[32] Henry Goddard had a deep fear of the masses, the 'seventy or eighty-six millions who might take matters into their own hands'.[33] In England, Sir Cyril Burt referred to ethnic groups as 'savages'.

We can conclude that the first premise of the IQ argument is either false or meaningless.

INTELLIGENCE AND SUCCESS

The second premise of the IQ argument—intelligence is a determiner of success in life—is a component of the *Meritocracy* myth. This is the view that people succeed in life on account of their merit. There are, of course, differences in the extent to which people succeed in life. In Australia 60% of the country's wealth is owned by 10% of the population; the richest 2,000 Australians own as much as the poorest 2.25 million. In America the top 1% of the population control just over 30% of the nation's wealth. In England the top 2.5% of the population control over 50% of the wealth. For most Latin American countries the figures are even more skewed. That there is differential success is undeniable; that intelligence is responsible for it is very deniable.

All the major proponents of the IQ argument subscribe to the meritocratic myth. Arthur Jensen quotes favourably E. L. Thorndike's view: 'In the actual race of life, which is not to get ahead, but to get ahead of somebody, the chief determining factor is heredity'.[34] Hernnstein says that the socialist slogan 'from each according to his ability, to each according to his need' runs up against the wall of human nature. Cyril Burt attributed the class structure of England to the differential distribution of intelligence in the society.[35] Richard Lynn, one of the Black Paper writers, and sponsor of Jensen's tour of England, claimed that the reason people lived in slums was that they had low innate intelligence.[36] The meritocratic thesis was first formulated by Thomas Jefferson as a relatively progressive doctrine. It stood in opposition to feudal and aristocratic views on how success in life was to be a consequence of the circumstances of one's birth. It was the explicit rationale for the pyramidal structure of public schooling in America—many primary schools, fewer country high schools and one State university. Jefferson referred to this process of selection and elimination as 'scrapping the heap'.

The thesis is idealistic and contrary to manifest evidence—could one believe that the Robber Barons were the most intelligent people in America, or that their descendants, who inherited the vast fortunes, were necessarily bright? The most interesting question is not whether it is true, but what possessed so many apparently reasonable people to believe it. Rather than deal with this, we will investigate the evidence against the thesis and against the second premise in the IQ argument. The definitive work here is that of Samuel Bowles and Herbert Gintis.[37] They have shown that IQ and success do correlate, but that this correlation masks two more important correlations. There is a direct relationship between years spent at school and economic success on the one hand, and a direct relationship between parents' income and economic success on the other. When each factor is considered separately to find out what was the most influential for economic success, the contribution of IQ score is close to negligible. The hard-core components of the meritocratic thesis are false. It is false that dumb kids from rich parents end up poor; it is false that bright kids from poor parents end up rich. A report of the British College of Surgeons is illustrative: 'Medicine would lose immeasurably if the proportion of such students [those from rich homes] were to be reduced in favour of the precocious children who qualify for subsidies from Local Authorities and the State purely on examination results'.[38]

INTELLIGENCE AND HERITABILITY

The third premise of the IQ argument—intelligence is highly

heritable—needs to be approached with a great deal of caution and a preparedness to engage in sophisticated discussion in genetics. At first glance, the premise is simple and straightforward; at a second glance this simplicity dissolves. The commonsense notion of heritability is that something is passed from parents to children. At this level we interpret the premise as saying that most of a child's intelligence is causally determined by his genetic endowment. In slightly more sophisticated terms this becomes 'intelligence as phenotype is mostly (80%) determined by genotype and only slightly (20%) by environment'. This, then, is the basis for seeing intelligence as fixed, and only superficially amenable to environmental and educative changes. It is this premise which explains the futility of massive intervention programmes. Now, there is great equivocation by Jensen concerning this premise. He says at one stage that people entering this mansion should leave their commonsense ideas of intelligence at the door. Later he repeats that his argument is being conducted at a scientific level and that we should be wary of the incursions of commonsense terms and interpretations into it (this notwithstanding the fact that he uses 'bright' and 'smart' as synonyms for 'intelligent' and 'dumb' as a synonym for 'unintelligent'). He claims that it is the science of population genetics to which he looks in order to establish the premise and at the same time to provide independent evidence for the construct validity of IQ tests.

The major problem with this argument is that the scientific notion of heritability and the commonsense one have *nothing* to do with each other. Jensen moves back and forth between these two unrelated senses: he gets the science wrong and then uses the commonsense notion to support his policy recommendations. In population genetics, once we specify a given population and a given environment, then heritability refers to the amount of variance in the phenotype due to variance in the genotype. It is a measure concerning variation in *populations*. It has nothing to do with individuals, with specific genotypes expressing or not expressing themselves as phenotypes. There is no such thing as heritability of a trait in general; heritability measures are always for specific populations in specific environments. Heritability and genetic determination are two completely different notions, although they are often run together by both lay and professional commentators. Jensen is aware of this, and goes to considerable pains to arrive at his 80% figure, a figure derived from population genetic studies (albeit mistaken ones). But he then switches over to a commonsense genetic determination discourse. To illustrate this, consider the following examples:

(i)   In a pure breeding population of tall poppies (all individuals have the same genetic composition, i.e., no genotypic variation) height is 100% inherited (i.e. is genetic) but has zero heritability (there is no genotypic variation of which height variation can be a function).

(ii) Place the above population in a nutrient deficient environment; height will be 100% inherited but all the poppies will be short.

(iii) Having a head is genetically determined, but heritability of the trait is zero—there is no variation in the phenotype.

Jensen *et al* use a *linear statistical model* for analysis of the contributions of different variables to intelligence. For an individual:

$$I = M + H + E$$

where I = intelligence; M = mean intelligence for population; H = variation due to heredity; and E = variation due to environment. There are good reasons why this model should be rejected, and replaced by a heredity/environment interactive model. Genes and environment interact from the very outset and phenotypic expression is a product of this ongoing interchange. Consider the very beginning of meiosis and sex cell division. DNA replication is a function of messenger RNA molecules in its 'environment', and these in turn are contingent upon the presence of particular amino-acids and are specified and determined by these acids. What we consider as 'genetic' at one level is 'environmental' at another. The genetic/environment distinction is yet another case where the clarity of common sense dissolves under the gaze of science. The polarity of gene/environment should be replaced by the dialectical coupling of gene and environment. The former considerably tortures nature.

Norms of Reaction are a more appropriate measure for biologists and population geneticists, who have an interest in intelligence, to be studying. These chart the changes in phenotype for a particular trait as a function of genotype variation and environmental variation. Daniels provides a representative norms-of-reaction graph which can be used to illustrate some important points:

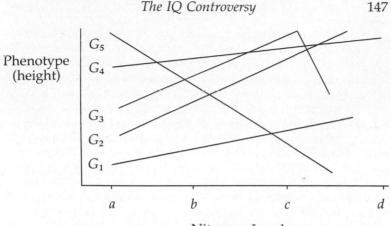

Nitrogen Levels

The case covers corn plants in different environments. For each of five genotypes (G_1 . . . G_5) the observed relation between phenotype (height) and environment (nitrogen level in soil) is plotted.

Some things which can immediately be read are:
(i) Phenotype is sensitive to both environmental changes and genotype changes; both are causes of final height. The notion of a causal division, where genes cause so much and environment causes so much, is a fallacy.
(ii) Examining the performance of genotypes in one environment gives *no* indication of their performance in another. In environment (a) $G_5 > G_2$. In environment (d) $G_5 < G_2$. The notion of a stability of genotypic dominance is also a fallacy. Punters have long expressed this in their adage 'horses for courses'.

We can exemplify these considerations by reference to a study done on the IQ scores of Jewish children. In European nuclear families the average IQ is 105; on Israeli kibbutzim the average is 115; in Middle-Eastern Arab countries the average is 85. Now, when the latter group move to a kibbutz, the average rises to 115, the average of the kibbutz. In terms of norms of reaction, this is to be expected. Without this analysis, then the Middle-Eastern children suffer all the disadvantages of being 'born dumb'.

An important consequence of this change to norms-of-reaction research is that the analysis of variance, that time-honoured pursuit of IQ researchers, has next to no value. It is always measured for a specific environment and genotype distribution. It takes vertical slices of the graph which cannot be interpreted without the whole picture being available. From a slice of the graph at (a) we cannot predict relative positions of the genotypes at (c). Analysis of variance as a technique arose as an alternative to causal analysis. For an individual, it asks how much their phenotypic deviation from the mean of the population is a product of their environment's deviation from the mean and their genotype's deviation from the mean. The analysis is thus a local analysis; it is for a specific population and specific range of environments. In norms of reaction, we are concerned with the functional relation holding between genotype and environment and their expression in phenotype. This allows prediction of trait performance in situations of environmental change (government interventions). Richard Lewontin traverses this terrain of population genetics and its putative connections with IQ research, and concludes: 'The simple analysis of variance is useless for these purposes and indeed has no use at all. In view of the terible mischief that has been done by confusing spatiotemporal local analysis of variance with the global analysis of causes, I suggest we stop the endless search for better methods of estimating useless qualities'.[39]

BURT'S TWIN STUDIES

Historically, the extensive 'studies' of Sir Cyril Burt have provided the bulk of the evidence for the 'IQ is 80% heritable' premise.[40] These studies were conducted over many decades and were translated into political and educational programmes —the Spens Report of 1949 establishing the 11+ exam in England was perhaps the most dramatic. Jensen described him as being 'the most distinguished exponent of genetical methods'. The logic of the twin study argument is that as we go from monozygotic to dizygotic twins, to siblings and to cousins, we should find a decreasing correlation of intelligence scores. Further, the IQ scores should be immune from environmental factors, so that twins reared apart should have substantially the same IQ. Burt's predictions were confirmed to three decimal points. Very impressive, at least until one goes over his results with a fine toothcomb and discovers numerous fabrications, fudges and inventions. His studies were largely thought experiments and his collaborators were figments of his imagination.

He was editor for many years of the prestigious journal *British Journal of Educational Psychology* and took this opportunity further to publicise and legitimise his views. He wrote articles and published them. When decency demanded that he should not, as editor, monopolise the journal, he merely published his own material over other people's names. These included the much-quoted correlation studies of IQ and occupation. Thankfully, this Watergate of intelligence theory is now being unearthed, prompted by the painstaking detective work of Leon Kamin.[41] He has reviewed other twin studies as well, and concludes that there is simply insufficient evidence to assign any non-zero heritability to IQ in any population.

The third premise of the IQ argument is in no better shape than the first two. There has been a considerable amount written about the fourth premise—that there is a significant gap between the mean IQs of blacks and whites and between the mean IQs of social classes.[42] It is not my intention to pursue this. There are a number of obvious points to be made: What is the relationship between mean IQ score and mean intelligence? What factors in the test situation affect the scores? What factors in the long history of domination and oppression affect the scores?

CAN INTELLIGENCE BE CHANGED?

The premises of the IQ argument are largely false or misleadingly simplistic. In addition, the conclusions of the argument can independently be shown to be false. At the surface level, IQ scores can manifestly be changed as a result of experience. The coaching effect is well known. P. E. Vernon, an advocate of the 11+ exam, was disturbed to find, in 1952, that coaching can raise IQ scores by as much as 14 points. One chief examiner suggested the enlightened policy of policing a uniform amount of coaching for each child; another administrator called for the firing of teachers who engaged in such perfidious practices.[43] There have been many intervention programmes which have raised IQs. The classic study is that of M. Skodak, and H. M. Sheels in 1949, which Sheels replicated some thirty years later.[44] Urie Bronfenbrenner has reviewed a large number of intervention programmes which have been efficacious in raising IQ scores.[45]

Following the intricacies of the intervention literature, at least as far as changing IQ scores is concerned, is really not of great interest. IQ scores are conventional, artefactual and abstracted

items. Whether they go up, go down or stay the same is largely
a conventional matter. Furthermore, it follows from the nature
of the scaling techniques used in determining IQ scores that:

(i)   For some groups' IQs to rise means that other groups'
      have to fall;

                              or

(ii) All raised IQs will be rescaled downwards.

This because it is determined *in advance* that the mean IQ of the
population will be 100 and the standard deviation will be 16.
Getting more IQ points does not in itself mean anything; in this
way it is somewhat like a salary rise. At a level beyond
appearances we might be interested in changing intelligence
rather than IQ scores. The ability of people to perform new tasks
and master situations is certainly changeable as a result of
changed involvement, motivation, interest and responsibility.
McIver Hunt has documented much of this, and his research is
the basis of his *Harvard Education Review* response to Jensen.[46]
The educational work of John Holt, Paulo Freire and others all
testify to the performance differences that experience can
generate and there is no reason to believe that this performance
change does not itself interactively generate a capability change.

The third conclusion of the IQ argument is that race differences in IQ scores are a genetic matter. Jensen writes that 'there are
no "black genes" or "white genes"; there are intelligence genes,
which are found in populations in different proportions, somewhat like the distribution of blood types. The number of
intelligence genes seems lower, overall, in the black population
than in the white'.[47] But the notion of heritability of differences
between populations is an absurdity. One cannot move from
within group heritabilities to between group heritabilities.
Richard Lewontin provides a succinct example to illustrate the
point.[48] First take two pure breeding corn strains, one tall, the
other short. Plant seeds from each. Within both lines, differences in height will be entirely environmental and heritability will
be zero. Between both lines (given similar soil) the height
difference is genetic. Second, take two open-pollinated strains
(genetically diverse) and grow in two environments, one
nutrient-rich, the other nutrient-poor. Within each line, height
differences will be 100% heritable (identical environments), but
between each line the differences are entirely environmental.
Thus we have a situation where heritability *within* each population is 100%, but the population differences are entirely environmental.

A fourth inference of the IQ argument is that intervention programmes are doomed to failure and should be abandoned. To say that this is false is too easy. Many intervention programmes are doomed to failure; but this is not a consequence of some mystical intelligence, it is a consequence of faulty analyses, poor politics and inadequate preparation and follow-up. Providing funds for Latin to be taught to aborigines in outback Australia (a real example) is a stupid form of intervention. Ivan Illich has argued cogently that schools are a hopeless vehicle for intervention strategies in poor countries. Intervention programmes that do not involve the families of individuals have been shown to have only short-term effects. In the final analysis, of course, the most efficacious intervention is the redistribution of wealth, capital and opportunities in a society. Short of that, we are largely involved in window-dressing.

CONCLUSIONS

What are some of the things which our account of epistemology, ideology and schooling can contribute to the IQ controversy?

(i) *Suspiciousness.* We have often stressed how one's understanding of an object affects the conceptualisation of it, research conducted upon it, the anomalies ignored in it. Broadly speaking, to hold a liberal-rationalist account of schooling (schools are concerned with the growth of knowledge, character-building and the alleviation of social ills) does not predispose us to be suspicious or too inquisitive about the growth and extension of the IQ racket. This is partly the explanation for the resounding silence of London Institute analyses of the IQ business.[49] Broadly speaking, to have a Marxist theory of schooling (that schools are about the reproduction of labour power, the inculcation of ruling-class culture and morals) is to have *a priori* suspicions about anything so widespread and effective in schools as IQ testing, the 11+ exam and tracking. The Marxist should be able to smell a rat here. But smelling a rat and catching it are different things. Part of the Marxist contribution is to provide the scholarship, research, categories and processing mechanisms for undermining the IQ argument. In the biological sciences Richard Lewontin, Steven Rose and Stephen Gould have all done good work in this direction. In educational, psychological and historical studies Walter Feinberg, Herbert Gintis, Samuel Bowles, Brian Simon and James Lawler have contributed much. We have repeatedly claimed that those who posit are themselves posited; that in a person's intellectual productions we expect to see, varyingly, aspects of their own predispositions, outlooks, class position. Not unexpectedly, this is the case in the contributions to the IQ controversy. One very interesting study has set about predicting the conclusions of intelligence research on the basis of the biographical characteristics of the researcher.[50] This is an interesting vindication of Niebuhr's claim about social science being akin to a Rorschach test.

(ii) *Historicity*. One of the central Marxist-Hegelian claims is that the understanding of an object, circumstance or institution involves examining its history, the process of its coming into being, the circumstances of its production. Thus, when faced with an IQ testing industry, we should initially seek to disclose its history. When this is done, something like the picture we gave in a thumbnail sketch will emerge. This is a history of constant, blatant use of so-called IQ tests to further the process of ruling-class control and hegemony over racial groups and the working classes. What is so clearly the case with the early work of Goddard and Thorndike becomes more difficult to detect as the decades roll by, until, of course, frauds such as Cyril Burt are unmasked and we are jolted once more back into the recognition that the leopard's spots really have not changed.

(iii) *Anti-biologism*. Any proposal which amounts to biological reductionism should be regarded as potentially ideological. Marx constantly opposed the materialists of his day who sought to reduce historical and social realities to biological ones —like the Italian materialist who thought that the presence of pasta in the diet was depressing revolutionary consciousness among his country-people. The attempt to reduce the complex social and political forces responsible for a person's IQ test performance to some attribute of the DNA molecule is absurd. Biological causal changes are certainly a reality; one ignores them at one's peril. But these chains are socially mediated by the time they reach the level of human affairs. In the field of sexual relations, vaginal or clitoral orgasms, large or small breasts or penises have few effects or implications in themselves. What effects they have is the result of the interaction of the biological with the social. Women reading standard analytic texts on the absence of vaginal orgasms being an indicator of failure to proceed to womanhood may well develop anxieties and self-doubts. These will very likely find behavioural expression; it is not however the absence of vaginal orgasm *per se* which brings this about. It is not biology, but socialised biology that is operative. The PKU gene manifests itself in mental defectiveness only in the presence of a particular amino-acid; remove the acid from a child's diet early enough, and PKU is no longer a 'low intelligence' gene.

(iv) *Anti-individualism.* A striking feature of the IQ argument is its individualism; its commitment to the thesis that it is the properties (in this case intelligence) of individuals which determine the social arrangement and places within it. This is seen in pure form when Burt talks of high-intelligence people from the lower classes rising to fill positions in the upper classes and low-intelligence people from the upper classes sinking to an appropriate level in the lower classes. This flotation theory of class is an absurdity. People are as they are by virtue of the social relations in which they engage and by which they are engaged. Compare the sixth thesis on Feuerbach: 'The human essence is no abstraction inherent in each individual. In its reality it is the ensemble of social relations'.

NOTES

1. *Harvard Education Review*, 1969, 39.
   The thesis has been elaborated in his *Genetics and Education*, New York, Harper & Row, 1973; *Educability and Group Differences*, New York, Harper & Row, 1972.
2. *I.Q. in the Meritocracy*, Boston, Atlantic Little Brown & Co., 1973.
3. 'Dysgenics, Geneticity, Raceology: A Challenge to the Intellectual Responsibility of Educators' in *Phi Delta Kappa*, January, 1972.
4. 'I.Q. Heritability and Human Nature', in *Boston Studies Philos. Sc.*, 32, 1976.
5. 'Reaction Time with Reference to Race', *Psych. Review*, 1895, 2, (5) Quoted in *Biology as a Social Weapon*, American Science for the People publication, Minneapolis, Burgess, 1977.
6. *Educational Psychology*, New York, 1903.
7. In I. Lakatos and A. Musgrave (eds.), *Criticism and the Growth of Knowledge*, Cambridge, C.U.P., 1974, p. 100.
8. *The Measurement of Intelligence*, Boston, Houghton Mifflin, 1916.
9. For the material in this section I am grateful to Stephen Yulish of the Education Department of the University of Arizona.
10. *The Measurement of Intelligence*, p. 11.
11. 'Intelligence and its Uses', *Harpers*, January, 1920, p. 233.
12. *Studies in the Nature of Character*, New York, Macmillan Co., 1928, p. 252.
13. 'Comparative Social Traits of Various Races', *School and Society*, 1921, 14.
14. J. McFadden and J. F. Daskiell, 'Racial Differences as Measured by the Downey Will Temperament Test', *Journal of Applied Psychology*, 1923, 7.
15. S. C. Kohs, 'Ethical Discrimination Test', *Journal of Delinquency*, 1922, 7.

16. E. Matthews, 'A Study of Emotional Stability in Children', *Journal of Delinquency*, 1923, *8*.
17. 'A Group Scale for Investigating the Emotions', *Journ. Abn. Psych. & Soc. Psych.*, 1921, *16*.
18. Quoted in David F. Noble, *America by Design*, New York, Alfred Knopf, 1979, p. 297.
19. Clarence Karier, P. Violas and J. Spring, *Roots of Crisis: American Education in the Twentieth Century*, Chicago, Rand McNally & Co., 1973.
    Clarence Karier, 'Testing for Order and Control in the Corporate Liberal State', in Ned Block and Gerald Dworkin (eds.), *The I.Q. Controversy*, London, Quartet Books, 1976.
    Walter Feinberg, *Reason and Rhetoric*, New York, John Wiley, 1975.
20. The distinction was first clearly formulated by K. MacCorquodale and P. E. Meehl in their paper 'On a Distinction between Hypothetical Constructs and Intervening Variables', in *Psych. Rev.*, 1948, *55*. Other significant contributions to the discussion have been J. R. Maze, 'Do Intervening Variables Intervene?', *Psych. Rev.*, 1954, *61*, (4); W. R. Roseboom, 'Mediation Variables in Scientific Theory', *Psych. Rev.*, 1956, *63*. In brief, a hypothetical construct refers to a real existing entity; an intervening variable refers merely to a relationship between two entities.
21. Harmondsworth, Penguin, 1973 (Orig. 1949).
22. 'Test Validation', in E. L. Thorndike (ed.), *Educational Measurement*, Washington, 1970. Quoted in *The I.Q. Controversy*, p. 469.
23. *Genetics and Education*, p. 77.
24. *Know Your Own IQ*, Baltimore, 1962, p. 8.
25. 'Intelligence as the Tests Test It', *New Republic*, 1923, *24*. See the 'Symposium on Operationism', in *The Psychological Review*, 1945, *52*, (5). It contains contributions from E. G. Boring, P. W. Bridgmann, H. Feigl and B. F. Skinner.
26. M. Neurath and R. S. Cohen (eds.), *Empiricism and Sociology*, Dordrecht, Reidel, 1973, p. 326.
27. Quoted in *The I.Q. Controversy*, p. 424.
28. See Peter Urbach, 'Progress and Degeneration in the IQ Debate', Pts. I, II in *Brit. Journ. Phil. Sc.*, 1974, *25* and *26*.
29. R. A. Champion, *Learning and Activation*, Sydney, Wiley, 1969.
30. For discussion of these terms and test theory generally, see Anne Anastasi, *Psychological Testing*, New York, Macmillan, 1961.
31. *The Measurement of Intelligence*, Ch. 1.
32. *J. M. Cattell: American Man of Science*, Lancaster, Science Press, 1947, Vol. II, p. 155.
33. *Human Efficiency and Levels of Intelligence*, Princeton, Princeton University Press, 1920, p. 97.
34. 'How Much Can We Boost IQ and Scholastic Achievement?'
35. 'Evidence for the Concept of Intelligence', in S. Wiseman (ed.), *Intelligence and Ability*. He admits that success is not just a function of intelligence, it is also determined by character!', p. 281.
36. *Black Papers, 2*.
37. *Schooling in Capitalist America*, London, Routledge & Kegan Paul, 1976.
38. Quoted in V. Navarro, *Class Struggle, the State and Medicine*, London, Martin Robertson, 1978, p. 76.
39. 'The Analysis of Variance and the Analysis of Causes', in *The I.Q. Controversy*, p. 192. On the same methodological point see D. Layzer, 'Heritability Analysis of IQ Scores: Science or Numerology?', *Science*, 1974, *183*.
40. The bibliography attached to Peter Urbach's double article contains a close-

to-complete listing of Burt's 'work'. He is one of thousands who took the work seriously.

41. *The Science and Politics of IQ*, Harmondsworth, Penguin, 1977.
42. See K. Richardson and D. Spears (eds.), *Race and Intelligence*, Harmondsworth, Penguin, 1973.
43. See Brian Simon, *Intelligence, Psychology and Education*, London, Lawrence & Wishart, 1971, Pt. I for a review of this material.
44. See *The I.Q. Controversy*, p. 488.
45. *Is Early Intervention Effective?*, Ithica, Cornell University Press, 1974.
46. J. McIver Hunt, *Intelligence and Experience*, New York, 1961. His reply to Jensen is in *Harvard Education Review*, 1969, 2.
47. *New York Times*, Aug. 31, 1969, p. 43.
48. *The I.Q. Controversy*, p. 98 ff.
49. There has been very little written by analytic philosophers of education on the IQ controversy. Peters, in his *Concept of Motivation* (London, Routledge & Kegan Paul, 1958, p. 112), says that 'intelligence' and 'goal-directedness' are logically inseparable concepts. Mark Fisher has an article, 'Intelligence', in the Philosophy of Education Society of Great Britain 1966 *Proceedings*. Commendably, he asserts that philosophers should question theories and concepts on other than logical or intra-theoretic grounds. But then he provides no historical or ideological analyses. Horses can be led to water, but they cannot be forced to drink. J. P. White, in 'Intelligence and the Logic of the Nature-Nurture Issue' (*Proceedings, Philosophy of Education Society of Great Britain*, 1974, 8, (1)), embarks on the hopeless task of locating the meaning of 'intelligence', although to his credit he does recognise that such meaning will not be given directly from common usage—we have to read between the lines. He does say that the IQ argument is ideology; but then, as he says that Freudianism, Marxism and Christianity are also ideologies—in that their central propositions cannot be proved or disproved—his designation is not very helpful.
50. J. J. Sherwood and M. Nataupsky, 'Predicting the Conclusions of Negro-White Intelligence Research from Biographical Characteristics of the Investigator', *Journal of Personality and Social Psychology*, 1968, 8 (53).

CHAPTER 9
ANALYTIC PHILOSOPHY OF EDUCATION

Analytic philosophy of education holds a position of dominance in teacher training institutions in the Anglo-Saxon world. It has been a powerful and influential presence in educational administration, curricula planning, books and journals. In the past two decades there has been no major curricula debate conducted without reference to the views of Peters and Hirst. Their work, along with the industry of many others, constitutes an imposing research programme in philosophy of education. It has been referred to as 'London Institute Philosophy of Education' and most recently by the apt acronym, APE. The argument of this book is directed against the APE research programme. It is a contribution to a broadly Marxist philosophy of education: a contribution which draws heavily upon the work of previous writers in this area.[1] This chapter will give some background to APE and locate it on a philosophical and ideological canvas. Then, three important components of APE will be outlined and criticised: its philosophical methodology; its epistemology; and its conception of schooling. APE is the educational representative of a liberal-rationalist world view which has political, economic, historical and cultural manifestations. It holds dear certain views about society, work, the State, the resolution of conflict and the role of ideas and the place of reason in the development of human history. APE, as the educational arm of this liberalism, was consciously locked into battle both with Progressivism and mindless Instrumentalism. It valued culture and the intellectual achievements of Western civilisation and was forthright in its belief that children should be initiated into these 'mansions'. It is, however, a mistake to see APE as a consciously conservative philosophy in the sense that the *Black Paper* authors were educational conservatives. Its concern for criticism, for the exercise of intelligence, for following the argument where it leads, for compulsion and authority only as temporary measures, all suggest that APE could see through the pretensions and follies of the conservative Right. Unfortunately, APE has in practice been a supporter of the status quo. By putting substantive questions about schooling, economics and science outside its purview, it has been at the mercy of implicit understandings of these substantive matters. These implicit understandings are the understandings of common sense, formed within the status quo. The argument between APE and Marxism is not just one of specific analyses, but rather a clash of research programmes, of orientations to the world and to the transformation of the world.

THE EVOLUTION OF APE

The history of a species needs to be located within the history of the genus, in this case philosophy of education. Taking a long view, Plato, Aristotle, Augustine, Aquinas, Locke, Rousseau, Kant and Newman were all philosophers who appended educational writings to their philosophical systems. In some cases— Plato and Newman for instance—these were fairly detailed and closely-argued works; but it is true to say that prior to the early twentieth century there was no identifiably separate entity labelled 'philosophy of education' under the canopy of either philosophy or education. With industrialisation and the implementation of compulsory mass education, there gradually developed the teacher training industry, centred around teachers' colleges. As Thomas Kuhn has well noted, intellectual paradigms require institutions, journals, finance and power if they are to take root and develop. Teacher training institutions provided the material necessities for the creation of the philosophy of education genus. In America, significant philosophers —A. N. Whitehead, William James, John Dewey, Theodore Brameld—wrote for and lectured to a wide audience of trainee teachers who were exposed to a variety of 'isms'—Realism, Essentialism, Existentialism, Catholicism—and encouraged to evaluate them and ascertain their educational consequences. At its worst, this was a kind of secular theology: a mishmash of history, educational ideas and idle musings about the good life and the nature of people. The National Society for the Study of Education Year-books of 1942 and 1957 encapsulate the best American contributions to this genus of philosophy of education. The harbingers of APE appeared in the '40s and '50s. First, C. D. Hardie's *Truth and Fallacy in Educational Theory* in 1942; second, Israel Scheffler's 'Towards an Analytic Philosophy of Education' in 1954;[2] third, D. J. O'Connor's *An Introduction to the Philosophy of Education* in 1957. These were inspired, on the negative side, by the unsavoury spectacle of PE of the old variety falling into academic disrepute, and becoming more and more removed from concrete concerns and debates of teachers. On the positive side, these harbingers saw themselves bringing to PE the analytic methodology of Wittgenstein, Austin and Ryle, which was creating the Revolution in Philosophy. They were concerned with the largely uncritical discourse, which often passed as educational theory. These were the explicit concerns of Scheffler's *The Language of Education* (1960) and B. O. Smith and R. H. Ennis' (eds.) *Language and Concepts in Education* (1961).

There are some good reasons for the provincial judgment that APE as a full-blown research programme began with the appointment of Richard Peters to the Chair of Philosophy of Education at the London Institute of Education in 1963, and the publication of his *Ethics and Education* in 1966.[3] In the Preface to the book he speaks of providing a 'few signposts' so that 'furrows' dug in the 'field' of philosophy of education might at least go in the 'right direction'. The important thing is that 'there should be a determinate structure on which students can train their critical faculties.' The determinate structure was the analysis of concepts in educational discourse; the determination of the 'logic' of educational argument and the justification of varied educational practices. Peters, and his early colleague Paul Hirst, had the might to establish the right direction for furrowing. They lectured to audiences of a thousand or more in undergraduate courses; they controlled the house journal *Proceedings of the Philosophy of Education Society of Great Britain* and, perhaps most importantly, they controlled and designed the graduate programmes which trained the first-generation advocates and teachers of APE. Soon these were taking up Chairs and senior positions in British provincial and colonial Education Faculties. They produced textbooks especially designed for undergraduate university students and college trainees. Indeed, one of the most popular Australian examples of the genre has a preface announcing the author's debt to R. S. Peters and P. H. Hirst and saying: 'If the only virtue of this book is to lead its readers on to work such as theirs it will have served a useful function'.[4] As these people supervised theses, made academic appointments and controlled provincial PE journals, they were in a position to ensure that APE grew in influence and stature away from the site of its first appearance off Russell Square. The positive heuristic of the programme was clear: go out and analyse concepts in educational discourse. Scheffler and Peters led the way with analyses of 'teaching' and 'education' respectively. Others followed on: R. F. Dearden analysed 'play'; Ivan Snook analysed 'indoctrination'; G. Vesey analysed 'learning'; a host of other figures analysed 'creativity'.[5] In Kuhn's terms, we had a decade of normal science activity in which there was very little debate about the foundations of PE among the APES. The negative heuristic of the research programme was equally clear. Philosophy is a second-order activity; it is concerned with reflective questions about scientific, religious, moral and other first-order activities. Other disciplines do the running; philosophers do the watching and analysing. In the words of Peters, philosophers are now 'more cautious about making pronouncements on matters which are not strictly philosophical in character'.[6] Hence analytic philosophers were not concerned to study the history, economics or sociology of schooling. So we have John White saying that the analysis of the concept of 'need' is a fitting and appropriate activity, but argument about which needs and whose needs are to be met in schooling is inappropriate. Israel Scheffler said that 'critical precision rather than doctrine is the essence of such philosophy.[7] Third class honours was the awful fate of any neophyte APE who wandered off into the field of substantive first-order discourse.

This brief sketch of the evolution of APE is, of course, not exhaustive. But it is sufficient to enable us to identify elements of APE which are amenable to our overall analysis of knowledge claims being the product of a process of theoretical production. We can see the raw materials being utilised by APE (educational discourse and debate, concepts of schooling and education); the means of production used (techniques of conceptual analysis); the pattern of productive relations (power associated with university Chairs and journal editorship); and the finished products (refined concepts, clearer arguments). The products certainly had exchange value in the sense that they could be negotiated for tenure and higher positions; it was to be hoped that they had use value in that they were to be utilised by the practising teacher. According to Scheffler, they 'cannot fail to deepen our understanding of what we do when we educate'.[8] For Peters and Hirst the products of analysis had a role to play in the *justification* of educational practices and proposals. They were engaged in curricula debate for which adequate analysis was a prerequisite.

Thus far we have given a largely internal account of the history of APE. But we know that purely internal accounts are not sufficient for explaining the rise and fall of research programmes or, in our terms, the development and overthrow of particular processes of theoretical production. With APE in particular, we need to look to external factors. In immediate terms it did provide PE with a sense of identity, purpose and

academic respect; it marked out a legitimate field in which PE
could lay claim to funds and positions in competition with
sociologists and psychologists. In wider terms it was consistent
with the liberal-rationalist ideology dominant in the social and
educational milieu. It takes over the uncritical common sense of
the everyday and canonises it. This is revealed in Scheffler's
image of teachers introducing students to the 'many mansions
of our heritage', and Peters' image of teachers as taking the role
of the priests who used to introduce successive generations of
individuals into the 'various aspects of a culture within which
the individual has eventually to determine where he stands'.[9]
Far from viewing this as a threat to the *status quo*, Peters indeed
overtly supports it. He sees our 'current political and cultural
institutions as embodying the very values of civilisation which
teachers should be striving to uphold and create'.[10] Authority is
necessary and must itself be 'institutionalised if it is to be
effective'. His earlier book, *Social Principles and the Democratic
State*,[11] is a very model of liberal rationalism applied to politics.
In another early work, *The Concept of Motivation*,[12] he says that
man in society is like a 'chess-player writ large' and that
explanations of behaviour are to be sought in terms of social
rules being followed. He cites some interesting examples where
this breaks down and we have momentarily to adopt a causal
model of explanation 'as with a married man who suddenly
makes an advance to a choirboy. In such cases it is as if the man
suffers something rather than does something'.[13] When faced
with the charge that all these positions were impregnated with
middle-class assumptions, Peters acknowledges it and says: 'All
I can say is, thank God somebody has got it right'.[14] Peters
articulates and defends a liberal world view; it is the world view
of the political theorist Michael Oakeshott, a person much
admired by both Peters and Hirst. This world view led Oakeshott
to title an essay on competing social interests: 'The Voice of
Poetry in the Conversation of Mankind'.[15] Paul Hirst chooses an
extract from this to conclude his 'Liberal Education and the
Nature of Knowledge' paper, saying that his words express
more succinctly than mine can precisely what it seems to me a
liberal education is and what its outcome will be. 'Education,
properly speaking, is an initiation into the skill and partnership
of this conversation in which we learn to recognise the voices, to
distinguish the proper occasions of utterance'. It is the world
view which inspired the English ruling class to carry on their
conversational diplomacy with European fascism in the '30s.[16]
But liberalism has always been an optional extra as far as

capitalism is concerned. In periods of boom and subsidence of class struggle, capitalism can afford to wear a liberal face; however, when crises occur, liberalism tends to be jettisoned. When Sputnik went up, child-centred education in the United States went down. The silicon chip technology and resultant massive unemployment; the concentration of capital into fewer and fewer hands; the need for the State to apply more and more coercive measures to ensure a compliant work-force and a resigned non-work-force—these might all be factors in the elimination of liberal-rationalist practices in the school system, and subsequently of the philosophy which advocates those practices. France and Australia have already seen large government enquiries into 'Education and Training for Industry'. It is liberal programmes which have gone to the wall as a consequence of these.

In the development of a research programme there has to be some internal reasons to claim people's allegiance; so also, in the elimination of a research programme there have to be internal problems and difficulties to allow external factors to be efficacious. Intellectual convictions are not to be discounted; the long history of religious and political martyrs testify to this. It is these internal weaknesses with which we are concerned here. First APE's methodology; second the concept of schooling it uses as raw material; and third its epistemology.

THE METHOD OF APE

Methodology was to be the long suit of the APE hand. Its three main cards were commitments to analysis as the proper method of philosophy, to a distinction between scientific and philosophical concerns and questions, and to the ideological, political and ethical neutrality of the method and hence of the products. Sadly, these leading cards have all been trumped.

(i) Analysis as a method of philosophy has been in full retreat since the halcyon days of J. L. Austin, G. Ryle and P. F. Strawson. The tide has ebbed; actually it had ebbed in philosophy proper prior to Peters' bringing his analytic canoe down to the beach to launch APE. APE has been paddling in a backwater. Why did the tide ebb? First, the quality of the practitioners dropped dramatically. J. L. Austin maintained that an issue's importance was not a consideration in determining whether philosophers ought to spend their time on it. Fortunately he dealt with uninteresting questions in an interesting manner which shed light on larger concerns. Unfortunately his followers at Oxford, for the most part, dealt with uninteresting questions in an uninteresting way which shed no light on any larger issues. The same, of course, is true of Wittgenstein, who dissociated himself from the Oxford analytic movement— despite many analysts' claiming him as their progenitor. An astute commentary is that, at Oxford, similar-looking techniques were being employed with the greatest skill, but without any deeper, or clearly philosophical, purpose. 'It was like exchanging a real clock for a child's clock-face which looks just the same at first sight but does not tell the time'.[17]

The second reason for the ebbing of analytic methodology was the growing conviction, often expressed by Popper, that the business of both science and philosophy is the search for truth, not the search for meanings. Meanings are interesting when they are embedded in correct accounts of the world. Philosophers ought to be facilitating the obtaining of the correct accounts. Popper, in his 'A Realist View of Logic, Physics and History', correctly gives an account of philosophic method which is diametrically opposed to everything APE stands for. He says: 'One should never quarrel about words, and never get involved in questions of terminology. One should always keep away from discussing concepts. What we are really interested in, our real problems, are factual problems, or in other words, problems of theories, and their truth'.[18] I endorse this view. It lies behind my repeated claim that analysis of concepts has a place *within* theories and is largely meaningless *across* theories. APES that set out to analyse 'intelligence' or 'learning' or 'ideology' are involved in a pointless exercise. Hirst speaks of conceptual analysis in Ryle's terms as 'logical geography'. It is concerned with 'distinguishing those patterns of terms which can be found when we do things with words'.[19] PE should be contributing to, and appraising, rival theories of learning, of intelligence and of ideology. For any putative analysis, we have to ask: Whose concept is being analysed? The geography metaphor is inappropriate. Mountains and valleys do have defined contours which can be mapped; their features impose themselves on us. Concepts in language and theoretical terms are simply not like this. Paul Feyerabend observed that analysis of usage will work best in a closed society that is firmly held together by a powerful myth, such as was the case in postwar Oxford.[20] There are many critical analyses of analytic philosophy available[21] and some of analytic philosophy of education.[22]

(ii) APE's second high card, the science/philosophy distinction, has been well and truly trumped. I have, in earlier chapters, referred to the inescapable interpenetration of physics and metaphysics, of science and philosophy. Roughly speaking, metaphysics enters science when statements of the General Conceptual Scheme governing the science are enunciated. Thus, Aristotelian physics is unintelligible and unworkable apart from Aristotelian philosophy of act and potency, of substance and accidents, of explanation in terms of principles. Newtonian mechanics is likewise inseparable from corpuscularian philosophy and so on. Peters, in the Introduction to *Ethics and Education* states succinctly a position which is plainly false:

A scientific question . . . is one that can, in principle, be answered by certain kinds of procedures in which observation and experimentation play a crucial part. But the clarification and discussion of the concepts used and of how they have meaning, and of the procedures by means of which these questions are answered, is a philosophical inquiry.

Peters' separatism is, of course, endorsed by Hirst—philosophy is one form of knowledge and science is another. Peters elsewhere makes the distinction in terms of science being a first-order activity and philosophy a second-order one. Science is talk about the world; philosophy of science is talk about talk about the world. A succinct statement of this position is provided by G. J. Warnock, who says: 'Philosophy is the study of the concepts we employ and not of the facts, phenomena, cases or events to which these concepts might be or are applied'.[23] But the distinction cannot be maintained. Quine calls the procedure of going from talk about objects to talk about descriptions of objects one of 'semantic ascent'. He recognises, however—and this is important—that science itself involves semantic ascent; scientific talk, debate, theory appraisal is multilevel discourse. All this becomes very clear when we adopt the 'science as theoretical production' model and make a distinction between the real object of science and the theoretical object. (It is unfortunate that Quine has not seen clearly this second distinction.) The raw materials of scientific production are already theorised materials, they are not real objects; when they are worked over into theoretical products they can be raw materials for another production process. Statements about the pressure of a gas are abstract raw materials for production of gas-law generalisations, which become raw materials for production of the kinetic theory, which is intelligible only within corpuscularian metaphysics.

(iii) The third high card in APE's methodology hand is the ethical and political neutrality one. This too has been trumped. Hirst displays it when he says that the content of a liberal education is determined in scope and content by knowledge itself; by the forms of knowledge and their harmonious hierarchical interrelations. Its great strength is that curricula decisions can be made free from 'the predilections of pupils, the demands of society or the whims of politicians'. Peters uses the metaphor of philosopher as spectator to convey the detachedness and neutrality which he sees as the hallmark of APE. Just as a spectator observes, 'so also does a philosopher detachedly ponder upon and probe into activities and forms of discourse in which he and others engage'.[24] This is a fictional position in both theory and practice; it is a position to which innumerable ideologists have laid claim. It is undoubtedly an attractive and seductive position; it frees one's conclusions from the taint of special pleading or the charge of subjectivism, bias or ideological distortion. I have previously rehearsed the Theory Dependence arguments of Kuhn, Hanson, Feyerabend, *et al.* which, while I think they are inextricably bound up with an empiricist epistemology (which takes individuals' perceptions and experiences as central to knowledge), nevertheless are sufficient to trump the detachedness to which APE cleaves. More importantly, if the first-order discourse embodies political choices, class interests and ethical prejudices, then the role of philosopher as portrayed by Peters cements these distortions. Far from being neutral, philosophy on the APE model is guaranteed to be political, at least to the extent that the first-order discourses are not value-free. To prove that the first-order discourses are not value-free requires an independent argument, some of the elements of which have been given in our discussion of ideology. Analysis takes language, everyday theory and common sense as given and fails to comprehend the ensemble as a product of certain practices which are historically contingent, and politically and economically ordered. As Marx suggested, in each age the ruling ideas are the ideas of the ruling class. For analysts to discuss political philosophy in terms of everyday notions of the State is to support those whose interest lies in people having a false account of the origin and function of that 'committee for managing the . . . affairs of the . . . bourgeoisie'. Richard Peters and Stanley Benn provide a clear instance of just such supposedly neutral analysis disguising substantive judgments of a conservative kind. They repeatedly use the metaphor of the State as an umpire, and reiterate the overwhelming need to accept authority because most social enterprises would be hopeless without it. Which States do they have in mind? Classes battle for control of the State; it is not a neutral observer. The history of the German, English and American States should make this apparent. The recent history of Chile and Zimbabwe make the State's neutrality even more mythical. Analytic political philosophy cements the ideological everyday conception of the State. This is replicated in Peters' analysis of schooling.

APES AND SCHOOLING

Peters, in the Introduction to *Ethics and Education*, states that one of the main issues with which the philosophy of education should be concerned is the analysis of the concept of 'school'. Before enlarging on his account we should note that he oscillates between giving an account of the concept of 'school' and giving an account of schools. That is, he slips back and forth between first-order and second-order analyses. Unfortunately, his first-order accounts tend to be flow-ons from his second-order ones. In this he is an idealist: he moves from what people think about schools, to what schools are. Hirst also oscillates. One article opens with the confident assertion that 'one of the central functions, if not the central function, of education is the introduction of pupils to those forms of thought and knowledge which we think peculiarly valuable'.[25] On the face of it, this is an empirical, first-order, substantive claim about the function of education systems in society. Elsewhere he maintains that his analysis is about what *should* happen in schools, not with what *does* happen. The equivocation is endemic.

In Chapter IX of *Ethics and Education*, Peters describes schools as institutions whose 'overriding aim should be that of education' which involves initiating the young into a worthwhile form of life.The schools share with churches and other institutions the 'function of preserving and transmitting the ultimate values of a society'. Their *raison d'être* is to 'transmit what a community values'. This is, of course, idealist in the technical sense. Peters acknowledges that some realism is necessary; that in Marx's terms, for a society to survive, it must first produce goods and reproduce labour power. Peters' view is that societies 'cannot be perpetuated unless many menial and instrumental tasks are performed and vast numbers of people are also trained in them'. The training and selecting of such people by the school is referred to as an instrumental and subsidiary function. Where this secondary function predominates over the primary educative function, we have instances of what he calls 'degenerate forms of a school'.

My claim will be that this conception of schooling is not only contrary to APE methodology—prescriptive and evaluative—but is radically mistaken.[26] Peters' primary and subsidiary functions are the reverse of what is the case in the real world. The selection and training of labour power is the main concern of a school system; education fits in where it can. Peters' reversal is an ideological reversal; it is a classic case of Marx's thesis that the ideological image of reality is that of the *'camera obscura'*, the upside-down image on the retina. The establishment of this claim is a matter for the history, sociology and economics of education.

It has been stressed in the early chapters that good theories depend in large part upon having adequate conceptualisation of their real objects. Joseph Priestly was unable to make real headway in chemistry because, although he had prepared and isolated oxygen, he had a confused and faulty conceptualisation of it. For him it was 'dephlogistated air'. Henry Cavendish was in a similar situation, referring to oxygen as 'dephlogistated water'. It was when Antoine Lavoisier described the gas as a separate and unique element—oxygen—that headway was made in the experimental and theoretical science of combustion. Analogously, the idealist conceptualisation of schooling with which APE deals prevents the resolution of anomalies and inhibits or misdirects research.

Peters is explicit about educational practices and policies following from his analysis. But the practices and policies are dependent upon the accuracy of the concept of education they use. 'The purpose underlying the conceptual analysis in this book is really to indicate the implications for teaching, for the curriculum, for relationships with pupils and for an educational community, of taking a certain view of education and of human development'.[27] There is equivocation here concerning what the 'certain view' is of. Is it actual schooling? Is it hoped-for schooling? If the first, it is mistaken; if the second, it is utopian and ideological. Either way, APE does not give people an adequate theory and appraisal of education. As is well known, faulty intelligence reports are harmless enough in peacetime; in a situation where education is under attack, they are disastrous. Clearly, his 'certain view' is a liberal view of schooling and society. This is a normative claim. The pretence of neutrality, to freedom from political and ideological commitment, is just that —a pretence.

EPISTEMOLOGY OF APE

Paul Hirst's 'Forms of Knowledge' thesis *is* the epistemology of APE. Hirst, a junior colleague of Peters at the London Institute, took the foundation Chair of Education at Cambridge. Peters expresses well how Hirst's theory of knowledge has laid the groundwork, and defined the terrain, for epistemological debate in the APE tradition. 'The writings of Paul Hirst, especially his "Liberal Education and the Nature of Knowledge" have been one of the formative influences in the development of philosophy of education during the past ten years. There is a sense in which anyone working in the field has to take up some stand with regard to the "forms of knowledge"'.[28] Indeed, further on in this passage he goes so far as to compare Hirst favourable with Plato. High praise indeed! To read down the list of contributors to the forms of knowledge debate confirms Peters' appraisal. It is a veritable roll-call of prominent APEs—Jim Gribble, Richard Pring, Allen Brent, John Watt, and so on. In Lakatos' terms, these have all contributed to the research programme of APE epistemology.

In this section I shall present the core theses of the programme as they occur in the original publication, chart some of the modifications to them, and then use considerations I have already developed in the philosophy of science to expose the major deficiencies of the programme.

The Early Account

Hirst is consciously stipulative in his approach. By no means does he provide an analysis of what *is* happening in schools but, rather, a statement of what *should* happen. He is an advocate and defender of *liberal* education, which he sees as being exclusively concerned with *cognitive* development. He allows that other things can and should go on in an educative process —emotional, spiritual and physical development for instance— but these lie beyond the compass of his interest. Liberal education is concerned with the development of mind. For Hirst this is tantamount to 'coming to have experience articulated by means of various conceptual schema' (*Education and the Development of Reason*, Pt. III, p. 12—subsequent page references are to this location). These schema he calls the 'forms of knowledge' and at this stage they are to be identified by four independent criteria:

1. Distinctive concepts.
2. Logical interrelations or conceptual structure.
3. Distinctive truth tests.
4. Distinctive methodologies for formulating the truth claims.

He has a propositional account of knowledge; the constituents of knowledge are propositions—the meaningful and the true ones. When applied to the population of propositions, the foregoing criteria mark out seven classes—mathematics, physical sciences, human sciences, history, religion, literature and the fine arts. There is some slight equivocation and ambiguity concerning both the criteria and the classes in the early formulation of the thesis. In one paper the 'distinctive tests' are omitted and consequently 'morals' appears as a form of knowledge.[29] 'Science' likewise is not differentiated into 'natural' and 'human' sciences. In another early paper, 'history' and 'human sciences' are collapsed into 'interpersonal understanding'.[30] I shall prescind from these minor perturbations of infancy and take his 'Liberal Education . . .' article as canonical for the early Hirst.

A more important equivocation in the formulation of his thesis concerns two senses of 'forms of knowledge' that he is using:

1. *Structural* sense. The clearest statement of this is when Hirst says that the forms of knowledge are thus the basic articulations whereby the whole of experience has become intelligible to man; they are the fundamental achievement of mind. A few pages on, he restates the view that the forms are the *means* or the *structures* or the *generating mechanisms* for the creation of knowledge.

2. *Propositional* sense. There is a suggestion that the forms are not the schema but what the schema generate, that is, the separate classes of true propositions. The clearest statement is where he says: 'The labels I have used for distinct forms of knowledge are to be understood as being strictly labels for different classes of true propositions'.[31]

A vast literature of intraparadigm discussion has been generated by the original claims of Hirst. It gave rise to a busy period of 'normal science'. Issues raised included: Are there eight rather than seven forms? Is geography a form of knowledge? Are we certain that religion is a form of knowledge? Is not literary criticism a form of knowledge? In the tradition of normal science a tertiary literature developed, exemplified by titles such as 'Norms and Forms' by John Watt, and 'Watt on Norms and Forms' by K. Simpson.[32] It can, and has been, pointed out against Hirst that:[33]

(i)   The putative classes of propositions do not have distinct concepts, concepts over which they have sole sovereignty. Indeed, the so-called categorical concepts of each form are not even separable. Physics, for instance, has high-level commitments of a metaphysical kind that are not distinguishable from commitments of philosophy or mathematics—indeed they are often the same.

(ii) The putative classes do not have either distinct structures or homogeneity of structures within them. There is a plurality of conceptual structures *within* mathematics; within theology; within biology; and so on. Consider, for instance, the deductive structures of dogmatic theology and Aristotelian physics, and contrast them with the inductive structures of biblical theology and Baconian physics.

(iii) The putative classes have to be recognised as distinct forms *in advance* of the application of the criteria. This is because over time the forms change, and yet we wish to maintain an identity between the early and later versions. We take it that both Aristotelian mechanics and Galilean mechanics belong to the form of science. This can be the case only if they are so recognised *prior* to the application of the criteria and, indeed, despite such an application resulting in their being fundamentally separate; as has been established in an earlier chapter, they have different ontologies, different forms of proof, and different evidential bases.

Hirst has acknowledged the cogency of much of these criticisms. His original position has suffered from an attrition process; the hard core has been whittled away. He gives up the criterion of categorical and unique concepts, the criterion of distinct conceptual structures, and the criterion of unique knowledge-generating mechanisms. The Archimedean point for the forms of knowledge thesis becomes the criterion of distinctive truth tests. If this is abandoned, then so also is the towering edifice of Hirstian epistemology. Should this happen, then the curricula theory, which so distinguishes APE and is so intimately connected with the Hirstian position, crashes.

The Truth Criterion

The distinctive truth test criterion has, itself, altered over time. To chart the metamorphosis is instructive. Originally we are told that 'the major forms of knowledge, or disciplines, can each be distinguished by their dependence on some particular kind of test against experience for their distinctive expressions'. In another work of the same period we are told: 'Such tests are perhaps best exemplified by the tests of observations in the sciences'.[34] This claim is altogether simplistic, inadequate, and indeed straightforwardly false. First, the distinctive expressions, the constituents of the General Conceptual Scheme of a science, are *never* tested singly. This has been established at some length in discussion of Lakatos. The testing of 'particular expressions'—force, momentum, gravity, inertial mass, and so on—is always parasitic upon testing of the framework or research programme with which they are associated. The particularist conception which has these expressions confronting the world naked and alone is a gross misrepresentation of scientific testing. Second, observation simply does not play the role assigned to it. It is the characteristic error of empiricism to think that it does. We have used Galileo to establish this all-important point. He laboured continually to establish the new mechanics and new astronomy *in spite* of the observations: we plainly *see* the sun revolving around the earth; we do not *experience* a constant wind from the east; objects dropped from the Leaning Tower are plainly seen not to land in a far outer western suburb of Pisa, and so on. In his *Two New Sciences* he proves on paper that the maximum projectile range is attained when the elevation of gun barrels is 45°; and asserts confidently that for all cases yet unseen that will be so. In the *Two Chief World Systems* he says: 'I am certain, without observation, that the effect will happen as I tell you, because it must so happen'. More generally, what Galileo is doing is an instance of the general recourse to idealisations, to ideal types in scientific testing. We assume that our laws and theories will be seen to hold, provided that the real world approximates to our constructed ideal one. Thus we assume elastic collisions, frictionless surfaces, perfect vacuums, *none* of which is ever seen or observed. All of this is by now fairly familiar. Empiricists who fail to distinguish the real from the theoretical objects of a science get into large-scale problems when they recognise this inevitable point about idealisation in science. Ernst Nagel and Carl Hempel are good examples of this dilemma. To their credit, however, they recognise the existence of a problem, whereas Hirst fails to do so. This, astonishingly, brings to light a major deficiency of APE's epistemology—its separation from philosophy of science. This is the more intriguing because Peters and Hirst claim Popper as an influence on them; this is the same Popper who constantly said that philosophy of science is to be at the focus of epistemology. All the standard anti-empiricist works were published prior to Hirst's article, yet he appears not to have cognisance of them. Russell Hanson's *Patterns of Discovery* was published in 1958; Thomas Kuhn's *The Structure of Scientific Revolutions* in 1962, the same year as Paul Feyerabend's 'Explanation, Reduction and Empiricism'. In a similar vein, Hirst ignores the long standing and influential epistemology of W. V. O. Quine, whose 'knowledge as a seamless web' thesis is so diametrically opposed to the forms of knowledge thesis. These lacunae in Hirst are witness to the dangerous isolation of APE philosophy from mainstream philosophic concern.

The truth test criterion is altered somewhat. In the 'Forms of Knowledge Revisited' paper, Hirst declines to specify just what is the content of the distinctive criterion. In another paper he says: 'It now seems to me that the use of the word "experience" has served only to confuse the issue, for it seems to me that fundamental tests in both moral and aesthetic matters are not made in any sense *against* experience. I would prefer to talk simply in terms of the objective nature of the tests and judgments involved'.[35] So, what is left at the conclusion of the attrition process is *objectivity*. But apart from manifesting the standard problems of objectivity, this theory does not have the capacity to carve out Hirst's distinct and irreducible seven forms of knowledge. Objectivity carries a heavy burden for Hirst: if no objectivity, then no rationality; if no rationality, then no liberal education. From the beginning, Hirst has specified two conditions for reasonable and rational truth claims:

(i)   they must be intelligible under publicly-rooted concepts;
(ii) they must be assessable according to accepted criteria.

Is Hirstian Science Rational Science?

The argument here will be that, given Hirst's characterisation of objectivity and rationality, then science is an irrational enterprise. If this argument succeeds, then Hirst is faced with an embarrassing dilemma: either the all-important nexus between education and the development of rationality goes; or else we condemn the Queen of the Forms to the educational wilderness. The first criterion of intelligibility under publicly-rooted concepts is obviously a stricture which is incompatible with the history of science. In all situations of scientific revolution or significant breakthrough, it is violated. This is the thrust of Paul Feyerabend's arguments. Hirst's criterion amounts to a policy of conservation; a policy which would cast Darwin, Galileo, Bohr and others into the limbo of unintelligibility. It supports Ernest Rutherford, who despaired of understanding the new physics of

Einstein, preferring to maintain his faith that the fundamental constituents of the world were like 'little billiard balls, preferably red and black'.[36] Hirst would also support the Continental physicists against Newton's introduction of the occult 'gravitational attraction' into the mechanical world view.

Had Hirst followed Popper's injunction, he could have tightened and clarified this first criterion by reference to a fairly well-rehearsed argument in the philosophy of science: namely that concerning the continuity or discontinuity of science. James A. McWilliams provides the quintessential continuist position: 'Dispassionate consideration of the case will reveal that Einstein has not superseded, or at least not replaced Newton—no more than Newton replaced Aristotle'.[37] Popper echoes this position when he asserts that even the most radical scientific revolution 'cannot really break with tradition'.[38] On the other hand we have Kuhn, Feyerabend and others who assert the discontinuist position. Alexander Koyré provides a clear statement of it. Speaking of Galileo, Kepler and others, he says: 'They had to destroy one world and replace it by another. They had to reshape the framework of our intellect itself, to restate and reform its concepts, to evolve a new approach to Being, a new concept of knowledge, a new concept of science—and even to replace a pretty natural approach, that of common sense, by another which is not natural at all'.[39] If the latter position is established then, given Hirst's first criterion, we have the history of science being declared irrational. We cannot consider this issue here.[40] We can once more, however, draw a negative conclusion regarding APE's methodology—namely, that its methodological *fiats* have put out of court an interesting investigation, the outcome of which bears crucially upon its central doctrine of rationality.

The second criterion of rationality is that judgments must be accessible by publicly-accepted standards or criteria. This is a formal statement whose content is minimal. We are given no account of what the publicly-accepted standards or methodologies are. In their absence we must fill in and discuss some of the well-known candidates:

(i) *Inductivism*—this is the view that to be rational in science is to accept only those propositions which describe hard facts or are reasonable generalisations from them. For well-known reasons, most cogently put by Popper and Kuhn, this leaves science irrational and impoverished.

(ii) *Falsificationism*—this is the view that to be rational in science is to change beliefs when evidence is against them. Again, for well-known reasons, put most cogently by Duhem and Quine, this leaves science irrational.

(iii) *Methodology of Scientific Research Programmes* (MSRP)—this is Lakatos' attempt to have falsificationism with just a whiff of inductivism, which we have reviewed extensively in Chapter 4. He sets out to rescue the history of science for rationality, and concludes with a fairly modest claim: 'Rationality tends to work much slower than people tend to think and even then fallibly'.[41] For Lakatos, 20/20 retrovision may be possible in identifying rational moves in science; 20/20 forward-vision is utopian. This is an important point for Hirst to take heed of. The MSRP is the most likely interpretation of rationality, in so far as the history of science comes out as rational when judged by it. But even it has no consequences for the rationality or irrationality of individual beliefs and activities. Paul Feyerabend sees that the MSRP 'describes the situation in which a scientist finds himself. They do not advise him how to proceed . . . Hence, one cannot *rationally* criticise a scientist who sticks to a degenerating programme and there is no *rational* way of showing that his actions are unreasonable'.[42] What I wish to establish from these truncated remarks is: first, that wise people disagree upon what the appropriate criteria are for the appraisal of scientific theories; second, that for all putative criteria, there is considerable doubt about the history of science being a rational history; thirdly, that there are no consequences to be drawn as to how individuals should or should not go about their affairs. With this established, we are then in a position to see how limp and naive is Hirst's repeated and crucial claim that 'it is a necessary feature of knowledge as such that there be public criteria whereby the true is distinguishable from the false, the good from the bad, the right from the wrong. It is the existence of these criteria which gives objectivity to knowledge; and this in its turn gives objectivity to the concept of liberal education' (p. 14). The success of our argument removes the foundations from Hirst's claim to establish liberal education upon an objective base, free from all considerations of interest and special pleading. It further shows that in *reality* APE's epistemology is down in the sullied arena of competing theories, each pushing a particular barrow. It gives the appearance that its educational barrow is being pushed from transcendental considerations removed from the arena, but this is purely appearance, not reality. The unveiling of appearances is a contribution to the critique of APE as ideology. If there are *no* forms of knowledge as characterised by Hirst then clearly his assertion that 'education is determined objectively in range, in structure and in content by the forms of knowledge themselves, and their harmonious hierarchical interrelations' (p. 2) becomes fantasy. The import of our criticism is that it is *ideological* fantasy.

Two other consequences of the overthrow of the forms of knowledge thesis are:

(i)   The APE account of the development of mind has to be rejected or re-argued. It is an account intimately fused to the forms of knowledge thesis. Hirst claims that to have a mind is to be able to articulate experience by means of the seven conceptual schema (p. 12); furthermore, without its structure all other forms of consciousness, including, for example, emotional experiences, or mental attitudes and beliefs, 'would seem to be unintelligible' (p. 11).

(ii) The APE account of the autonomous individual has to be rejected or re-argued. It is also intimately fused to the forms of knowledge thesis. The development of the requisite autonomy is a key feature of the educational practice sanctioned by APE; indeed, it is a prerequisit for their very model of an educated person. R. F. Dearden, another prominent APE, writes of autonomy and the forms of knowledge as follows:

> The forms of understanding would be important for autonomy, and even partially constitutive of it, in at least two ways. First in terms of content they contribute much to the background perspective from which choices, decisions, opinions and so on are made or formed in our society. Secondly, these 'basic forms' supply the general criteria in terms of which the validity of various claims is to be assessed (p. 72).

Given the crucial role played by the conception of autonomy in APE's battle with Progressivism, we can appreciate the political consequences of this additional implication of the overthrow of the forms of knowledge thesis.

NOTES

1. See Kevin Harris, *Education and Knowledge*, London, Routledge & Kegan Paul, 1978; T. M. Norton & B. Ollman, *Studies in Socialist Pedagogy*, New York, Monthly Review Press, 1978; J. Karabel & A. H. Halsey, *Power and Ideology in Education*, New York, Oxford University Press, 1977; Paulo Freire, *Pedagogy of the Oppressed*, Harmondsworth, Penguin, 1972; Peter Stevens, 'Ideology and Schooling', *Educational Philosophy and Theory*, 1976, *8*, (2); S. Castles and W. Wüstenberg, *An Introduction to the Theory and Practice of Socialist Education*, London, Pluto Press, 1979. Special mention should be made of unpublished work of Jim Walker of Sydney University, who has developed in fine detail the outlines of a specifically historical-materialist philosophy of education and who coined the APE acronym.

2. *Harvard Educational Review*, 1954, 24, (4). Reprinted in his *Reason and Teaching*, London, Routledge & Kegan Paul, 1973.
3. London, George Allen & Unwin. The book had four impressions in the first two years and numerous ones thereafter.
4. J. Gribble, *Introduction to Philosophy of Education*, Boston, Allyn & Bacon, 1969.
5. The nadir of this tradition can be seen in works such as H. Schofield, *The Philosophy of Education*, London, Allen & Unwin, 1972. He attempts analyses of 'culture', 'conditioning', 'value', among others.
6. 'The Philosophy of Education', in J. W. Tibble (ed.), *The Study of Education*, London, Routledge & Kegan Paul, 1966, p. 59.
7. *Reason and Teaching*, p. 10.
8. *ibid*. p. 17.
9. R. S. Peters (ed.), *A Recognisable Philosophy of Education*, London, Routledge & Kegan Paul, 1969, p. 17.
10. *Ethics and Education* concludes with the statement: 'The most worthwhile features of political life are immanent in the institutions which we in fact have'. This illustrates well how Peters does in fact slip into substantive claims about the world. Because these are unexamined, they are typically conservative and typically wrong.
11. London, Allen & Unwin, 1959. (With S. I. Benn.)
12. London, Routledge & Kegan Paul, 1958.
13. *ibid*. p. 10.
14. *The Times Educational Supplement*, 1971. Quoted in David Adelstein, 'The Philosophy of Education or the Wisdom and Wit of R. S. Peters', in Trevor Pateman (ed.), *Counter Course*, Harmondsworth, Penguin, 1972, p. 137.
15. *Rationalism in Politics and Other Essays*, London, Methuen, 1962.
16. See accounts in Laurence Lafore, *The End of Glory*, New York, Lippincott, 1970.
17. Alan Janik and Stephen Toulmin, *Wittgenstein's Vienna*, New York, Simon & Schuster, 1973, p. 259.
18. *Objective Knowledge*, Oxford, Clarendon Press, 1972, p. 310.
19. 'Language and Thought', Philosophy of Education Society of Great Britain, *Proceedings*, 1966, p. 72.
20. P. K. Feyerabend, 'How To Be A Good Empiricist', in P. H. Nidditch (ed.), *The Philosophy of Science*, Oxford, University Press, 1968, p. 32.
21. P. K. Feyerabend, 'Linguistic Arguments in Scientific Method', *Telos*, 2, (1), 1969.
    Ernst Gellner, *Words and Things*, London, Gollancz, 1959.
    Anthony Skillen, *Ruling Illusions*, Hassocks, Harvester Press, 1977.
22. See Abraham Edel, 'Analytic Philosophy of Education at the Crossroads', in J. F. Doyle (ed.), *Educational Judgements*, London, Routledge & Kegan Paul, 1973.
    Colin Evers, 'Analytic Philosophy of Education: From a Logical Point of View', *Educational Philosophy and Theory*, 1979, 11, (2). See also David Adelstein, *op. cit.*
23. *English Philosophy Since 1900*, Oxford, University Press, 1958, p. 167.
24. *Ethics and Education*, p. 15.
25. 'Language and Thought', *op. cit.*, p. 63.
26. See Kevin Harris, 'Peters on Schooling', *Educational Philosophy and Theory*, 9, (1), 1977.
27. P. H. Hirst and R. S. Peters, *The Logic of Education*, London, Routledge & Kegan Paul, 1974. Introduction.

28. P. H. Hirst, *Knowledge and the Curriculum*, London, Routledge & Kegan Paul, 1974, Introduction.
29. 'Educational Theory', in J. W. Tibble (ed.), *The Study of Education*, New York, Routledge & Kegan Paul, 1966.
30. 'Modes of Knowledge and Experience', in *The Logic of Education*.
31. 'Modes of Knowledge Revisited', in *Knowledge and the Curriculum*, p. 87.
32. Much of this literature can be found in the pages of *Educational Philosophy and Theory*.
33. 'The Distinguishing Features of Forms of Knowledge', *Educational Philosophy and Theory*, 1971, 3, (2).
34. *Logic of Education*, p. 62.
35. 'Literature, Criticism and the Forms of Knowledge', *Educational Philosophy and Theory*, 1971, 3, (1), p. 16.
36. Cited in Stephen Toulmin, *Human Understanding*, Oxford, Clarendon Press, 1972, p. 286.
37. 'Aristotelian and Cartesian Motion', *New Scholasticism*, 1943, 17.
38. 'The Rationality of Scientific Revolutions', in R. Harré (ed.), *Problems of Scientific Revolution*, Oxford, Clarendon Press, 1975, p. 82.
39. *Metaphysics and Measurement*, London, Chapman & Hall, 1968, p. 21.
40. See John Krige, *Science, Revolution and Discontinuity*, Hassocks, Harvester Press, 1980.
41. In Imre Lakatos and Alan Musgrave (eds.), *Criticism and the Growth of Knowledge*, Cambridge, C.U.P., 1920, p. 174.
42. *Against Method*, London, New Left Books, 1975, p. 185.

CHAPTER 10

MARXISM AND EDUCATION

Marxist theory of education is, in the first instance, a theory of the history, structure, content and functioning of compulsory State schooling. It is a theory about schools and their function in society. In the second instance, Marxist theory of education will be about specific features of schooling. These will be theories concerned with curricula, learning arrangements, authority patterns, and so on. Here we find Marxist psychology, sociology and history. At this level we expect not only theories about educational practices, but also theories about mistaken accounts of those practices. In other words, here we expect accounts of ideology to feature. In the third instance, Marxist theory of education will be about what things could, might and should happen in schools, vis-à-vis curricula, relationships with the community, teacher-pupil interactions, and so on. For good reasons, this third and normative aspect of theorising will be the last feature to be considered. There are some introductory remarks which need to be made before commencing our exposition.

1. Normative and Factual Theories of Education
The first two levels of Marxist theory of education are factual theories—factual in the sense of giving an account of what *is* the case concerning schooling. For the most part, 'theories' of education are normative affairs. Many confusions arise from the failure to recognise this distinction. When people ask what one's theory of education is, they usually expect a reply along the lines of what one would like to see happening in schools; what one thinks the aims of schools should be; whether schools should be child-centred or subject-centred, and so on. We might preface an answer by saying that we are existentialists, and schools should therefore be concerned with allowing students to recognise their radical subjectivity and to overcome the fear and trembling which attends upon their experience of autonomy. Others might preface their reply by saying that they are Christian Essentialists, and schools should therefore be concerned with promoting knowledge of the Good Life and encouraging students to recognise their fundamental dependence upon the Ground of their Being. Others will say that they are Herbartians

or Naturalists or Montessorians or Steinerians or something else, and draw whatever are the appropriate conclusions about what schools should be doing. These normative theories of education are similar to theologies. They are visions of what is *good* for people, what people really *need*, how society *ought* to be structured, what *human nature* is, and so on. In their sophisticated form they are the outcome of '*Ism-ism*' philosophy of education. In their less sophisticated form they are the outcome of shallow, commonsensical musings. This is what we see in New South Wales Education Week slogans—'Education Builds a Nation', 'Education for New Horizons', 'Education Builds Bridges of Understanding', 'One World Through Education'. As with most theologies, these normative theories of education have little concern with the concrete historical analysis of existing social realities. We can say of these endeavours what Marx said of religiosity, that it 'acts as a soporific on those whom it feeds with its sentimental mash'.

Normative theorising is for the most part utopian theorising and is just as pointless. Galileo refused to be drawn into it. When Simplicio, in the second day of the *Dialogue Concerning the Two Chief World Systems*, asked him to say what would happen in the space occupied by the Earth if the Earth were to be annihilated and what happened in the same space before the Earth was created, he gracefully declined to answer, deferring to the superior knowledge of his adversary on these matters.

Hirst and Peters ostensibly share this same concern with anti-utopianism, but their programme is as utopian as the most utopian. Peters says that he is concerned with what would happen in schools *if* a certain view of education were taken; thus his criticism of the Progressivist Plowden Report from the standpoint of Liberal Rationalism. Hirst explicitly says that he is not interested in what *is* happening, only with what *should* happen upon adopting his forms of knowledge thesis. Despite their denigration of 'nature of man'-type theorising in education, they are not above having recourse to it in criticising substantive and normative proposals put forward by their protagonists. Peters' view of human nature is a Hobbesian one. This is revealed when, in criticising Dewey and the progressives, he said: 'The view that civilisation is a brittle crust, containing with difficulty irrational yearnings, made no impact on Dewey in spite of his active interest in the rise of Nazism as a threat to democracy'.[1]

Marx said at the very beginning of his writing (1843), in rejecting utopian socialist schemes, that 'we do not attempt dogmatically to prefigure the future, but want to find the new world only through criticism of the old'.[2] This was his 'ruthless criticism of everything existing'. It is the kind of caution and realism that Francis Bacon enjoined when he said that 'for nature to be commanded, she must first be obeyed'. What people should or should not do cannot be removed from what it is possible for them to do. Dialectics exposes the real limits of situations and then makes proposals for the transcending of them. As an ancient proverb has it, to walk forward we must have one foot on the ground; so also in educational theorising.

2. Practice and Ideology

Any factual theory of education will need to recognise the distinction between what people are doing and what they think they are doing; between the realities of an age and the illusions of an age. Appearances and self-understandings are not to be ignored, they are indeed part of the reality to be explained. Take a recent historical example: J. F. Kennedy was a jingoistic, war-mongering capitalist whose foreign policy repeatedly led America to the brink of destruction; perhaps eventually he will be universally acknowledged as such. Clearly, then, there were two realities in the early '60s—what Kennedy was and what most people in America thought he was. Which is real?—both are. A person's subjective understanding of the necessity of clean hands is as real as their compulsive hand-washing. Both need to be explained. What Marxism says is that appearances do not explain the reality. This has implications for research methodologies such as ethnomethodology, phenomenalism, participant observation, and so on. Einstein had some salutory advice: 'If you wish to learn from the theoretical physicist anything about the methods he uses, I would give you the following advice: don't listen to his words, examine his achievements'.[3]

Our account of the real processes will of course be theory-dependent: the real is not immediately given. This is the conclusion of earlier chapters on philosophy of science. But as I have argued, to admit that there is no neutral standpoint is not to say that rival theories cannot be compared and evaluated. They can be.

3. Real and Theoretical Objects

Aristotle correctly observed, in his *Nicomachean Ethics*, that we should not seek for more precision in a science than the nature of its object allows. In providing a theory of schooling, we have to deal in generalities and make simplifications in order to understand dominant features of the system. Failure to recognise this leads to debate fragmenting and people no longer seeing the forests because of the trees. This is a common enough point in natural sciences. In order to get workable equations for planetary motion we 'smooth' out their orbits and assume them to be ellipses. When Boyle plotted his data for pressure and volume relationships he got an array of points generally heading in a straight direction. There was no function that would fit them all. A line of best fit was drawn through them and it was then obvious that the volume of a gas varied inversely with the pressure upon it. Copernicus said of his heliocentric calculations: 'If only I can be correct to ten minutes of arc, I shall be no less elated than Pythagoras is said to have been when he discovered the law of the right-angled triangle'.[4] All of this is clarified if we keep in mind that, although science is about the world (its real object), the objects of scientific knowledge are abstracted theoretical objects.

The real social world is chaotic and complicated. There are numerous competing causal chains interacting. To understand it, to appropriate it theoretically and intervene practically, we must of necessity begin with simplified models and theories. This point is worth making, as many unnecessary arguments are generated by a failure to appreciate it. A commonplace type of argument in response to a claim about schooling is to point to some out-of-town school where what has been claimed doesn't apply. This has little theoretical interest. It is analogous to a point at some remove from a line of best fit. We do need to note it and keep it under observation, just in case the exception might prove the rule, but of itself it is of no moment. John Dewey totally failed to understand the crucial role of idealisation in science when he rejected the class analysis of American society.[5] There are assuredly bad and inadequate class analyses—Marx's own *The Eighteenth Brumaire of Louis Bonaparte* is a model for the criticism of vulgar and faulty class analysis—but they are not faulty or unscientific *by virtue* of being abstract and hypothetical, as Dewey claims. What generates this mistake is the empiricist failure to appreciate the distinction between real and theoretical objects of a science.

4. Eclecticism

Marxism is not the preserve of Marxists; Marxist theory of education can incorporate research and analysis done outside the tradition. Copernicus, indeed, took over and utilised many of Ptolemy's celestial measurements and data. Christian theology has at various times utilised Aristotelian, Platonic, Hegelian and other frameworks for its expression. Marxist theory of education will freely draw upon phenomenological studies of the school and classroom in order to appreciate the school experiences of children. It will freely draw upon the work of radical historians such as Joel Spring and Clarence Karier to appreciate the actual responses of the State to the demands that capital has made upon schooling. No Marxist theory of education could fail to appreciate and learn from the experiences and analyses of Paulo Freire concerning his pedagogical work with the working class and peasants of Brazil. All such inputs are raw materials which will be processed by Marxism in the production of its own theory of eduction. Many, of course, will have to be reworked in order to 'fit' into the production process. For example, I have used a motif of the Jesuit Bernard Lonergan throughout this work. He speaks of the problem of a 'communal flight from understanding' arising from the 'very fabric of a civilisation'. In a loose, pre-scientific, everyday sense we can appreciate what he is attempting to express. When Marxists utilise, or translate, Lonergan's problem it becomes one of 'ideology' arising from 'social practices controlled by a society's ruling class'. Similarly, when Peters speaks of the necessity to 'keep the wheels of industry turning', Marxists translate this into 'the necessity to reproduce labour power'.

There are, of course, limits to eclecticism. I agree with Lakatos that any research programme which merely runs along saying 'me too' has nothing to contribute. In the evaluation of competing research programmes, approbation is given to those that can initiate new and significant research, and have some of their novel predictions confirmed. Some aspects of the methodology and ontology of competing research programmes can be fatal to Marxism if ingested. Copernicus took into his heliocentric astronomy aspects of Ptolemy's theory: the fundamental distinction between the celestial and sublunar regions; the perfection of circular motion; the existence of crystalline spheres in which the planets adhered and moved. All of these impeded development of the Copernican world view; it was Galileo's task one hundred years later to expel most of these foreign bodies. This century, Marxism has been Freudianised, Existentialised, Positivised, Hegelianised, Christianised, and much more. Much of this has taken the cutting edge off the analysis Marxism can provide. In the same way the Social Democratisation of the

European Marxist parties took the cutting edge off working-class struggles for control of the political sphere.

MARX'S SOCIAL THEORY

To state a truism, any theory of schooling is going to be dependent upon a theory of society. Schools are locked into a social structure; an understanding of schools will depend upon an understanding of this structure. They may give the appearance of being independent institutions, but this is mere appearance. They are not independent institutions.

It is one the principal claims of Marx's theory that for a society to continue in existence it must produce materials and reproduce people. Children in a society of hunters and gatherers have to learn to be hunters and gatherers; children in a society of cultivators have to learn to cultivate fields. There is *biological* reproduction and the birth of biological *individuals*. But the reproduction and formation of the individual into a human *subject* is a matter of *socialisation* into the language, knowledge, competencies, structures and ideologies of the society. To introduce some refinement into this picture I will speak about a 'mode of production' (MP) to refer to the way in which material production is arranged and controlled in a society. I will use the term 'social formation' (SF) to refer to the ongoing ensemble of activities, rituals, beliefs and institutions which collectively form a society. Marx's thesis is that the MP is the chief determinant of the SF and that changes in the MP generate changes and realignments in the SF. This, in brief, is the working principle of historical materialism.

An MP consists of productive forces and relations of production. *Productive forces* consist in a determinate structure of (a) direct producers (labour power), (b) raw materials (ultimately nature), and (c) means by which (a) and (b) are brought together —technology or instruments of production. The pair (a) and (c) constitute the 'means of production'. The *relations of production* refer to relations of ownership between the productive forces and the workers or non-workers.

The productive forces and relations of production interact. In Marxist writings this is known as the 'first law of sociology'— the necessity of conformity between the productive forces and the relations of production. The former are recognised by Marx as the leading factor, as they are the first to undergo change. Tools and techniques of production are constantly changing and being perfected; the relations of production, buttressed by customs and laws, are more resistant to change. After certain decisive changes in the productive forces, it is necessary that productive relations change.

The political, cultural and economic history of countries which had the 'Green Revolution' thrust upon them is illustrative of the foregoing thesis. Rockefeller-developed High Yield Variety rice and wheat is more sensitive than indigenous varieties. It requires the right proportion of irrigation, drainage, fertilisers and pesticides. To reap the multiple harvest, and to prepare the land for sowing several times a year, farm machinery is required, together with transport and storage facilities. HYV seeds necessitate capital for their utilisation. Banks will lend only to rich farmers, who in turn increase rents and buy out peasant holdings. Ironically, foodstuffs have to be exported to pay for American fertiliser and machinery. Thus the much hailed and lauded Green Revolution brings displacement from the land, increased poverty, unemployment and death. It is a pity that school texts do not present this side of the story.

Marx distinguished five historical modes of production: primitive community or Asiatic, slave, feudal, capitalist and socialist. Three of these—slave, feudal and capitalist—are *antagonistic* modes of production. That is, there is private ownership of the means of production; the workers do not own their material or the means of their labour. This is the basis for *class* division and class rule in society.

The *capitalist* mode of production (CMP) is specified by: (i) the major means of production being privately owned by a comparatively small minority of the population; (ii) labour-power, or the capacity to work, being also privately owned and saleable on the market; (iii) the owners of the means of production buying labour power and putting it to work; (iv) the bulk of production being concerned with commodities, things which have a use value and an exchange value; (v) commodities being exchanged or sold in order to realise profits for their owners.

People not only produce and enter into relations of production; they also live in families, establish legal and ethical systems, form social and political organisations, create churches, develop languages. For Marx this domain, or superstructure, is not independent of the mode of production. This is sometimes referred to as the second law of Marxist sociology: the law of necessary conformity between mode of production (base) and superstructure. This law should be regarded as a heuristic; it suggests a relationship for investigation. At different times in the Marxist tradition it has been given an utterly mechanical interpretation whereby all elements of the superstructure are a direct response to factors in the economic base. For many aspects of culture in many social formations this vulgar Marxism is quite sufficient—metropolitan cultures imposed upon colonised people, for instance. However, this second law has been given richer and more subtle interpretations.[6] The metaphor of separate piles sunk into muddy ground and connected across the top by a platform is helpful. In one sense, the piles (economic base) determine the platform (superstructure); in another important sense the platform enables the piles to maintain their configuration. This allows interaction between the two aspects: an interaction which is important in situating the place and function of schooling in an SF.

This theory of social structure which we have been outlining is basically an exposition of Marx's famous 1859 Preface to his *Contribution to the Critique of Political Economy*. Modes of production give rise to classes in social formations. These classes are objectively in conflict, their interests are antagonistic. There are three dimensions to class struggle:

(i) *Economic:* this is the struggle for control over the means of production, the process of production and the products created. In CMPs it is concerned with appropriation of surplus value.

(ii) *Political:* this is the struggle for control of State and State power.

(iii) *Ideological:* this is the struggle for the 'hearts and minds' of those in the SF. It is preferable in liberal-democratic SFs that ends can be achieved by consent, rather than by coercion. In World War One it was better for the ruling interests of England and Australia that people went to war for 'God, King and Country' than that they had to be conscripted. In *The German Ideology* Marx correctly observes: 'The ideas of the ruling class are in every epoch the ruling ideas. That is, the class which is the ruling material force of society is at the same time its ruling intellectual force'.[7]

The State has a crucial role in all aspects of class struggle. It is required by the ruling class of an SF to protect it against itself, against its tendency to exploit to elimination the labour power it buys. Consider here the extermination of Congo negroes and Brazilian Indians by English rubber companies. The State is required to protect the ruling class from the predatory interests of the other ruling classes (consider World War One). Above all, it is required to protect the ruling class's property rights and social relations against the exploited classes. An instance of this is the legitimising of British occupation of Ireland in the eighteenth century and attendant laws against poaching and theft. The institutions of the State can be separated broadly into two categories:

(i)   Repressive State Apparatuses: here control is exercised by direct force—police, army, courts, prisons.

(ii) Ideological State Apparatuses: here control is exercised by non-direct, intellectual means—churches, schools, cultural organisations, trade unions. (See Althusser on this.)

The importance of the recognition of class and class struggle for Marx's social theory is that it avoids the temptation of a mechanical form of functionalism. There is conflict, fluidity, antagonism in the economic, political and ideological domains. In most SFS the CMP does not function in a rigorously determined manner. The State can be influenced by the non-capitalist classes. Dominant ideologies need not be hegemonic; they can be partially exposed and occasionally penetrated by resistant ideologies or nonconformist and revolutionary ideologies. This is an important consideration in arriving at an adequate account of schooling. It is not just Marxists, of course, who assert that public schooling has a political, ideological and economic function. John Stuart Mill, in Chapter 11 of *On Liberty*, wrote of State education establishing a 'despotism over the mind' in order to please the dominant power in government.

POLITICS OF SCHOOLING
The Marxist thesis is that schools are primarily concerned with the production and reproduction of labour power in an SF; and this in a manner that ensures the stability of the productive relations. That is, schooling legitimises the existing system of privilege, power and resources. Schools create competencies; they also create and procreate a public knowledge; this knowledge has a political function. As the Tom Paxton song asks:

> What did you learn in school today
> Dear little boy of mine?
> What did you learn in school today
> Dear little boy of mine?

> I learned that Washington never told a lie,
> I learned that soldiers seldom die,
> I learned that everybody's free,
> That's what the teacher said to me,
> And that's what I learned in school today,
> That's what I learned in school today.

The family used to be the site for the reproduction of labour power because production took place within the family unit. With development of productive forces, say from the hand loom to the power loom, we have a change in the site of production from the home to the factory. Consequently, the production of labour power became increasingly a State function, highlighted in the nineteenth-century move to universal and compulsory education. Educators in this early period were less coy about their motives than many today. A British administrator wrote in the early part of the century: 'The great object to be kept in mind in regulating any school for the instruction of the labouring class is the rearing of hardy and intelligent working men, whose character and habits shall afford the greatest amount of security to the property and order of the community'.[8] At the turn of the century, a us Federal Commissioner of Education, when addressing the question: 'Why Educate the Children of the Common Laborer?' wrote: 'For your own well-being and the well-being of your children, the children of all must be educated. If you wish property safe from confiscation by a majority composed of communists, you must see to it that the people are educated so that each sees the sacredness of property'.[9] At the same time, a report on public education in Australia was quite frank in asserting: 'An educated community is on the whole more moral, more law-abiding, and more capable of work than an uneducated; and therefore the State is justified in enforcing education that it may economise its revenue and develop its resources . . . it holds out to the employer the prospect of an eventual supply of steady and instructed workmen'.[10]

The prospect of a supply of steady and instructed workmen certainly had a wide appeal among industrial bosses. In 1841 a textile manufacturer wrote to the Massachusetts Board of Education saying: 'I have never considered mere knowledge . . . as the only advantage derived from a good . . . education . . . workers with more education are more orderly and respectful in their deportment, and more ready to comply with the whole-some and necessary regulations of an establishment'.[11]

In the usa and the uk this early history of schooling is well documented. It is worth noting that it was *not* just capitalist interests th'at were calling for it nor, indeed, benefitting from it. Schools were the site of struggle. The apologetic tone of the foregoing quotations derives from the fact that capitalists did *not* universally see their interests as being served by schooling. State schooling, after all, had to be paid for from the surplus value that labour produced; it was State expenditure and as such it was opposed. The capitalist class view then was no different from today's with regard to State expenditure on welfare and services—it is seen as diminishing the proportion of the surplus-value cake available to itself. On the other hand, the organised working class was itself demanding access to education, to the three Rs. Where schooling was decentralised, as in the USA, the possibility of working-class control of education was greater, but even here, of course, it had to compete with churches, local businessmen, and so forth. The more centralised the school system, the more subordinate working-class interests were to the interests of capital. These latter interests were served by both the hidden curriculum and the explicit curriculum. American and English texts of the period were full of praise for resignation and contentment with one's station in life. It was a great tragedy that when the working class demanded and fought for education they received capitalist education.

The view that knowledge and education were politically biased was widespread. Sarah Trimmer, a much prescribed English author, wrote books stressing the importance of a poor child's knowing his station in life and not moving from his place of birth or from the station into which he had been born. Texts for use in Irish schools were chosen to ensure that 'whatever was of dubious tendency has been carefully excluded, while the merits of vaccination . . . the nature of Savings Banks . . . and a variety of knowledge useful to the peasantry are to be included'.[12] 'English Literature' was on the whole synonymous with 'Ruling-Class Ideology'—an ideology which was sexist, racist and anti-socialist. For example, the whole genre of *Boy's Own* and *Girl's Own* literature, the literature of John Buchan, Dornford Yates, Ian Hay and Enid Blyton abounds with goodies bashing up Jews, Bolshevists, Blacks, pigtailed opium-smugglers and the like. George Orwell long ago laid bare the political choices contained in so much children's literature.[13]

The politics of literacy has been a topic of keen interest in recent times.[14] A Vermont history text has America declaring war on Spain because 'the American people could no longer tolerate Spanish treatment of the Cuban people'. Ruth Elson, in *Guardians of Tradition*,[15] has said that Alexander Pope's dictum 'Whatever is, is right' was as recurrent a motif for American texts as was 'It is the Lord who maketh poor and maketh rich'. The politicisation of curricula is still with us of course. American schools in the '60s were still teaching the doctrine of Manifest Destiny in history courses. Objective tests were set with items such as: 'Westward expansion was the result of M . . . D . . .'. A popular text acclaimed the unique mission of American society: 'From its earliest beginnings, its people have been conscious of a peculiar destiny, because upon it have been fastened the hopes and aspirations of the human race, and because it has not failed to fulfil that destiny or to justify those hopes'.[16] A New South Wales economics text has a chapter on 'Income Differentials' where it is stated, falsely, that high income is a function of: first, length of hours worked; second, danger associated with work done; third, training required for job. In 1978 the Queensland Government banned the Jerome Bruner *inspired* MACOS (Man: A Course of Study) syllabus from its primary schools, and also the SEMP (Social Education Materials Project) syllabus from its secondary schools. These liberal courses were seen as undermining the accepted values of the State concerning homosexuality, the family, abortion, socialism, and so on. The State Premier, Mr. Bjelke-Petersen, announced: 'The emphasis today must be on technical training'.[17]

The politicisation of syllabi poses a problem for Paul Hirst's contention that 'curricula descend from the forms of knowledge and their harmonious interrelationships'. One obvious reply is to give the factual ground to the opposition, but retain the normative ground. Hirst can agree that curricula and public knowledge reflect the struggle for power and hegemony among rival classes in society, but he can insist that this should not be so; that his 'Liberal Education' statement is not about what *actually* happens in schools, but about what *should* happen. But even in Hirst's ideal situation, he is still dealing with forms of knowledge that are, to varying degrees, politicised. History, economics, literature, science embody political, ethical and ideological commitments.

LABOUR IN THE CMP
Marxist theory requires that there be some connection between the schooling process and characteristics of work in an SF. What are the dominant characteristics of labour in the CMP?

(i)   Control is out of the hands of the worker. People do not
      have significant control of the what, when and where of
      their productive activity.

(ii) The production process is fragmented; there is a social
      and a technical division of labour. This is an increasing
      tendency in the development of the CMP. It arose with
      the cult of efficiency and the need to control labour.
      Frederick Taylor, early in this century, gave the process
      the full support of 'scientific management theory'. His
      first proposal was to separate mental and manual labour;
      to this end he reported to Congress in 1912: 'I can say,
      without the slightest hesitation, that the science of
      handling pig-iron is so great that the man who is fit to
      handle pig-iron as his daily work cannot possibly under-
      stand that science . . . the man who is fit to work at any
      particular trade is unable to understand the science of
      that trade'.[18] Taylor, the social scientist, was an ideologue
      of the 'de-skilling' of labour, a process which is much
      written on and which is now reaching its zenith.[19]

(iii) Motivations and rewards for work are, in general, ex-
      ternal to the work done. People work for wages, not
      intrinsic satisfactions.

(iv) Rewards gained for labour are uneven.

(v)   Competitiveness, rather than co-operation, is the basic
      relationship among capitalists (striving for profit) and
      among workers (striving for work and promotion).

(vi) Submissiveness and conformity are traits required by the
      authoritarian organisation of work and by the fact that
      individuals are increasingly, in Marx's terms, 'append-
      ages of the machines' they operate.

It is obvious that cognitive skills and capacities are increasingly *less* important for most occupations in the CMP. We
are witnessing the proletarianisation of white-collar workers
and professionals. An understanding of the forms of knowledge
has little connection with selling shirts, assembling radios,
harvesting corn and operating a switchboard. Ivar Berg's work
confirmed the fact that for most jobs there was little correlation
between people's performance in it and the amount of education they had received.[20] In reviewing the famous *Equality of
Educational Opportunity* report by James S. Coleman and others,
Christopher Jencks, Professor of Education at Harvard, wrote:
'Despite much popular rhetoric there is little evidence that
academic competence is critically important to adults in most

walks of life'.[21] His critic, Charles Silberman, is simply mistaken when he says that educational requirements will continue to increase, reflecting the long-term trend towards the substitution of brain-power for muscle-power.[22]

The silicon-chip revolution has done away with much muscle-power but it has also made significant inroads into areas of skilled operations. The PLATO computerised teaching network operating out of the University of Illinois has the potential to obliterate thousands of teachers. A small handful of people spend their days writing hundreds of programmes, and teachers at far-flung terminals become child-minders and equipment supervisors. Medical specialists are now devising programmes for the diagnosis and treatment of innumerable disorders of various systems, which a much less trained doctor or para-medical professional can use with patients. Mechanical harvesters can, completely unaided, drive themselves around a farm harvesting a crop. Not only are jobs done away with, but rural skills and knowledges are discounted. The micro-computer revolution based upon the silicon chip heralds one of the great crises of human history. It is a clear instance of Marx's thesis about developments in productive forces (technology) causing massive readjustments in productive relations and social relations more generally. Who has control of its application in education is a vital issue.

What, then, are the non-cognitive attributes which people require for performance of work in the CMP? People must be such as to:

(i)   Acquiesce in the lack of control they exercise over their productive activity.
(ii) Acquiesce in the fragmentation of their productive activity.
(iii) Acquiesce in the alienation of their productive activity.
(iv) Acquiesce to, if not endorse, a competitive ethic.
(v)   Be rule-oriented.

Beyond these, for the system to function, the real relations in which people are engaged must not become universally apparent. Ultimately, the fact that labour creates surplus value which is then appropriated has to be hidden in some manner. As a popular cartoon has it, the worker cannot know that he is giving the boss $80 a day so that the boss can order him around. The wage form of capitalist employment generates apparent relations of work, status and power. Varied ideologies then cement and

justify these apparitions. Marxist social theory is in part con
cerned with penetrating these appearances and laying bare the
material relations in which people are involved.

SCHOOLS AND PRODUCTION OF LABOUR POWER

In the first section of this chapter we have pointed out that
historically there has been a clear connection, both in practice
and in theory, between schools and the production of labour
power suited to the CMP. The State both mediates and controls
this connection. The development of knowledge, skills, abilities,
temperaments and attitudes are all part of the school's role in
the reproduction of society's *productive forces*, labour power
being one component of these. But *productive relations* have also
to be reproduced. This is largely the ideological function of
schooling. The dominant ideology is expressed, lived and,
indeed, examined in schools.

In schools:

(i) Students are kept ignorant of whole domains of knowledge and terminology. Americans learn more about the
Presidents than they do about their own long, bloody
history of class struggle. Generals McArthur and Eisen-
hower are remembered for being famous World War Two
generals, not for being the people who turned machine-
guns on thousands of starving veterans demonstrating in
Washington in 1932. In England, Constitutional History
pushes Labour History out of curricula. Although 'working class' is a permissible phrase in Australian schools,
'ruling class' is comparatively taboo. This is part of the
systematic cultivation of 'social amnesia'.

(ii) Only partial connections are formed and only partial
analyses are made. Japanese expansion into China is
unacceptable aggression and imperialism, which the
Western democracies could not stand idly by and tolerate
American occupation of the Philippines; Dutch occupation of Indonesia; British occupation of Hong Kong,
Malaya, Borneo, Singapore; French occupation of Indo-
China; Portuguese occupation of Timor and Goa, are all
just part of the normal and acceptable nature of things.
Workers who withdraw their labour are called 'strikers',
and this is identified with disrupting production, if not
'holding the country to ransom'. Capitalists who take
their money out of a country, or who invest it in non-

productive enterprises, are equally disrupting production, but this is never mentioned. Industrial legislation is
necessary for the former; knighthoods and positions in
Government are rewards for the latter. Connections
between record unemployment figures on page 1 of a
newspaper and record company profits on page 31 are
not made.

(iii) In countless ways, students are imbued with respect for
authority figures; they are taught to accept contingent
circumstances as being necessary; they learn the appropriate rationalisations and justifications of the social
formation they are in. These rationalisations can be
religious (Calvinism), philosophical (Liberalism), scientific
(IQism), or permutations and combinations of all these.

How do schools bring about the reproduction of productive
forces? As a first approximation, they reproduce labour power
by reproducing in the school the conditions of labour power in
the social formation. As Alvin Toffler remarks: 'The most
criticised features of education today—the regimentation, lack
of individualism, the rigid systems of seating, grouping,
grading and marking, the authoritarian role of the teacher—are
precisely those features that made mass education so effective
an instrument of adaptation for its place and time'.[23] Thus we
find that:

(i)   The control of the learning process is largely outside the
control of the learner.
(ii) The learning process is fragmented both socially (stream-
ing, tracking) and technically (subjects).
(iii) Motivations and rewards for learning are in general
extrinsic to the learning process—marks, grades, certificates, position in class, teacher approval.
(iv) Rewards are unequal; for someone to succeed others
have to fail, and this has to be accepted as a necessary
fact of life. Jules Henry describes the case of Boris and
Peggy in a fifth-grade arithmetic lesson.[24] Boris' failure to
answer the teacher's question makes it possible for Peggy
to succeed; his depression is the price of her exhilaration;
his misery the occasion for her rejoicing. Although the
classroom incident is unexceptional to us, and indeed we
should in all likelihood praise the teacher for good
control, to other cultures this is not so. The wringing of

success from soneone's failure is *not* a necessary universal human characteristic.

(v) Competitiveness, rather than co-operation, is the bas type of relationship among pupils. Schools are one of the few social institutions where co-operation is called 'cheating'.

(vi) Rule conformity is highly valued. Robert Dreeben is only one of thousands to remark that 'the school's main contribution to learning lies in the area of social norms'[25] and that this is not *just* a didactic matter but equally an osmotic one. The structure of schooling and the tasks that children are engaged in produce normative changes.

Another way of expressing this is that in formal schooling, students are placed in the situation of an educational exchange which prefigures the capitalist exchange. The structure of schooling prefigures the productive relations in which students will find themselves. They receive from professional, certificated teachers certain commodities, namely their own transformation into suitable and appropriate labour power, the type and amount of which is attested to by grades and certificates. The cost to students is not just monetary, but essentially involves willingness to participate in the process, and the preparedness to be appropriately transformed. What they receive has an exchange (at least while there are employment opportunities), and it has, to varying extents, a use value. The exchange value and use value are determined largely by the market-place. Degrees in classics once had a high exchange value—they no longer have. When traditionalists speak of the intrinsic worth of subjects they are referring, on our model, to one form of use value.

The importance of conceptualising schooling in this manner is that it clearly links intellectual and ideological achievements to a base in social practices and in particular relations among individuals. These practices are not just confined to schools but are continuous with those in the wider society. Similarly, they generate appearances so we have varied sets of apparent relations covering real relations.

EFFECTIVENESS OF SCHOOLING

There is no doubt that schools are, on the whole, effective in doing what they do; namely reproducing a society's reproductive forces and productive relations. There is now a massive stock of documentary evidence supporting this claim. Schooling

a vehicle for social mobility; no matter what is done in the
ool sphere, there is very little change in the overall distribu-
on of power and wealth in society. In England, Douglas and
others concluded that 'middle-class pupils have retained,
almost intact, their historic advantage over the manual working
class'.[26] Christopher Jencks and his collaborators at the Harvard
Center for Educational Policy Studies have shown in a massive
study that there is inequality of educational opportunity. Moreover, where there is equality of education, there are still
preserved the standard patterns of social and financial inequality.[27] This is the same picture as that painted by Bowles
and Gintis in their numerous researches.

Louis Althusser, the French philosopher, gives an over-
determined and perhaps too rigid picture of the social function
of schooling, but one which nevertheless approximates to the
real situation. He uses a pyramidal image of masses of children
from all classes and backgrounds coming into infant school and
absorbing knowledge and techniques wrapped in ruling-class
ideology for the duration of their stay, which is itself determined
by the social class from which they came. They are ejected into
production at various levels; those who reach the summit
becoming 'unemployed intellectuals . . . agents of exploitation
. . . or professional ideologists (priests of all sorts, most of whom
are convinced "laymen")'.[28]

The conscription issue in Australia in the 1960s provided good
informal evidence for the thesis being argued. Conscription for
service in Vietnam applied on a lottery basis to twenty-year-
olds. Only the smallest handful refused to register at all on the
grounds that the State had no right to mount the exercise; a
slightly larger group registered but were conscientious objectors
on political grounds; a still larger group registered but were
objectors on pacifist and moral grounds; the overwhelming bulk
of twenty-year-olds (the present writer included) duly registered
their names. Despite between 12 and 15 years of education, 12 to
15 years of being initiated into the forms of knowledge, and into
the 'skill and partnership' of that 'conversation begun in the
primeval forests and extended and made more articulate in the
course of centuries', school graduates did not know their
economic elbow from their political nose. It was a directive of
the State Education departments that if the Vietnam war was
discussed it had to be in an 'even-handed' manner. In one
particularly scandalous case, the clerical headmaster of a
Methodist college was dismissed from his position for advocating to final-year students that, if they were pacifists, they

should register as conscientious objectors, such action is
consistent with Christian principles.[29] The 'boundary c
ditions' for human life are set by political-economic conditions
such conditions being largely determined by the ongoing
struggle between those who create wealth and those who
expropriate it. It is a peculiar thing that those who advocate that
'education should be for life' simply exclude political economy
from the sphere of life. At the height of the Vietnam War, the
New South Wales Education Week slogan was: 'Education
Builds Bridges of Understanding'! Manifestly, as Paulo Freire
reiterates, education is always a political event.

As with anything else, there is inefficiency in schooling; there
are contradictory tendencies within it; it does other things
besides carrying out its main function. This is the paradox of
Catholic schools: some of the most regimented and repressive
institutions produce some of the most radical and liberated
people. The skills required for reading Rudyard Kipling also
enable one to read George Orwell's 'On Shooting an Elephant'.
Teaching the virtues of democracy in History classes can spark
an interest, and perhaps a demand, for democracy in the school.
The scientific skills and knowledges required for the maintenance of capitalist production also enable the rigorous moni-
toring and analyses of its exploitation of nature and its pollution
of the environment. The bookkeeping skills necessary to be a
functionary in the Commonwealth Bank of Australia may also
enable a connection to be made between its $136 million profit in
1979 and its refusal to grant salary increases to staff in the same
year. As Freire said of the Catholic Church, 'Christ led me to the
people and the people led me to Marx'. Whether the recessive
side of the contradiction is enlarged is dependent upon factors
outside the school situation. If wide-ranging censorship is
exercised, then Orwell may not be available; if the police patrol
schools, then demands for pupil government may not be raised;
if all scientific research is State controlled, then we may have no
science of pollution; if companies do not publish balance sheets,
then profit and salary connections may not be made.

There is, however, another side to this picture. Work being
conducted at the Birmingham Centre for Contemporary Cultural
Studies has underlined the non-monolithic nature of schooling,
and has drawn attention to the plurality of ideologies competing
for dominance within it. These studies cause revision of the
fairly straightforward picture painted by Althusser, and by
Bowles and Gintis. The work of Dan Finn, Paul Willis and Stuart
Hall has stressed that an adequate theory of schools must grasp

connections between schools and other sites of social
relationships, the most important of these being the family,
work, and the formal political sphere.[30]

Perhaps the best research conducted here is that by Paul
Willis, contained in his *Learning to Labour: How Working Class Kids
Get Working Class Jobs*.[31] He identifies the inculcation of con-
formist ideology and the dominance of traditional social relations
and practices in the schools. Importantly though, he identifies
and charts the structures and practices of working-class
children's non-conformist culture and practices *within* the
school. The dialogue of a group discussion by the 'lads' on
teachers runs as follows:

Joey: . . . the way we're subject to their every whim like. They want something
    doing and we have to sort of do it, 'cos, er, er, we've just, we're under
    them like. We were with a woman teacher in here, and 'cos we all wear
    rings and one or two of them bangles, like he's got one on, and out of the
    blue, like, for no special reason, she says, 'take all that off'.
PW: Really?
Joey: Yeah, we says, 'One won't come off', she says, 'Take yours off as well'.
    I said, 'You'll have to chop my finger off first'.
PW: Why did she want you to take your rings off?
Joey: Just a sort of show like. Teachers do this, like, all of a sudden they'll make
    you do your ties up and things like this. You're subject to their every
    whim like.[32]

The 'lads' develop a consistent and entrenched oppositional
stance. There is a caged resentment which stops just short of
open confrontation, a resentment expressed in the countless
little things which annoy teachers and frustrate school organisation and discipline. They develop a style of ritualised re-
sistance. They are proud of themselves and their achievements
when contrasted to the 'ear 'oles', or the school group whom
they see as being toadies and conformists. Speaking of one of
the 'ear 'oles' (those who always listen and never do anything),
Joey says: 'We've been through all life's pleasures and all its
fucking displeasures, we've been drinking, we've been fighting,
we've known frustration, sex, fucking hatred, love and all this
lark, yet he's known none of it'.[33] When speaking of their own
children in response to a teacher's claim that they will be
unmanageable, Joey replies: 'They wouldn't. They'll be outspoken. They wouldn't be submissive fucking twits. They'll be
outspoken, upstanding sort of people'.[34]

Willis recognises that this counter-school culture is ambiva-
lent; it has weaknesses as well as strengths. It is horribly sexist;
women are basically things for men to masturbate into. 'After
you've been with one like, after you've done it like, well they're

scrubbers afterwards.'[35] It is also horribly racist. But it does have the potential for carrying over into shop-floor politics and organisation. It can generate a shop-floor militancy and solidarity.

EDUCATION AND UNEMPLOYMENT

What mixed joy a Marxist might derive from studies such as Willis' depends upon there being a shop floor on which the lads can find employment. This is increasingly less likely. The silicon-chip revolution has decimated the labour power required for social production. Capitalists have always exploited technology in order either to eliminate or to weaken the position of labour in production. The silicon chip is by far the greatest weapon which has ever been used in the pursuit of this end. The job market has collapsed like a pricked balloon. In IBM's new Australian factory, a mere fifty workers using new computerised assembly procedures will produce 76% of Australia's total market in electric typewriters. This market itself will collapse as new word-processing machines eliminate over 80% of typing staff across the country. One white-collar employment agency estimates that the first generation of word-processors have displaced 20,000 typists in Sydney alone. One insurance company reduced staff by 30% in two years and saved $133,000 in wages. The effect spreads—less office space is required, fewer desks, fewer carpets, a smaller maintenance staff, and so on.[36] In Australia in 1978 over one-third of all the unemployed ($\approx$ 8% of the workforce) were teenagers, this being nearly one-quarter of the teenage population in the labour market. Naturally, job selection is increasingly on political grounds. Willis' 'lads' will swell the ranks of the dole queue, not the shop floor; they will become the lumpenproletariat, not the proletariat. The Australian pattern is, in varying degrees, replicated in all the advanced industrial nations.

There is a fiscal crisis of the State, and a structural unemployment crisis. Increasingly, there will be a small percentage of people whose labour time is virtually priceless and a vast percentage whose labour time is basically worthless. This development in the CMP has forced a reorientation of the so-called great Educational Debate. In the '50s and '60s, during a period of capitalist expansion and optimism about employment, the British debate was about Progressivism and Traditionalism. This was the halcyon era of the Plowden Report. There was a liberal-democratic consensus about educational aims. A Depart-

ment of Education and Science report in 1967 on pupils overcoming the deprivation of family poverty could assert: 'Better
education is the key to improved employment opportunities for
young people in these districts'. The Newsom Report of 1963[37]
could confidently say that 'the future pattern of employment in
this country will require a much larger pool of talent than is at
present available . . . the need is not only for more skilled
workers . . . but for a better educated and intelligently adaptable
labour force'.[38] The employment assumptions upon which these
reports are based—'there are jobs available if only people could
be trained'—no longer hold. These same assumptions lay
beneath liberal–progressive opposition to the *type* of work available to school-leavers. In the early '70s John Holt was remark-
ing: 'It is a waste of time and money, as well as a cruel
deception, to talk of providing good education for children if the
central experience of their adult lives is going to be pointless,
stupid and stupefying work'.[39]

Contradictions within the State over the role of schooling are
ample testament to the close links it bears to the economic base.
More money spent on schooling diminishes the amount of
surplus value available for appropriation. Pressure from the
capitalist class, and indeed from the working class, has always
been to make the expenditure efficient in the creation of
productive labour power. After the silicon chip, productive
labour power is needed less and less. In social democracies, the
political consequences of eliminating schooling for the bulk of
the working class would be too disastrous for the State to
contemplate. Apart from anything else, it flies in the face of a
popular conservative explanation of unemployment, namely
that it is the consequence of poor education. In 1977 the
Organisation of Economic Co-operation and Development produced a study of the Australian education system and its
relation to work. It concluded that the 'real solution' to the
problem of youth unemployment lay in a closer connection
between education and job opportunities.

What are the possible responses of the State to this situation?

(i)   It can lower the expectation that people have of obtaining
      a job upon completion of an education. If people don't
      expect anything then they won't be disappointed. In-
      deed, a 1975 report to the Trilateral Commission in the
      USA (an adjunct of the Rockefeller Corporation), when
      dealing with the *Crisis of Democracy*, said: 'A programme
      is then necessary to lower the job expectations of those
      who receive a college education . Another Rockefeller

adjunct, Exxon Oil, made billions of dollars' profit that year.

(ii) It can reintroduce streamed education but this time, instead of the bottom stream being marked out for menial work, it will be marked out for no work. An Australian trade union leader, Bob Hawke, has advocated just such a scheme. The bottom stream will be schooled in hippy, low-energy, subsistence living, and the State will provide tracts of land on which they can idle their time away.

(iii) It can further erode work conditions by bringing in part-time work schemes. Universities are moving in this direction—replacing full-time staff by armies of part-time staff. At one stroke we move from one person employed and five unemployed to six persons employed—unfortunately, at the salary of the one.

CONCLUSION

Education is an important arena for people concerned with establishing a socialist society. Socialism is not achieved by simply changing economic relations; it requires the changing of hearts and minds, the development of an informed and critical consciousness among people. There are valuable aspects of our tradition and our culture to which children ought to be systematically introduced; there are also exploitative, repressive and mystificatory aspects of our tradition which should be exposed for children, and against which they should be encouraged to struggle. The epistemology and theory of ideology advanced in this book is meant as a contribution to the task of socialist pedagogy. A central element of this task is class theory, and the identification of the inroads of class interest into the corpus of knowledge, culture and ideology in which we move and have our being. Philip Agee's reflections are pertinent here; at the end of many years as an operative for the CIA he said:

The key to adopting increasingly radical views has been my fuller comprehension of the class dimensions of capitalist society based on property or the lack of it. The divisions were always there, of course, for me to see, but until recently I simply failed to grasp their meaning and consequences . . . But by getting behind the liberal concept of society, that concept that attempts to paint out the irreconcilable class conflicts, I think I have grasped an understanding of why liberal reform programs in Latin America have failed.[40]

Socialist pedagogy attempts to teach in schools what Agee had learnt in the embassies of Latin America. The detail of how this is done is not my present concern. It will be a difficult task, involving new theories and new practices. It will involve identifying and countering the ideologies that are constitutive of the liberal conception of society—in philosophy of education, this is the work of Richard Peters and Paul Hirst. Although education is important for socialism, it is certainly not sufficient. The forces of capital are massive and have to be counteracted in the political and economic arenas. This is a daunting task for teachers, but one which they have to face.

NOTES

1. R. S. Peters (ed.), *Dewey Reconsidered*, London, Routledge & Kegan Paul, 1977, p. 120.
2. Robert C. Tucker (ed.), *The Marx–Engels Reader*, New York, Norton & Co., 1972, p. 13.
3. *On the Method of Theoretical Physics*, Oxford, 1933, p. 5.
4. A. R. Hall, *The Scientific Revolution*, Boston, Beacon Press, 1962, p. 63.
5. *Liberalism and Social Action*, New York, Putman's & Sons, 1935. Quoted in in W. Feinberg, *Reason and Rhetoric*, New York, Wiley, 1975, p. 212.
6. See, for instance, Raymond Williams, 'Base and Superstructure in Marxist Cultural Theory', *New Left Review*, 1973, 82.
7. Marx–Engels, *Selected Works*, Moscow, Progress, 1969, p. 47.
8. Quoted in Gerard Macdonald, 'The Politics of Closed Curricula', *Brit. Journ. Educ. Tech.*, 1973, 4, (1).
9. Quoted in W. Feinberg, *Reason and Rhetoric*, p. 35.
10. Quoted in Michael Gallagher, 'Political Economy of Schooling in Australia', Sydney, Transnational Cooperative, 1979.
11. Quoted in Michael Katz, *The Irony of Early School Reform*, Cambridge, Mass., Harvard University Press, 1968.
12. Macdonald, 'Politics of the Closed Curricula', p. 25.
13. *Collected Essays, Journalism and Letters of George Orwell*, Sonia Orwell and Ian Angus (eds.), London, Secker & Warburg, 1968, Vol. I, pp. 460 ff.
14. Martin Hoyles (ed.), *The Politics of Literacy*, London, Writers & Readers Coop, 1977.
    Carol and Lars Berggren, *The Literacy Process: A Practice of Domestication or Liberation*, London, Writers & Readers Coop, 1975.
    Sylvia Ashton-Warner, *Teacher*, New York, Simon and Schuster, 1963.
15. University of Nebraska Press, 1964.
16. Allen Nevins and Henry Steele Commager, *The Pocket History of the United States*, New York, Pocket Books, 1956, p.v. Quoted in *Reason and Rhetoric*, p. 195. For more on the doctrine of Manifest Destiny in American consciousness and historiography, see Frederick Merk, *Manifest Destiny and Mission in American History*, New York, Vintage, 1963.
17. John Freeland, 'Class Struggle in Schooling: MACOS and SEMP in Queensland', *Intervention*, 12, 1979.
18. Quoted in Samuel Bowles, 'The Integration of Higher Education into the Wage Labour System', *Union Radical Political Economists*, 1974.
19. Harry Braverman, *Labor and Monopoly Capital*, New York, Monthly Review Press, 1974.
20. *Education and Jobs: The Great Training Robbery*, New York, Praeger, 1970.

21. 'A Reappraisal of the Most Controversial Educational Document of Our Time', New York Times Magazine, August 10, 1969. Quoted in Charles Silberman, *Crisis in the Classroom*, New York, Vintage Books, 1971, p. 67.
22. *ibid.*
23. *Future Shock*, London, Bodley Head, 1970, p. 361.
24. *Culture Against Man*, Harmondsworth, Penguin, 1972, p. 243.
25. *On What is Learned in School*, London, Addison–Wesley, 1968, p. 55.
26. J. Douglas *et al.*, *All Our Future*, London, Davies, 1968. See also A. B. Atkinson, *Unequal Shares*, Harmondsworth, Penguin, 1972.
27. Christopher Jencks, *Inequality*, Harmondsworth, Penguin, 1975.
28. *Lenin and Philosophy*, New York, Monthly Review Press, 1971, p. 155.
29. To be fair, it was not the Church that dismissed him, but a lay council consisting of some of the most prominent members of Australian society, led by a person who wields considerable power over public broadcasting in Australia.
30. Dann Finn, Neil Grant, Richard Johnson, 'Social Democracy, Education and the Crisis', in *Cultural Studies*, 10, 1977.
31. Farnborough, Saxon House, 1977.
32. *ibid.* p. 11.
33. *ibid.* p. 16.
34. *ibid.*, p. 12.
35. *ibid.* p. 44.
36. Keith Windschuttle, *Unemployment*, Harmondsworth, Penguin, 1977, p. 36.
37. Quoted in *Cultural Studies*, 10, p. 180.
38. *ibid.* p. 181.
39. *Freedom and Beyond*, Harmondsworth, Penguin, 1973, p. 168.
40. *CIA Diary*, Harmondsworth, Penguin, 1975, p. 564.

SELECT BIBLIOGRAPHY

ALTHUSSER, L., *Lenin and Philosophy*, New York, Monthly Review Press, 1971.

----, *For Marx*, London, Alan Lane, 1969.

ALTHUSSER, L. and BALIBAR, E., *Reading Capital*, London, New Left Books, 1970.

AMSTERDAMSKI, S., *Between Experience and Metaphysics*, Boston, Reidel, 1975.

ARISTOTLE, *Metaphysics*, Richard Hope (trans.), Ann Arbor, University of Michigan Press, 1968.

ARONSON, J., 'The Legacy of Hume's Analysis of Causation', *Studies in the History and Philosophy of Science*, 2, 1971.

ASHTON-WARNER, S., *Teacher*, New York, Simon & Schuster, 1963.

AYER, A. J., *The Problem of Knowledge*, London, Macmillan, 1956.

BACON, F., *Novum Organum*, in E. A. Burtt, *The English Philosophers from Bacon to Mill*, New York, Random House, 1939.

BERG, I., *Education and Jobs: The Great Training Robbery*, New York, Praeger, 1970.

BERNSTEIN, R., *Praxis and Action*, London, Duckworth, 1972.

BERNSTEIN, R. (ed.), *John Dewey: On Experience, Nature and Freedom*, New York, Liberal Arts Press, 1960.

BHASKAR, R., *A Realist Theory of Science*, 2nd edit., Hassocks, Harvester Press, 1978.

BINNS, Peter, 'The Marxist Theory of Truth', *Radical Philosophy*, 4, 1973.

BLACKBURN, R. (ed.), *Ideology and Social Science*, London, Collins, 1972.

BLOCH, Ernst, *On Karl Marx*, New York, Herder & Herder, 1971.

BLOOR, D. C., 'Are Philosophers Averse to Science?', in D. O. Edge & J. N. Wolfe (eds.), *Meaning and Control*, Tavistock, London, 1973.

----, *Knowledge and Social Imagery*, London, Routledge & Kegan Paul, 1976.

BOWLES, S. and GINTIS, H., *Schooling in Capitalist America*, London, Routledge & Kegan Paul, 1976.

BRAVERMAN, H., *Labour and Monopoly Capital*, New York, Monthly Review Press, 1974.

BUCHDAHL, G., *Metaphysics and the Philosophy of Science*, Oxford, Blackwells, 1969.

BURTT, E. A., *The Metaphysical Foundations of Modern Physical Science*, London, Routledge & Kegan Paul, 1924.

CAMPBELL, D., 'Evolutionary Epistemology', in P. A. Schilpp (ed.), *The Philosophy of Karl Popper*, La Salle, Open Court, 1974.

CASTLES, S. and WÜSTENBERG, W., *An Introduction to the Theory and Practice of Socialist Education*, London, Pluto Press, 1979.

CHALMERS, A., *What Is This Thing Called Science?*, Brisbane, Queensland University Press, 1976.

COHEN, R. S., 'Dialectical Materialism and Carnap's Logical Empiricism', in P. A. Schilpp (ed.), *The Philosophy of Rudolf Carnap*, La Salle, Open Court, 1963.

COPLESTON, F. C., *History of Philosophy*, New York, Doubleday, 1964.

COUNTS, G. S., 'Dare Progressive Education be Progressive?', *Progressive Education*, 1932, 9. Reprinted as *Dare the School Build a New Social Order?*, New York, John Day, 1932.

CROMBIE, I. M., *An Examination of Plato's Doctrines*, London, Routledge & Kegan Paul, 1962.

CURTHOYS, J. and SUCHTING, W., 'Feyerabend's Discourse Against Method: A Marxist Critique', *Inquiry*, 20, 1978.

DALE, R. *et al. (eds.)*, *Schooling and Capitalism*, London, Routledge & Kegan Paul, 1976.

DALLMAYR, F. R., 'Marxism and Truth', *Telos*, 29, 1976.

DANIEL, N., 'I.Q. Heritability and Human Nature', *Boston Studies in the Philosophy of Science*, 32, 1976.

DEARDEN, R. F., HIRST, P. H. and PETERS, R. S. (eds.), *Education and the Development of Reason*, London, Routledge & Kegan Paul, 1972.

DEWEY, J., *Philosophy and Civilisation*, New York, Minton Balch, 1931.

————, *Liberalism and Social Action*, New York, Putnam's & Sons, 1935.

————, *Democracy and Education*, New York, The Free Press, 1966.

DICKSON, D., 'Science and Political Hegemony in the Seventeenth Century', *Radical Science Journal*, 8, 1979.

DREEBEN, R., *On What is Learned in School*, London, Addison–Wesley, 1968.

DUHEM, Pierre, *The Aim and Structure of Physical Theory*, P. P. Wiener (trans.), Princeton, Princeton University Press, 1954.

EDEL, A., 'Analytic Philosophy of Education at the Crossroads', in J. F. Doyle (ed.), *Educational Judgments*, London, Routledge & Kegan Paul, 1973.

EDWARDS, R. C. *et al.* (eds.), *The Capitalist System*, Englewood Cliffs, Prentice-Hall, 1972.

EINSTEIN, A., *The Evolution of Physics*, New York, Simon & Schuster, 1966.

EVERS, C., 'Analytic Philosophy of Education: From a Logical Point of View', *Educational Philosophy and Theory*, 11, (2), 1979.

FEIGL, H., 'Empiricism at Bay', *Boston Studies in Philosophy of Science*, 14, 1974.

FEINBERG, W., *Reason and Rhetoric*, New York, John Wiley, 1975.

FEYERABEND, P. I., 'Problems of Empiricism', in R. G. Colodny (ed.), *Beyond the Edge of Certainty*, Englewood Cliffs, Prentice-Hall, 1965.

––––, *Against Method*, London, New Left Books, 1975.

FINN, D., GRANT, N. and JOHNSON, R., 'Social Democracy, Education and the Crisis', *Cultural Studies*, 10, 1977.

FISK, M., 'Idealism, Truth and Practice', Monist, 59, (3), 1976.

FRAZIER, N. and SADKER, M., *Sexism in School and Society*, New York, Harper & Row, 1973.

FREIRE, P., *Cultural Action for Freedom*, Harmondsworth, Penguin, 1972.

––––, *Pedagogy of the Oppressed*, Harmondsworth, Penguin, 1972.

––––, *Education for Critical Consciousness*, London, Sheed & Ward, 1974.

––––, *Pedagogy in Progress: Letters from Guinea–Bissau*, London, Writers & Readers Coop, 1979.

GALILEI, G., *Dialogue Concerning the Two Chief World Systems*, Stillman Drake (trans.), Berkeley, University of California Press, 1962.

GAUKROGER, S., *Explanatory Structures*, Hassocks, Sussex, Harvester Press, 1971.

GOTTLIEB, R. S., 'A Marxian Concept of Ideology', *The Philosophical Forum*, 6, (4), 19.

HALL, A. R., *The Scientific Revolution*, Boston, Beacon Press, 1962.

HAMILTON, P., *Knowledge and Social Structure*, London, Routledge & Kegan Paul, 1974.

HANSON, N. R., *Patterns of Discovery*, Cambridge, University Press, 1958.

HARDING, S. G. (ed.), *Can Theories Be Refuted?*, Boston, Reidel, 1978.

HARRÉ, R., *Matter and Method*, London, Macmillan, 1964.
HARRÉ, R. (ed.), *Problems of Scientific Revolution*, Oxford, Clarendon Press, 1975.
HARRIS, K., *Education and Knowledge*, Routledge & Kegan Paul, 1978.
HARRIS, N., *Beliefs in Society*, Harmondsworth, Penguin, 1971.
HEMPEL, C., 'Carnap and the Philosophy of Science', in P. A. Schilpp (ed.), *The Philosophy of Rudolf Carnap*, La Salle, Open Court, 1963.
————, *Aspects of Scientific Explanation*, New York, Macmillan, 1965.
HERNNSTEIN, R., *I.Q. in the Meritocracy*, Boston, Atlantic Little Brown & Co., 1973.
HIRST, P. H., *Knowledge and the Curriculum*, London, Routledge & Kegan Paul, 1974.
————, 'Liberal Education and the Nature of Knowledge', in R. F. Dearden *et al.* (eds.), *Education and the Development of Reason*, London, Routledge & Kegan Paul, 1972.
————, 'Human Movement, Knowledge and Education', *Journal of Philosophy of Education*, 13, 1979.
HOLTON, G., *The Scientific Imagination*, London, Cambridge University Press, 1978.
HOYLES, M. (ed.), *The Politics of Literacy*, London, Writers & Readers Coop, 1977.
HUME, D., *Enquiries into Human Nature*, L. A. Selby-Bigge (ed.), Oxford, Clarendon Press, 1888.
————, *A Treatise of Human Nature*, L. A. Selby-Bigge (ed.), Oxford, Clarendon Press, 1888.
JACOBY, R., *Social Amnesia*, Boston, Beacon Press, 1976.
JANIK, A. and TOULMIN, S., *Wittgenstein's Vienna*, New York, Simon & Schuster, 1983.
JENKS, C., *Inequality*, Harmondsworth, Penguin, 1975.
JENSEN, A. R., 'How Much Can We Boost IQ and Scholastic Achievement?', *Harvard Educational Review*, 1969.
————, *Genetics and Education*, New York, Harper & Row, 1973.
KAMIN, L., *The Science and Politics of I.Q.*, Harmondsworth, Penguin, 1977.
KANT, I., *Critique of Pure Reason*, Norman Kemp Smith (trans.), London, Macmillan, 1964.
KARABEL, J. and HALSEY, A. H., *Power and Ideology in Education*, New York, Oxford University Press, 1977.
KATZ, M., *The Irony of Early School Reform*, Cambridge, Harvard Univ. Press, 1968.
KARIER, C., VIOLAS, P. and SPRING, J., *Roots of Crisis:*

American Education in the Twentieth Century, Chicago, Rand McNally & Co., 1973.

KOLAKOWSKI, L., *Marxism and Beyond*, London, Paladin, 1971.

KOSIK, K., *Dialectics of the Concrete*, Boston, Reidel, 1976.

KOYRÉ, A., *Metaphysics and Measurement*, Cambridge, Mass., Harvard University Press, 1968.

KRIGE, J. M., *Continuity and Discontinuity in the Historiography of Science*, Hassocks, Harvester Press, 1980.

KUHN, T., *The Structure of Scientific Revolutions*, Chicago, University of Chicago Press, 1962.

–––––, 'Notes on Lakatos', *Boston Studies in the Philosophy of Science, 8*, 1970.

LAKATOS, I., *Proofs and Refutations*, Cambridge, University Press, 1976.

–––––, *Collected Works*, Vol. I, *Methodology of Scientific Research Programmes*, J. Worrall and G. Currie (eds.), Cambridge, Cambridge University Press, 1978. Vol. II, *Mathematics, Science and Epistemology*, J. Worrall and G. Currie (ed.), Cambridge, Cambridge University Press, 1978.

LAKATOS, I. and MUSGRAVE, A. (eds.), *Criticisms and the Growth of Knowledge*, Cambridge, Cambridge University Press, 1970.

LAKATOS, I. and ZAHER, E., 'Why did Copernicus' Research Programme Supersede Ptolemy's?', in R. S. Westman (ed.), *The Copernican Achievement*, Berkeley, University of California Press, 1975.

LECOURT, D., *Marxism and Epistemology*, London, New Left Books, 1972.

LENIN, V. I., *Materialism and Empiro-Criticism*, Moscow, Progress Publishers, 1947.

LICHTHEIM, G., *The Concept of Ideology*, New York, Vintage, 1967.

LOCKE, J., *An Essay Concerning Human Understanding*, John W. Yolton (ed.), London, Dent & Sons, 1961.

LONERGAN, B., *Insight*, New York, Longmans, 1957.

MacDONALD, Gerard, 'The Politics of Closed Curricula', *British Journal of Educational Technology, 4, (1)*, 1973.

McMULLIN, E. (ed.), *Galileo Man of Science*, New York, Basic Books, 1967.

–––––, 'Empiricism at Sea?', *Boston Studies in Philosophy of Science, 14*, 1974.

–––––, 'History and Philosophy of Science: A Marriage of Convenience?', *Boston Studies in the Philosophy of Science, 32*, 1974.

MANNHEIM, K., *Ideology and Utopia*, London, Routledge & Kegan Paul, 1960.

MARKOVIC, M., 'The Problem of Truth', *Boston Studies in the Philosophy of Science*, 5, 1966.

————, *From Affluence to Praxis*, Ann Arbor, University of Michigan Press, 1974.

MARX, K., *The Poverty of Philosophy*, Moscow, Progress, 1955.

————, *Capital*, Moscow, Progress, 1956.

————, *The Economic and Philosophic Manuscripts of 1844*, Dirk Struik (trans.), New York, International Publishers, 1964.

————, *Grundrisse*, Martin Nicolaus (trans.), Harmondsworth, Penguin, 1973.

————, *Critique of Hegel's Philosophy of Right*, Cambridge, Cambridge University Press, 1972.

MARX, K. and ENGELS, F., *Selected Works*, Moscow, Progress Publishers, 1969.

————, *The Holy Family*, Moscow, Progress, 1956.

MOORE, E. C. (ed.), *Charles S. Peirce: The Essential Writings*, New York, Harper & Row, 1972.

NIDDITCH, P. H. (ed.), *The Philosophy of Science*, Oxford, Oxford University Press, 1968.

NIEBUHR, R., *Moral Man and Immoral Society*, New York, Scribners, 1932.

NOBLE, D. F., *America by Design*, New York, Alfred Knopf, 1979.

NORTON, T. M. and OLLMAN, B., *Studies in Socialist Pedagogy*, New York, Monthly Review Press, 1978.

PATEMAN, T. (ed.), *Counter Course*, Harmondsworth, Penguin, 1972.

PETERS, R. S., *Ethics and Education*, London, Allen & Unwin, 1966.

————, 'The Philosophy of Education', in J. W. Tibble (ed.), *The Study of Education*, London, Routledge & Kegan Paul, 1966.

PETERS, R. S. (ed.), *The Concept of Education*, London, Routledge & Kegan Paul, 1967.

————, *A Recognisable Philosophy of Education*, London, Routledge & Kegan Paul, 1969.

————, *Dewey Reconsidered*, London, Routledge & Kegan Paul, 1977.

PETERS, R. S. and BENN, I. S., *Social Principles and the Democratic State*, London, Allen & Unwin, 1959.

PHILLIPS, D. C., 'The Distinguishing Features of Forms of Knowledge', *Educational Philosophy and Theory*, 3, (2), 1971.

PLATO, *Theattetus*, in F. M. Cornforth (trans.), *Plato's Theory of Knowledge*, London, Routledge & Kegan Paul, 1935.

————, *The Republic*, H. D. P Lee (trans.), Harmondsworth, Penguin, 1955.

————, *The Meno*, W. Guthrie (trans.), Harmondsworth, Penguin, 1956.

POINCARÉ, H., *Science and Hypothesis*, New York, Science Press, 1905.

POPPER, K., *Conjectures and Refutations*, London, Routledge & Kegan Paul, 1963.

————, *The Logic of Scientific Discovery*, London, Hutchinson, 1972 (Original 1934).

————, *Objective Knowledge*, Oxford, Clarendon Press, 1972.

PRATTE, R., *Ideology and Education*, New York, David McKay, 1977.

QUINE, W. V. O., *From a Logical Point of View*, New York, Harper, 1953.

RAVETZ, J. R., *Scientific Knowledge and its Social Problems*, Harmondsworth, Penguin, 1973.

ROTENSTEICH, N., *Basic Problems of Marxist Philosophy*, New York, Bobbs-Merrill, 1965.

RUBEN, D.-H., *Marxism and Materialism*, Hassocks, Harvester Press, 1977.

SCHEFFLER, I., 'Towards an Analytic Philosophy of Education', *Harvard Educational Review*, 24, (4), 1954.

————, *Conditions of Knowledge*, New York, Scott, Foresman, 1965.

————, *Reason and Teaching*, London, Routledge & Kegan Paul, 1973.

SCHILPP, P. A. (ed.), *The Philosophy of John Dewey*, Evanston, Northwestern University Press, 1939.

SELIGER, M., *The Marxist Conception of Ideology*, Cambridge, Cambridge University Press, 1977.

SILBERMAN, C., *Crisis in the Classroom*, New York, Vintage Books, 1971.

SIMON, B., *Intelligence, Psychology and Education*, London, Lawrence & Wishart, 1971.

SKILLEN, A., *Ruling Illusions*, Hassocks, Harvester Press, 1977.

STACHEL, J., 'A Note on the Concept of Scientific Practice', *Boston Studies in the Philosophy of Science*, 17, 1974.

STEVENS, P., 'Ideology and Schooling', *Educational Philosophy and Theory*, 8, (2), 1976.

SUCHTING, W., 'Marx's *Theses on Feuerbach*', in J. Mepham and D.-H. Ruben. (eds.), *Issues in Marxist Philosophy*, Hassocks, Harvester Press, 1979.

TARSKI, A., 'The Concept of Truth in Formalised Languages',

in J. H. Woodger (ed.), *Logic, Semantics and Metamathematics*, New York, Oxford University Press, 1956.

TIBBLE, J. W. (ed.), *The Study of Education*, London, Routledge & Kegan Paul, 1966.

TOULMIN, S., *Human Understanding*, Oxford, Clarendon Press, 1972.

TRIBE, K., 'On the Production and Structuring of Scientific Knowledges', *Economy and Society*, 2, 1973.

TUCKER, R. C. (ed.), *The Marx–Engels Reader*, New York, Norton & Co., 1972.

URBACH, P., 'Progress and Degeneration in the IQ Debate', *British Journal of Philosophy of Science*, 25, 26, 1974. (In two parts.)

WARTOFSKY, M., 'Metaphysics as Heuristic for Science', *Boston Studies in the Philosophy of Science*, 3, 1964–1966.

————, *Ludwig Feuerbach*, London, Cambridge University Press, 1978.

WATKINS, J. W. N., 'Metaphysics and the Advancement of Science', *British Journal for the Philosophy of Science*, 26, 1975.

WEIGEL, G. and MADDEN, A., *Knowledge: Its Values and Limits*, Englewood Cliffs, Prentice-Hall, 1961.

WILLIAMS, R., 'Base and Superstructure in Marxist Cultural Theory', *New Left Review*, 82, 1973.

WILLIS, P., *Learning to Labour: How Working Class Kids Get Working Class Jobs*, Farnborough, Saxon House, 1977.

WINDSCHUTTLE, K., *Unemployment*, Harmondsworth, Penguin, 1979.

PROPER NAME INDEX

SUBJECT INDEX